The Many Tongues of Literacy

The Many Tongues

of
Literacy

Ray B. Browne

Bowling Green State University Popular Press
Bowling Green, OH 43403

Dedicated

to

My thousands of colleagues around the world

and at home

to

Christopher Geist

Carl Holmberg

Anne Kennedy

Marilyn Motz

Jack Nachbar

Michael Marsden

Jack Santino

Contents

Preface

Democracy and capitalism though seeming symbiotic partners that work well together contain antagonistic stress in regard to power and powerlessness and, especially, in regard to education. Democracy insists that politically and humanistically everyone is equal to the rights of education. Capitalism, on the other hand, since it thrives on some people being more equal than others, demands only that education be widespread and sufficiently advanced to drive the machine of its own making. In many ways a well-informed people is a threat to capitalism.

The result of the two competitive tracks is great stress on education, one that the people in the education business have not been able to harmonize successfully. Throughout the eighteenth and nineteenth centuries, the conflict was muted because of two constants in the development of both thrusts into human associations and behavior. Those constants were educating and education, each appealing to the "good," honest, up-lifting and ideal in life. But, both bastions have been breaking down through the years.

Religion has long been suspect as the business of the quack, charlatan and crook, who exploited one of the most vulnerable aspects of the human being. Lately the suspicion has been made flesh in the spectacular examples of such people as televangelists Jim Baker, Jerry Falwell and Jimmy Swaggert and scores of others whose venality has shown itself in their unprincipled exploitation of the public.

The crumbling of the house of religion left the citadel of education. Now, however, with the disclosures that various colleges and universities have been robbing the government and administrators have been siphoning off vast funds from the educational budget—at the expense of the taxpayer and the student—the final citadel has crumbled. It has become clear that education—which has always been packaged as a treasure—has become merchandise, something to be sold for the benefit of educators' personal gain. The highest levels of administration manipulate moneys for their own personal and professional gains. Teachers insist that their personal fortunes be foremost in the business of education, no matter how much the children suffer.

Education has become the glitzy product that everybody trades in. Talk is inexpensive. Politicians and educators realize that there is much to be gained by paying lip service to developing the minds of our

i

students—and older citizens. But students are not the primary concern of those people in power, no matter how they protest that they are. Power and control—the acquiring and protecting of perks—are. It is almost as though the American Dream and the implementing of it have shifted. Being mortal we recognize the we must eventually pass on power and control. But being unwilling to admit mortality we withhold power as long as possible. The American Dream almost promises eternal power.

We care so little for children that we make them pawns in our tug of war for power. Literacy—our professed goal for everyone—is a battle of turf. Professors do not want to teach; they want released time for learning to teach what presumably they already know. Foundations and research groups subsidize non-teaching while educators teach themselves how to not-teach. Administrators give up teaching because administrating has become more important and beneficial. Government fights over who is to control education—the White House, Congress, Department of Education, National Endowment for the Humanities, governors, state legislators, teachers unions. All power blocks seem more interested in controlling education, in dictating its directions, than in guaranteeing its development and success.

Education is always the first casualty in a financial set-back. Children cease being loved citizens of tomorrow and become instead small adults whose future must be sacrificed for the immediate benefit of the ruling adults. All such "frills" as music and sports programs must be eliminated, even while after working hours we devote our time assiduously to sports and music programs. Parents often entrust to baby-sitters whose impact is going to be far below what one would expect parents to demand. Educators abuse their classes, often arguing—correctly or incorrectly— that it is far more important to have happy teachers who teach small classes than to work hard themselves and demand dedicated application on the part of the students.

The failure of education has derived in part from the fact that the education we must advance has become so complex that people are unable to grasp it for the teaching. Thus people are driven into specialization, even while experience has convinced us that over-specialization frustrates and blunts the aims of education.

All education depends on fluency of communication, on people understanding the message no matter what language it is spoken in. Fluency levels the playing field and more nearly equalizes the game because it allows all people to understand the rules and techniques. To paraphrase Thomas Jefferson on education, a democratic people that is not fluent in the media of communication cannot create a society that will stand. Fluency means communication in a thousand media— the total media of existence. All such media speak various languages that contribute either to a cacophony of sounds or a thousand intelligible languages. We must examine them all and see how they can contribute to the needed education that is requisite to modern life.

To succeed in this examination we must first of all examine our own mind-set. If it is firmly set, intractable, closed—it needs to be opened. It needs to be affectable by new ideas and new concepts. And new approaches to the phenomena of life.

Education and democracy thrive only on newness and growth. Wrestling with modernity's problems with the attitudes of the past guarantees inadequacy and failure. An open mind is the classroom of progress. Politicians, administrators, educators and students need to keep the mind open. Foremost, however, parents and adults must keep the mind receptive to new ideas and new ways of doing things. Ultimately, of course, it is from them that all educative power flows. In the final commitment the fate of education rests in their hands.

This commitment is both a sacred and very real trust. Adults cannot afford to waste or abuse it. Ultimately the fate of America, and indeed of the world, rests in our hands.

Introduction

Learning the Unknown Tongues

In our day of ever-expanding and ever-rushing media of communication battering us on all sides and our ever-increasing sensitivity about the communicative roles of all phenomena of life, we might become confused and worried about the languages of these media, the voices they use to communicate with us, if we do not know them. We might also become confused about the various other objects and artifacts of life around us which speak constantly to us. We might, in reaction, tend to close out some of the avenues of communication, because we might overlook some of the languages that are really obvious but perhaps not familiar.

We realize that there is a written and spoken language, the language we are familiar with and comfortable using. We might be inclined to tune out some of the other languages. In so doing we deny ourselves access to many other media and messages, all of which affect the world around us whether we know it or not and by affecting our culture touch upon our lives. The similarity is in music where we might listen to a particular instrument, say the flute, when the full richness of the orchestra is being ignored. One cannot be concerned with only one instrument of communication without ruling out many others.

Since the purpose of languages is communication—the transmission and reception of messages—we realize that the electronic media have their languages as well as do the conventional tongues we are familiar with. But as our awareness of the role of language increases we become more and more aware that all the phenomena of life, both past and present, both animate and inanimate, both great and small, have their languages of communication. They have their vocabularies and syntax, the organization of communication. In these organizations we need fluency in the messages the languages are communicating in. We must have *literacy* in those languages if we are to understand the world.

In some instances we call lack of knowledge in a particular medium lack of training or skill. Perhaps such a designation is apt. For example, many of us do not know anything about how to change the firing mechanism in our automobile, or even how to change a tire. That perhaps is properly called lack of skill. But not to know the principle of internal

1

combustion or the dynamics of wheel usage is actually illiteracy in these areas. If we know nothing about the cause of earthquakes or thermal springs, we are illiterate in geology. If we know nothing about the dynamics of music, then we are illiterate in that medium. When we say, "I know nothing" about so and so, we are really confessing illiteracy in the medium. We undoubtedly know the area under consideration and probably have some efficiency in its use, but we do not understand its communicative skills, we are not fluent in its language of communication. What we need is more than the skill to handle the item. We need fluency in its language of communication, the waves of communication emanating from some particular object or phenomenon.

Lack of skill or ignorance in how to fully handle an artifact is less than illiteracy, and literacy is more than mere skill in or knowledge of it. Literacy is fluency, ease, understanding in the language of communication used by a particular item or phenomenon in its rays of outreach. In other words, the language in which it speaks.

On the conventional level language consists of sounds and symbols which have been standardized to identify certain aspects of life. Language is sounded symbols, symbols communicated by conventional marks and sounds. Thus, the sound represented by the letters kol means the black carbonated mineral that is mined from the earth. Kild means the state of being uncomfortably below normal temperature. Joining the sounds and symbols of identified objects or states of being constitutes the sentences and longer utterances which make up our oral and written communication. The relationships of symbols one to another constitute the grammar and syntax of a language. In conventional language, this is clear and generally understood.

There are, however, languages emanating from all phenomena and artifacts of life. Poets have long commented on the "language" of nature and thought they understood it. They anthropomorphize it, make it speak their language instead of their understanding its, and letting it speak its own piece. To nineteenth-century English poet Thomas Gray nature appealed even from the grave: "E'en from the tomb the voice of nature cries, E'en in our ashes live their wonted fires." To the American artist James McNeill Whistler, nature reserved her voice for the artist: "Nature sings her exquisite song to the artist alone, her son and her master— her son in that he loves her, her master in that he knows her." Both artists were writing of the phenomenon of nature without being more than the slightest fluent in the language of nature. They were speaking of their perceived reception of the communication of nature but really being illiterate in the real communication. Others, before and after, have of course heard other and strikingly different communications from nature. According to Aesop, mountains give birth to rodents: *"In the Mountains of Labour* he chronicles the birth of a mouse." A huge gap appeared in the side of the mountains. At last a tiny mouse poked its little head out of the gap, a strange concept of nature also reported by Phaedrus and Horace. Thus, to one and all nature speaks a private language understood in its cultural and personal aspect. But such communication is personal and far from the core of what nature really communicates. Not to understand, or to misread, the communication of nature is to underread its message.

Many persons have looked upon numerous other phenomena and lamented the lack of communication between them and us. "Oh what a story that could tell if it could only speak," we often say. What a story the battlefield at Gettysburg could tell if it could talk. What a sad story the bedroom across the street from the Ford Theatre in Washington where Lincoln died could tell if it could articulate its observations. What a tale of changes in the earth the Grand Canyon could report if it could talk. What stories Vatican Square, the Parthenon, Lancelot's sword, the Winchester Cathedral, the underground garage at the Watergate hotel in Washington could tell if they had voices. Historians, musicologists, artists, archeologists, folklorists, classicists all recognize the innate languages in the many phenomena but often merely cry out in their ignorance without trying to discover the Rosetta stones that translate the various languages into a language intelligible to us all. But clearly languages of the Tower of Babel must be distinguished and understood.

Archeologist M.K. Shuman, for his part, is reading the civilization of the early Mayans at least partially by looking at their present-day culture. Historians for a long time have known that the everyday culture of the past is vital to our understanding of the civilizations that have preceded our own. Increasingly this popular culture is forming the backbone of the study by all kinds of cultural historians like Daniel Boorstin and Peter Burke, by people interested in vernacular housing like John A. Jakle, Bastian and Meyer and scholars interested in "Reading Landscape," as the title of one books goes that uses as its thesis: "Landscape in recent years, . . . has stood as a surrogate for more politicized notions of nationhood (a displaced expression of sentiments of attachments which are denied expression elsewhere) and as a source of spiritual strength, a 'moral therapy'" (Pugh 1).

An excellent example of cultural history at its best is the 1990 PBS eleven-hour documentary named *The Civil War,* which calls upon every aspect of vernacular culture available of America (and Europe) at mid-19th century. This documentary shows beyond doubt that to understand the Civil War we must live the daily lives of Billy Yank and Johnny Reb as well as Prudence Mather and Jane Jones, and their cultures. We can learn most fully by participating either vicariously through documents or really through experiencing living parks.

4   The Many Tongues of Literacy

Historian of art Alan Gowns has argued that every artifact—especially every piece of art—contains within it, when it is properly and fully understood the essence of the civilization in which it was created or used. Every artifact is a microchip of its civilization waiting to be read. Everything has its language of expression.

Everything has been communicating since creation but often not heard. Trees, for example, may be merely "minutely articulate" to New Zealand crime writer Ngaio Marsh (*Off With His Head*, 1957, 1) but to others their voice is loud and clear. Rain forests, giant redwoods and trees throughout the world cry out that without their chemical assistance humanity perishes. Those voices are being increasingly heard and heeded.

The voices of the artifacts and phenomena of life have been like radio beams that have filled the air waves long before we learned how to capture them. The age-old philosophical-physical argument about whether a tree falling in the forest with nobody around to hear would make a sound is, of course, mere sophomoric foolishness. The various elements of life have always made communicating sounds and gestures. They have spoken their languages since their creation. The trouble was that nobody was listening to be communicated with. Nobody was literate in the language of that communication.

Before we could become literate in a particular form of communication we, of course, had to realize that there was a medium of communication. At first we felt that communication involved the use of sound, despite the fact that observation had long since demonstrated that the first means of communication was gestures, "body language," and other means of non-verbal communication. But sounds are our "body language," and other means of non-verbal communication. Some cultures demand more articulation in "body language" than others. Italians and other Southern Europeans are famous for their gestures and other forms of body language. Perhaps Arabs even more than Italians speak with their bodies as well as with their mouths. One authority on the subject says that "so intimately related are speech, gesture and culture, that to tie an Arab's hands is tantamount to tying his tongue. Whatever an Arab has to say in words must, in a sense, be accompanied by a series of graphic illustrations with his hands and body," as the series of accompanying photographs will illustrate. They have at least two hundred and fifty recorded gestures and undoubtedly scores of others— on both a folk and popular level—that are local and unrecorded.[1]

But sounds are our major and most obvious means of communication. People make sounds and communicate. Animals make sounds and communicate, though for a long time we felt that animal sounds were meaningless nonsense and were dedicated to enriching the lives of *homo sapiens*. According to this logic, birds sing because they want to provide human beings with pleasure. Lions roar to frighten people. Bighorn

From Barakat, Robert A., "Arabic Gestures," *Journal of Popular Culture*, VI, 4, 1973, p. 793.[1]

sheep butt their heads against each other's in order to amuse the occasional mountain climber who observes them. English poet Thomas Gray summed up the human feeling when he talked of "dumb driven cattle." Cattle might not be overly intellectual, but they are hardly without sounds of communication. Some mammals might be show-offs whose duty it is to amuse people, but even the stage requires language for its actors. Most people will agree that not all the world's a stage for all animals dedicated to delighting mankind.

We have finally discovered that animals have their own reasons for their forms of communication. Nearly all have reason to communicate with other members of their kind. All mammals of the whale genus, for example, have their languages—including highly complicated songs—with which they communicate at short and long range. Wolves have a complicated system of verbal and non-verbal communication. And so on. What applies to macromammals undoubtedly applies to the microanimals as well. Crabs too have their language.

What is true of animate objects is equally valid for inanimate objects. Just as the snake in Eden had a story to tell about its most famous seduction in history, so too did the tree that produced the fruit that introduced Eve to the world. But as all language is symbolic and represents the objects and actions of the world, inanimate objects that have witnessed action, participated in it or been the result of it have the fullest and strongest voices of communication. Paintings, photographs, music, architecture, cooking, driving cars, shearing sheep, highways, windows, lawn race tracks, pots and pans, fashions, fads, etc. all have their languages of communication that they share among themselves and with the *homo sapiens* who also inhabit the world. Each has its own vocabulary, its own syntax and speaks in a voice particular to its breed.

The need is for us to become literate in what they say. In other words, to speak their languages. We are not here talking about hearing strange wee voices communicating to us from beyond the grave, beyond the sky, or beyond reality. But real, tangible voices speaking from mouths that have means of communication.

In many ways learning their languages is much simpler than learning other real recognized verbal languages of other peoples. Even the simplest non-native language has thousands of words, sounds and combinations. Eskimo, for example, has 37 different words for the Atlantic salmon, and 6 for different kinds of snowfall. The more sophisticated languages have hundreds of thousands of words and combinations. English, perhaps the richest of all languages so far, has 2 million words, and nobody can even estimate the number of communicable subtleties and nuances.

Instead of being confusingly complex, the various artifacts of life communicate in some ways much more simply. Although they speak in their own tongues, their own languages, each statement is filtered to every individual in his own language, his own experience, his own culture. The important languages are dialects of a larger language. All dialects ultimately blend into a kind of UR language, that is a general *lingua franca*, which transcends the spoken languages of various people and speaks one intelligible to all who will learn.

The arch in buildings, though it has a long history before being taken over and spread throughout Europe by the Romans, for example, is generally modelled after the Roman style regardless of where it appears. In an English walled city it obviously means something different from what it means in a city in Kansas. But the sameness is there in both—the common language—and the language of the arch. If people want the depth of the meaning of this language, they must look beyond the surface.

In fact it is the sameness of the language which strengthens the language and points out the two ways the arch must be understood: comparatively-internationally and humanitarily.

If one is to understand fully the languages of the arch—to continue with that example—he must understand them comparatively. The similarity of the arch to Kansas and English civilizations is the root language, the symbol, the motif, formula and convention it shares world-wide. To each person its speaks a personal, cultural language. If the receiver of the language is to understand fully what the language means, he must learn that language in its cultural context. What the arch means throughout America and what it has meant for the last 500 years; what it means to the English and the English culture and what it has meant for the last thousand years.

Ideally, the viewer resorts to the *lingua franca* provided in the arch and compares it to the uses it has had around the world from the years of its invention in Classical Rome. The arch is compared through cultures and nations both in contemporary and historical times. Thus, the listener learns the political and military symbolism, the architectural reasons and implications, the place of the Roman arch in civilization.

All these aspects place a heavy communication burden on the artifact. It is heavy and pregnant with the voices and actions of external civilizations. In Kansas and around the world the arch speaks in dialects of an international language that traces on the oscilloscope its trail through the world. That is quite a lot. But there is more burden on the listener.

The sound trail so far outlined is really less than half the voice of the arch. That voice is intrinsic to the arch, its communicator. The other half, at least to human beings, especially those who would understand mankind in his world, is the internal, the human communication. What have the architect, the plumber, the soldier, the politician, the housewife, the woman and the man on the streets thought about the arch? How has it affected their lives?

Increasingly, people are learning to "read" the many artifacts—the countless "arches"—surrounding us. For example, in an excellent article, "The Archaeology of Slave Life," Theresa A. Singleton talks about how from a "careful analysis of tangible material remains—broken pottery, mortar, food bones, tools, buttons, and beads . . . —archaeologists are able to piece together information on how African-Americans spent their daily lives, built their homes, prepared their food and crafted household equipment and personal possessions" (155). The author, and many others working in these artifacts, should have been bolder. She quotes from James Agee and Walker Evens, *Let Us Now Praise Famous Men: Three Tenant Families* (1941; reprint, Boston, 1969, 3), who recognized the value of non-verbal communication. "If I could do it, I'd do no writing at all here. It would be photographs; the rest would be fragments of cloth, bits of cotton, lumps of earth, records of speech, pieces of wood and iron, phials of odors, plates of food and of excrement." Agee and Evans are getting at the point. If one is fluent in these media of communication one does not need writing. With such fluency one can hear and read; without it one must remain partially or wholly ignorant of the message.

Clearly the answer to the questions of how the various media of communication have affected people's lives is not simple. It is as complex as the lives of the many people who have been affected—and as difficult to fathom and understand. There is only one way to approach the answer thoroughly and effectively—with the key of the humanities. Much is to be learned through the traditional approach to the conventional humanities, the popular culture. What are the humanities and what are the popular humanities, the popular culture?

The answer requires an in-depth study throughout all possible means of communication among and to all kinds of people.

Chapter One

Understanding the Babel

Our earliest ancestors had to come to realize through experience that there was some kind of relationship between their physical environment and their thinking, lifestyle and fate. In their earliest centuries of development sometimes their caves were warm, sometimes cold; eventually they found that skins—or other physical objects—kept them warm when they otherwise would be cold. When nature brought animals around or kept them away, they adjusted their eating habits and either feasted or famished. From the earliest they discovered that they had to communicate with one another if they wanted to make their efforts the most effective.

Records of hominids' efforts to communicate go back at least 100,000 years. In 1964 the Hungarian archaeologist Laszlo Vertes published a photograph of a mammoth's tooth, found near Tata, Hungary, that had been carved and bevelled on one side by man and painted with red ocher on the other. The tooth obviously had been used for some kind of communication among people. From a Cro-magnon rock shelter at Blanchard, France, comes a small shaped bone somewhat similar to the earlier Tata plaque. This bone shows evidence of having been scratched deliberately with 29 sets of marks with some purpose in mind. "It was almost as though someone, 25,000 years before the development of writing and arithmetic," says Alexander Marshack, archeologist at the Peabody Museum of Archeology and Ethnology at Harvard University, "was keeping a record of some process or series of events and was structuring it in a manner that he could 'read.' " The markings, it was discovered, corresponded to the changing phases of the moon.

In a later and different world, in western South America, the Incas developed their culture without writing. Their language was Quechua but a large element was the quipu, a collection of cords with knots tied in them, similar to a tangled mop head. The quipu was so easily manipulated that it could almost literally have been used as a common language among the Incas, especially in counting and in keeping records.

These three examples—among thousands of other possible ones—demonstrate that the past—as well as the present—long thought to be capable of speaking to us only in the written word, is filled with messages

9

that need only to be "read" to be understood. These messages reveal
that long before our time—before, during and after the age of myth—
people came to know and adjust to their surroundings or they perished.
What they were doing would now be called reading the physical and
cultural surroundings and adjusting to them.

Reading the environment and reacting to its unalterable demands
is becoming more and more imperative today as the world population
explodes in numbers and in consumption of non-renewable natural
resources and we realize more dramatically that we have only one planet,
with its limited resources and finite flexibility to survive physical abuse.
Either we learn to read the physical world around us and respond to
our reading or, it is becoming more and more apparent, we lose the
world and ourselves. Like the dinosaur and hundreds of thousands of
other species before our time, we read the environment or we perish.
We must and we can.

Scientists are learning to read the laws of science more accurately
now than they did in the past. Historically they often read nature in
order to exploit it rather than to work in harmony with its laws. Now,
however, more and more are learning to work in conformity and harmony
with nature's laws. Humanists, for their part, throughout history have
been more concerned with the human being than with the physical well-
being of the physical surroundings. The universe, to them, has been
largely a homo-centric place. Sometimes—as in the Romantic period
in England and the United States—literary people have formed
movements to synchronize themselves with nature. But this living in
harmony with the surrounding world was largely an emotional attitude
based upon sentiment rather than rationality. In fact, the Bible has taught
the Judeo-Christian world that man, being the special creation of an
all-wise God, was superior to and should "conquer" the physical world,
including both animals and environment. If the world did not shape
up properly, then it should be brought round to the desired
configurations. If animals did not bow to man's desires, they should
properly be brought to heel or destroyed. Such thinking led to peculiar
perverted observations. Eighteenth-century English thinkers, for example,
detested mountains as warts on the face of the earth that should be avoided.
Classical Greeks and Romans before the English had viewed mountains
as the home of the gods. Eighteenth-century British—because they could
not rationalize mountains in their perfectly logical world construct—
thought they were the home of monsters and fearful creatures.

To these same eighteenth-century British and Americans the world
was also a place filled with wonder. To American Puritan minister
Increase Mather, for example, the world vibrated with *Illustrious
Providences* (1684), as the name of one of his many books reveals. This
manuscript was as near as Mather could get to scientific proof of the

existence of supernatural forces on earth. To thinkers of the time it was necessary to bring some kind of order to the chaos that seemed to exist. The philosophical concept of a Great Chain of Being created and rationalized a natural order that ran from the lowest form of life—rocks— skyward in a kind of linkage through mankind to the angels and ultimately to the highest, God. This ordering made logic of the seeming jumble. Mankind's curiosity about the chaotic world led to the establishment of animal exhibits, zoos, trips to distant countries and other efforts to see—and through seeing to establish dominance over— the world. Always the words "to claim" new lands and "to conquer" weaker people and animals have been driving forces. They motivated the Greeks to investigate the borders of their limited seas, the Mongols to flare out from the East to the West and Captain James Cook to begin his voyage around the earth (1768).

Thus the drive of Columbus to claim the Indies for Spain when he mistakenly "discovered" the New World, although if he was any kind of competent sea captain he must have been familiar with the ways which would have shown him that one does not reach India by sailing West. Thus the claim of the early European settlers in America to take over the land and to conquer the Indians. Thus the drive of the British settlers in Australia and New Zealand to take over the land from the aborigines. Thus the American drive to get to the moon before anybody else did. The adrenaline of power and possession has motivated mankind from the earliest.

Nineteenth-century Americans changed their attitude about nature from hard-headed rationalism to sentimentalism. Mountains became objects of veneration, glens and meadows became "friends" and lovers. Natives became romanticized into noble savages. Such writers as novelist James Fenimore Cooper created characters like Natty Bumppo who "read" nature though they were unlettered in conventional books. Fifty years later Ralph Waldo Emerson and Henry David Thoreau, to name only two of hundreds, read nature through the lenses of their own desires.

Such romantic love for nature was a sentimental effort to understand and read it. The American Renaissance figures gave way to writers and observers who actually knew the landscape and read it in order to survive. Thus we had the actual pioneers—Daniel Boone, for example, and the author of pioneer and frontier stores, James Fenimore Cooper—the literary people who followed them—Hamlin Garland and Willa Cather, for instance—and the naturalists who rounded out the view of nature— Theodore Dreiser and Frank Norris, who found, in the latter's terms, that scientific naturalism drives everything into despair and defeat, and nature is indifferent to man's needs and desires. The Romantics had seen nature as smiling and sympathetic. The naturalists saw her as indifferent at best and hostile at worst.

Though all these efforts were personalized attitudes about nature and mankind and have been generally proven naïve and innocent, they were at least man's efforts to "read" nature, to understand the language of the physical world in order to adjust to it. It was a man-centered and man-mediated universe, but it was also man-curious and man-willing, wanting to learn the physical environment. After a slow and belated start, humankind was trying to open the book on the vocabulary of language and nature, at least in the babbling, nursery stage of understanding.

In the last couple of decades of the 20th century the school of nature has undergone remarkable changes in curriculum and students, has opened up new dimensions, new vocabularies, new languages and new urgencies on numerous subjects:

Computers have created a world of communications and their own language;

Mathematics has created international communications which demands its own numiacy;

Ecology has made us aware of man's interrelationship with the physical world. There is now a flurry of activity to save from total destruction the rain-forests in Africa, Central and South America which are being ravaged by the staggering amount of 100 square acres every minute of every day, with the resulting dire consequences to man's atmosphere. There is a desperate rush to prevent extinction of our animal life; the drive began with the exotic species and now has spread to include virtually all.

Awareness of animal feelings and rights has brought new attitudes about the treatment of other species by man; and concern with animals has demonstrated that they have languages which they use to communicate to one another and that we must learn those languages if we are to benefit from what animals know.

New attitudes toward buildings and housing have given us new concepts of space and of the physical world.

Pollution has taken on a new language and a new urgency; after the nuclear explosion at Chernobyl and the melt-down at Three Mile Island and the accumulation of atomic wastes throughout the U.S., we recognize that the voice of pollution is nothing less than the language of survival.

Tourism, recreation, museums, air travel and many others—all have opened new obligations. Tourism has been developed to the art of conservation of natural resources and a thrust toward cleaning up the environment.

This horizontal and vertical in-depth understanding of the interrelationship of all things in nature has clothed the Great Chain of Being concept in a basic humanism or understanding of life that hitherto has been lacking. Scholarly and popular media are filled with studies of all kinds of living organisms from corals to whales and reveals the obligations that the human being—by self-acclamation the most intelligent and responsible of all animals—owes to the whole world. "Perceiving nature as a rich and varied collection of living things linked one to another and to their substrata or inorganic environments," says cultural geographer Robin Daughty, "rejects the notion of nature as merely a stage or backdrop for human initiative and enterprise."

To be more accurate, Daughty should have insisted that all forms of life must be perceived as organic and social continuums. To get at the complexity of life we are now studying the social organizations in all kinds of animal communities—the predators as well as the prey: lions, deer, coyotes, gorillas, wolves, whales, dolphins, bees, ants, termites— as well as primitive people, in order to see what we can and must learn from them in order to copy or reject certain aspects so that human society can possibly benefit. The models in these other societies might prove beneficial to our own. But to get the most out of them we have a lot of learning, or relearning, to accomplish.

One of the curses laid upon mankind at his expulsion from Eden, according to the Biblical historian Josephus, was loss of ability to communicate with animals. Apparently before the Fall, Man had a direct communication with other animals. Satan tempted Eve in the form of a talking serpent that she understood. Communication between earliest Mankind and other animals seems evident. In *The Dragons of Eden*, Carl Sagan speculates that such communication was symbolic—gestural, guttural, communication to assist in the hunt and in protection. Gradually this communication has grown less immediate, as through the ages the communication system among *homo sapiens* has become more and more sophisticated, abstract and mathematical, and consequentially more distant from other animals (104).

Some people until recently have looked upon the ability to communicate among themselves as one characteristic which demonstrates man's superiority over other animals. But such an attitude merely reveals mankind's arrogance and unwillingness to learn new means of communication. A mild example of this is our reluctance to learn the languages of people other than ourselves. But the problems of resisting new languages is more profound—and more difficult to remedy. Sagan speculates that our unwillingness derives from a fear of branching out to the complete world—a fear that holds among us all—and regrettably academics—today: "Our difficulties in understanding or communicating with other animals may arise from our reluctance to grasp unfamiliar ways of dealing with the world," he says. Some of the means of communication among most animals are, indeed, very different from our own. For example, Sagan suggests that dolphins and whales communicate with one another by a rich and elaborate set of clicks, which so far have proved too elaborate for man to understand. One explanation is that "a dolphin does not 'say' a single word for shark," Sagan thinks, "but rather transmits a set of clicks corresponding to the audio reflection spectrum it would obtain on irradiating a shark with sound waves in the dolphin's sonar mode" (Sagan 113-114).

The skill of communication among some animal species is nothing short of astonishing. Mothers and offspring of all species, of course, must learn to communicate in order for the offspring to live. But some other degrees of finesse in communication strain credibility. Each year a million penguins crowd the sandy shores of Patagonia for their nesting. At first the males come ashore and reestablish their nests. A month later the females swim in. Males and females have mated for life. Not having seen their males for over six months, the females must locate them. Each does that by listening to the individual call of her mate among the cacophony of half a million calling males. How this is done is still a mystery, but apparently all females find their lifetime mates each year.

Such systems of communication are so alien to the experience of Mankind that there is no wonder it creates anxiety and apprehension. At least we recognize that there is much in the way of communication in the animal world that we do not know.

But the borders of fear are gradually being eroded as we realize that mankind must learn to talk with the animals and the physical surroundings again, as Rex Harrison as Dr. Doolittle urges in the play by the same name by Hugh Lofting. We are slowly realizing that we have been talking to animals, and they to us, for thousands of years. Dogs, long ago separated from wolves by training, talk to us and we to them, and they to sheep, as they tend the flocks and as they hunt birds and bark them up or "point" them out to us. Some animals have sophisticated languages. Whales and monkeys, for example, have regional dialects which do not communicate to groups outside their regions and dialects. The sophisticated intricacies of communication among all animals have yet to be understood. But they obviously are more complex than we know at this time.

One of the more interesting was aired on NBC Evening News, Dec. 23, 1990, when Garrick Utley ran a short tape on an art exhibit and brisk sale of works being held at the Phoenix, Arizona, zoo. These paintings which sold $40,000 worth had been painted by an artist named simply Ruby. Ruby, the adulating public was surprised to learn, is an elephant at the Phoenix Zoo, which when given paint brushes with different colored paints on them touches the canvas apparently with design. Though all the canvases might be classified as, Utley remarked, "Jumbo Impressionism," all differ one from another. Ruby, it seems, prefers bright colors for her painting.

Ruby behind her easel. Phoenix Zoo Photo by Dick George. Used by Permission.

Could we conclude from this chance encounter with elephant art—perhaps the first of more to come—that this particular animal has something she wants to say, some message she wants to communicate to people through her art, or was she painting under the assumption that her works would be exhibited at an elephant art gallery? Perhaps we have never given other elephants the opportunity to express themselves in art and there is a new world of art waiting for its chance to be seen. Ruby seems to be doing in one medium what other animals seem to want to do in other media. It is interesting that the people in charge of Ruby, assuming that they know the artist's wishes, have dedicated the income from the art works to saving the elephant in Africa.

Some animals in the wild have developed sophisticated and advanced forms of communication. Researchers among primates—Jane Goodall, for example among chimpanzees—have discovered the complexity of language among man's cousin-animals and their ability, like ours, to learn other languages. Beatrice and Robert Gardener, psychologists at the University of Nevada, and others, for example, have demonstrated that chimpanzees they have worked with have developed working vocabularies in English of 100 to 200 words. Like human beings the chimpanzees are inventive of neologisms. One chimpanzee named Washoe, for example, seeing a duck for the first time signaled the word "waterbird." Lana, another subject-chimpanzee, seeing an orange for the first time but knowing only an apple, gestured "orange apple," and Lucy, another chimpanzee being taught English, after tasting a watermelon for the first time called it "candy drink" or "drink fruit" (Sagan 117).

After reporting dozens of cases where animals have shown remarkable intelligence, considering our inability to recognize it, Sagan half whimsically questions: "How smart does a chimpanzee have to be before killing him constitutes murder? What further properties must he show before religious missionaries must consider him worthy of attempts at conversion" (127)? Those days may not yet be impending, but two or three things are becoming more and more clear. One is that the story in the Bible of Adam's naming all the animals in his world and God's command to him to go out and establish dominance over all the animals in the physical world were signs of man's insecurity even then. In naming the animals, Adam gave mankind nominal and therefore real control of the animals. The second obvious conclusion is, that man's development of zoos and animal cages, which began in England in the 17th century was an effort to demonstrate to animals and to the worried public that Mankind was in control of all.

Though pictures of wildlife drawn or painted on walls of caves and other stone faces go back thousands of years, wildlife art, that is the picturing of wildlife safely "caught" on canvas, is not old. The first exhibited in France was apparently *Tiger Devouring Gavial* (*gavial*, a kind of crocodile), by Antonine-Louis Barye, was exhibited in the Paris Salon exhibition of 1831. At the time animals were looked upon as competing with mankind for survival and preeminence and therefore viewed as powerful antagonists, consequently were all the more appreciated when depowered by the medium in which they were presented. That is, transformed from life to canvas animals were much more under man's control.

The third point that is becoming clear about man's relationship with animals is that the British development of the concept of a Great Chain of Being, in which all elements of reality from the lowest—rocks— to the highest—God—was a rationalistic way to put and keep animals underfoot and subordinate. Only lately have we legitimized the concept of animals' rights. Now we assign them, in familiar terms in our own species, "life, liberty and the pursuit of happiness," and have made dramatic changes in the way we treat animals.

But this attitude is not accepted as genuine among all artists and critics. Some, at least, look upon Man's current respect for animals and animals' rights as a sentimental fad and transitory. "I think there are fads in emotions," says a Yale University researcher and professional animal trainer, "and right now the ideologically sound emotions to have toward animals is guilt," and therefore the need to compensate for past transgressions against them. Perhaps she is right, for the feeling of guilt, though transitory, is one of the most powerful motivators in the human psyche. So, powerful positive results may come from this guilt-drive. Paul Soderberg's feeling in *Art-Talk* that "The Environmentalism movement is just that, a movement, a fad" (17), is, the world must hope, dead wrong. Viewing concern with the fragile environment as a fad is like seeing Russian roulette as a mere game when four of the chambers of the revolver are loaded with live ammunition.

After the oilspill of the *Exxon Valdez* in Prince William Sound, sculptor Kent Ullberg sculpted a dying eagle, *Requiem for Prince William Sound*, and proposed it as an icon to be viewed by every skipper before boarding his ship for the outward voyage. The proposal was not greeted enthusiastically, and sculptor and sculpture-critics bemoaned the fact that the public passes up sculpture for the more immediately communicating media of television and newspapers. Naturally. There should be no surprise there. Television and newspapers are media of communication in which the public are more fluent than in sculpture. There is no criticism there. The need is for people to become more fluent in sculpture. But the petty sour-grapes attitude exhibited by Ullberg and his associates is not the way to promote and develop such literacy. Such pique demonstrates all too clearly that Ullberg does not want to buy into the world but wants instead for the universe to buy into his world.

One wonders how much longer such a shortsighted view will be held among some people.

Despite such glitches as that of Kent Ullberg, apparently *homo sapiens* are finally reaching a level of maturity which allows all of earth's creatures—and the earth itself—to assert rights equal to our own, and to join the extended family of man in the brotherhood of existence.

Perceiving the flora and fauna of nature as the ultimate extended family unit is fundamental to an understanding of the total environment. The necessary beginning of this realization is understanding the Babel of languages "spoken" in this large and varied extended family and household.

The buzz word in media studies these days is *mediated*. Phenomena and actions are transmitted and changed through the media. Just as things are communicated through the media, people are themselves mediated back to the media. People are mutated through the media and people mutate the media. If a television program is not liked—does not have the desired mediating effect—it changes or goes off the air. If a particular fashion in clothing does not catch on, it is discontinued. An unpopular style of architecture—generally after a long and costly period of unpopularity—finally is fazed out and replaced by another. Culture is in a constant state of mediation and counter-mediation, of cause and effect, of creation and recreation.

These new fields of inquiry have developed new linguistic vocabularies, to be sure, but they have done more than that. They have established new languages—new worlds, as it were—in which people spend most of their working time, and nobody knows how much of their non-working and sleep time. Such worlds demand new literacy in their languages.

Literacy is an umbrella term which covers all forms of communication. *Literacy* means communication—the ability to receive and also to send messages. Thus literacy in the English language means not only to be able to read but also to write. The ability to "read" another "language," say television, is therefore the ability to understand what television is saying and also to "speak," that is to be conversant in television. Both abilities assume the ability to "understand," that is to know what is happening and why.

There are, of course, dozens of fields in human experience which demand communication and literacy. The most obvious are in those media which communicate; signs and symbols, icons, print, electronic, the various media of human experience.

But we are coming more and more to recognize that all phenomena have the language to and do in fact communicate by "speaking" in their own language. In an inanimate way, for example, many geographers, according to cultural geographer Sona Karentz Andrews, "consider maps as the language of geography" (quoted in Zonn 12) . She should have said that maps are the vocabulary, but language is more than vocabulary. On the Sun Bowl football broadcast Jan. 1, 1991, the El Paso Chamber of Commerce commercial urged people to go out at daybreak and "talk with the tree." Another commercial, sponsored by the Natural Gas Industry on TV in 1991 urged people to "Listen to the trees. They're trying to tell us something about pollution." Thus we are coming more and more to realize that animals speak not only to us but also to themselves. Inanimate objects also talk. Man-made structures—buildings, dams, highways, automobiles, wrestling matches, games, all phenomena—communicate with us who look at them and try to "read" their effects. The assumptions of some people have led us a long way toward this goal. One book is named, *How to Speak Furniture with an Antique American Accent*, by James B. Siegel. A furniture company advertises, "One chair says it all."

Collectively artifacts and art encode a whole civilization. Talking about art as the record of history, William H. Truettner remarked: "To read these images to westward expansion closely is to discover essential truths about the cultural basis of national identity."

Art historian Alan Gowans insists that each and every individual work of art—or artifact—has its own messages, its own communication content. Each if properly understood can tell us the story of the culture in which it was created and used. Thus, each item contains a book— or library—of information encoded in its language. Our task is to understand the language, and to discover the Rosetta Stone that will provide translations of the many languages being used around us by all forms of life and results of that life.

Historically, understanding of the common written language was called *literacy*. But literacy is an old-fashioned anachronistic word which should give way to more useful terms. *Mediacy* is now liked by people in the various media. Though useful, this word has its limitations, since *mediacy* is most applicable to the specific electronic media. Perhaps *fluency* is the more comprehensive and appropriate term. It means skill in handling a language and therefore is applicable to any form of communication, not just the media- or print-produced.

Such a changed definition of the term releases the old-fashioned concept, and the people who use it, from many of the blind and unconscious restrictions and exclusions which have controlled their thinking in former years. In the past literacy has had an elite class consciousness used as a form of exclusion. Literate people who wanted to protect their positions in society could claim that any degree of fluency in whatever language still did not measure up to the person's degree of "literacy." To speak English and French, for example, might or might not be sufficient. The inclusion of Latin might or might not be enough.

We all remember how 17th century playwright Ben Jonson tried to prove the superior playwright William Shakespeare his inferior by declaring that Shakespeare had "little Latin and less Greek." Had Jonson known Hebrew or some other exotic classical language, that language would undoubtedly have been necessary for literacy. The stuff of one's being dictates the outlines of literacy in others.

Thus "inferior" people, especially those who use any conventional language with a slightly different accent from one's own, could be called illiterate. *Illiterate* equaled *dumb, ignorant, socially unacceptable, undesirable.* Now, of course, that definition of literacy is being changed, sometimes explosively in armed uprisings by people who no longer tolerate being excluded, sometimes by the more peaceful erosion of usage and by the vote of democracy. But people will not be arbitrarily excluded from the treasures of fluency.

The test of literacy has always served as a power base. For centuries people have feared the negative result of writing, or of any other new means of communicating. Sagan recounts the myth of Throth, the Egyptian equivalent of the Greek Prometheus, as recounted by Plato in *Phaedrus*. In ancient Egyptian the phrase that equals the written language means "The Speech of the Gods." In the myth, Throth, who invented writing, is rebuked by Thamus, a god-king, who says:

> This discovery of yours will create forgetfulness in the learners' souls, because they will not use their memories; they will trust to the eternal written characters and not remember of themselves. The specific which you have discovered is an aid not to memory, but to reminiscence, and you give your disciples not truth, but only the semblance of truth; they will be hearers of many things and will have learned nothing; they will appear to be omniscient and will generally know nothing; they will [have the] show of wisdom without its reality. (233-4)

At a much later date anthropologist Claude Levi-Strauss correctly had grounds for feeling that writing was invented for the exploitation of man by man. Of course it has been used as a repressive device. The art of writing can be a put-down and keep-out exercised by the cognoscenti, to whom it provides the mechanism for a priesthood to impose itself on a public which either does not know the secret or can be intimidated by its use. Literacy, that is, in an established medium. It is always used against any new medium. It was levied against photography, and especially against cheap everyman cameras, against television, and is now being inveighed against computers. Self-defined literacy has always allowed certain people to control the past and the present through withholding or disclosing, and interpreting information. The tradition is carried on now through the use of such class-laden, snobbish terms as *literacy, taste, class, quality* (which has nothing to do with the integrity of an item), all of which being personal, artificial terms which operate on a sliding scale and change as needed, are unquestionable and absolute.

A society that is kept "illiterate" in name or reality is one for which the power brokers can manipulate the past as well as the present. But a basic tenet of democracy is equal opportunity of fluency for all, and this fluency once having been acquired has wrested control of the distortion of history and of the present from those powerful literates who have maintained watch over it.

This new kind of literacy is fluency in communication. Fluency in communication creates a more level playing field for all people to play on—women, ethnics, rich, poor, homosexuals, pro-abortionists, pro-lifers, blacks, etc. It generates a new respect for all aspects of life, for various kinds of people, for the environment, for animals, for the act of living. But in order to develop this new respect for the physical environment and in living itself, one needs to be literate in several media. This *intermediacy* or *crossmediacy* creates new awareness of the interrelatedness of communication among the various phenomena of life. As such, it folds various literacies back on themselves, and thus enriches each one individually and all collectively. As such, it is a healthy counterforce in society today against the tendency to separate and autonomize various aspects of life and culture.

Politically and socially, various aspects of society—as well as countries and political units—are demanding autonomy and self-control. These developing "third world" segments are powerfully on the move to establish their own dignity and value. Such separateness often leads to suspicions of others and hostility towards them. One possible move to counter these suspicions is to raise the power and respect for fluency in communications in all media.

These moves toward separateness come at the time when people in the elite and popular humanities are pleading for greater understanding of, and therefore the greater power of, the humanities. The humanities, many people believe, can provide bridges over the various chasms separating the many thrusts in literacy. More is required than the humanities in the conventional sense of the term. But this, again, is mainly a matter of definition. Historically the humanities have been felt to be those aspects of society which tend to bring out the elite biases in us, as British poet-essayist Matthew Arnold said in the nineteenth century. Nowadays we recognize that such exclusive feeling about the humanities is not only outdated but in fact is hostile to the proper development of the elements in life it names and professes to promote. Such a definition excludes most of society and keeps in power those who have established ascendency. Such snobbishness no longer washes. It is time that we all realize that the humanities depend not only on attitude, if at all, but mainly on communication. Any commentator on the humanities must be someone who is fluent in the various media of communication that involve aspects of the humanities and can communicate an understanding of them. So in effect, the humanities tend to equal fluency, which equals literacy.

One of the new thrusts in the humanities is in cultural geography, which is not a new subject at all but is increasingly reasserting its importance as an area which, because of its concern with people on the land (as well as in the city), deals with important and discreet aspects of culture. Specialists and generalists are establishing new roles in the discipline. For example, the importance of the geographical approach in studying the world situation was reasserted by one of the leading cultural geographers, Wilber Zelinsky, when he insisted that "Nationalism is the reigning passion of our times," and that regardless of the importance of political economic phenomena a social-psychological approach (cultural geographic) is profitable for studying this nationalism.

Another study, *Seeking New Horizons*, outlines the deteriorated state of American education as cited by the National Commission on Education:

Our nation is at risk. The educational foundations of our society are presently being eroded by a rising tide of mediocrity. If an unfriendly foreign power had attempted to impose on America the mediocre educational performance that exists today, we might well have viewed it as an act of war. We have, in effect, begun committing an act of unthinking, unilateral educational disarmament. (Castner 38)

In less militaristic terms, we might agree with the Commission that through our actions, if not our will, we are imposing upon ourselves an educational system that is starving and killing our geographical literacy. The general complaint is that our schools build from top down rather than from the bottom up. They teach advanced geography before they establish geographical literacy. The schools teach maps and mapping, parallels, meridians, compass reading before they establish a vocabulary in which to teach these concepts.

Other approaches begin with the assumption that a new language is being created and used. In *Reading Landscape: Country-City-Capitol*, the editor, Simon Pugh, and the authors of the individual essays of the collection work under the belief that "Landscape in recent years...has stood as a surrogate for more political notions of nationhood." The point, unstated by the editor and authors, is that this notion of nationhood must be read into the landscape, countryscape, cityscape and capitolscape, and out of it.

Smaller areas of landscape speak to portions of our existence more modest than nationhood. In *The Look of the Land*, John Fraser Hart suggests, "perhaps nothing tells so much about the values a man holds as the kind of house in which he chooses to live" (153). Thus, as Pierce Lewis states, "If a people changes its collective mind about its houses, there is a good chance it has changed its mind about many other things as well" because housing is one of the many bits of our conspicuous consumption and through it, as Hart says, the dweller "is able to demonstrate his artistry, advertise his beliefs, and flaunt his wealth." The dweller becomes a part of his dwelling; in every sense of the term we are what we live in. Our surroundings become a language all their own, in which we must become fluent. Without fluency in these media nothing can be fully learned.

With fluency, on the other hand, much can be understood. But the term *media* needs to be made more expansive and inclusive. "The working definition of 'medium' is far more comprehensive and eclectic than that usually given for 'mass media'," quite properly says cultural geographer Leo Zonn. "Instead," he continues, "the term should encompass any mechanism that has the capacity to convey information—in this case, information about 'place'."

The language of landscape—place—in western civilization goes back in literature at least to Theocritus, Pliny, Columella and Virgil. In physical events it reaches back to other people who may have properly or improperly read it and benefitted or suffered from the reading: the Ptolemies in their world of sand and river, Hannibal's elephants crossing the Alps in the Second Punic War, the Romans in Britain, the Chinese and their Great Wall, the Mayans and their civilization built in the climatic wrong part of the world (fl. 600-9000), down to the Americans in the Dust Bowl of the 1930s, the space probes of the 1980s and 1990s and the threats to our environment—like Three Mile Island, Chernobyl, destruction of the rain forests, etc.—during the 1990s.

In paintings of countryside, obviously, there are interpretations and messages. Thus English artist J.M.W. Turner (1775-1851) in his landscapes spoke various languages to people with different political stances. In other times pictures of the British Lake District, the American Hudson Valley and the Great West spoke in different voices one from the other.

Perhaps one of the strongest affirmations of the language of landscape is the present-day inclination of British cultural geographers to give it a Marxist reading and interpretation. One of the earliest and firmest advocates of such readings was the late Raymond Williams, who felt, with some justification, that the countryside was a political microcosm which the British elite used as a reflection of and model for colonialism and imperialism.

Such reading of the rural landscape no doubt makes a worthwhile point. But it can be perverted into absurdity, especially if portions of the whole communication and its inhabitants are overlooked or ignored.

Perhaps, instead, our understanding of the language of nature is increasing at a rate that most people find difficult to keep up with. For example, the comments and concepts by Theodore Adorno, quoted and endorsed by Pugh, in the book cited above are typically inadequate:

> The song of birds is judged beautiful by nearly everybody. No sensitive person of European background, for example, fails to be moved by the song of a robin after a shower of rain. All the same, there is something frightening lurking in the song of birds, which is not really a song but merely a response to natural necessity . . . The ambivalence of natural beauty can be traced back to the ambivalence of myth.

The naiveté or incomplete knowledge about nature revealed in this comment demonstrates the danger in half-literacy or half-illiteracy in understanding the communication of nature. The song of birds, like the talk of other animals, is the language they use to communicate with one another, not just "a response to natural necessity." Only an emotional child would feel that a robin sings only for his human audience and that always for robins the song is meant to be more esthetic that utilitarian. To feel that is to assume that the beautiful spots on the leopard skin are grown only for the pleasure created by it on the back of the lady who steals the fur from the animal for her own coat, or that God spotted the leopard only for woman's delight.

Such nonsense is, of course, hoary with age and tradition. Eighteenth-century British philosophers were arrogant enough to congratulate God on His thoughtfulness and foresight in placing mankind's nose in its present position so that it would be where needed when he developed eye glasses. Later philosophers have used as evidence of God's wisdom and kindly intentions toward man His creation of an air which is heavy enough to support airplanes; and in perhaps the ultimate extreme His creation of deserts throughout the world so that thoughtful and introspective people could have places of retreat for their contemplations of the world! That was indeed a heavy price to pay for contemplation. Perhaps the so-called "retreat" so common today among academics as places to escape to in order to get away from it all, are not unreasonable affordable substitutes for the desert. This is obviously a myth of some strength, and according to perceptive American novelist Herman Melville in *Moby Dick* the power of myth is "appalling," and we know that the power of self-delusion is even more staggering. In the eyes of mankind God's wisdom has no bounds! It suffuses present-day cultures. Surely we have made it comprehend all human sillinesses.

These nonsensical readings of nature make all the more compelling the need for people to become literate in the languages of life surrounding us so they can read for themselves. Illiteracy leads to abuse of ourselves and of nature, even possible destruction of mankind and the earth.

We are frustrated and frightened on every front by our inability to read all of the pressing messages. The feeling is that the near-disastrous melt-down at Three Mile Island resulted from the engineer in charge's inability to read and understand all the gauges lighting up before his eyes. Designers who create the electric monsters apparently never intend to use them themselves or for other people to use them. Air Force fighters have so many lights and gauges engaging the pilot's eyes that he cannot possibly learn to fly the plane fully. Repair people who are experts in the latest computer hardware and software spend most of their time trying to have on-the-job training and fail. That is why the manufacturers provide 800 telephone numbers for people who own and repair. Most of the specialist repair people are constantly on the phone to the 800 number. And your average Joe owner when he or she dials the number gets so much jargon that he or she is only further bewildered. "The gap between the people designing technology and those who buy it just keeps getting bigger and bigger," says David Kelley, a product designer who ought to know, as he works developing his material in Palo Alto, California.

Literacy on the part of the people who write the instructions would also help. *Newsweek* quotes one of the more bizarre examples of instructions which comes from a Sharp Electronics' manual for a home fax machine: "The Remote Transfer Passcode can be used in Extension Telephone Function. To transfer a fax call from an extension phone to the UX-170 for reception. This function, the call is transferred to the UX-170 by pressing the passcode number and * key at the extension telephone. The passcode is a one-digit number, selected from 0 to 9. To change the Passcode, redo the entry operation. To check the Passcode, print-out and refer to the Program List (see p. 76). If an incorrect number is entered during the procedure, press the * key and repeat entire procedure."

Admittedly, companies are trying to have these instructions in English translated into real English, but with the various lunges forward in creation and modification occurring every day, there is probably no hope that instructions will ever keep up with creations.

Literacy, on the other hand, leads to understanding, respect for and harmony with mankind and the earth—if, that is, literacy is properly understood. To be most helpful, it needs to be rethought and deepened as a concept. We can do that perhaps best if we go back to one of the meanings of the term literacy—being well-versed, knowledgeable, and learned, not merely able to read and write. This means being fluent in the use of a "language," that is any medium of communication, not just print literature, and surely not just elite print literature.

This book is a tentative exploration—a McLuhanesque probing, if you will—into reexamination of the tenets of literacy with some suggestions about recasting those tenets and definitions. In many ways it may be a Marconi-radio-like signal in the invention of new awareness of the various fields of communication. What is further needed is more realization of the ramifications of the new concept of literacy and incorporation of that concept—with its implications—into society. The old concept of literacy as fluency in print media locks more people out of literacy than admits them in. With the continued rise in media of communication other than print, using print as the only medium of literacy will continue to do more harm than good as the disparity between print and other media of communication broadens.

The new reading of *literacy* as *fluency* in other media, however, will open up the concept and admit more media not yet developed. It will demonstrate further the already perfectly-clear but sometimes unadmitted fact that fluency in one medium stimulates fluency in others. Fluency encourages curiosity, interest and carry-over fluency. If one knows the conventional language French, say, in addition to English, it is easier to learn Spanish, or some other language. If one understands the language of architecture, to cite another example, it is easier to learn the language of special arrangement of objects and people. If one is fluent in house-customs, it is easier to come to learn body rituals. And so on.

The more languages one knows—a second, third or tenth—the easier it is to become fluent in others. Thousands of examples abound around us in every aspect of life. Always, to be sure, prominent in this stimulation of fluency stands the written word, the print language, which because of its prominence in the past continues to influence and to benefit from the many tongues of literacy. Such a confluence of tongues can create a tower of learning reaching toward the sky before the languages are made confusing and the tower becomes a Babel of more dangerous non-communication. If the problem is approached now, possibly the many tongues can be made understandable by all.

Among all these tongues, all of culture—throughout the world—becomes the beneficiary. But only if the concept is recognized by all levels of society—adults, teachers and students—so that the many tongues are accepted with dignity by all. It will not do having students accept the concept while their elders, the teachers and other members of adult society, resist it. Nor with only students and teachers accepting it. There is too wide a schism between educators and society now. Tax-payers, teachers and students must dignify the various media of communication and make them generally acceptable if they are to work anywhere near their potential, and we are to benefit from that potential.

"Only that which is connected to life will be remembered for life," astutely observes Rustum Roy, professor at Pennsylvania State University and member of the National Academy of Engineering (NAE). Many Humanities educators are even in less contact with reality. Roy argues that scientists, believing in their natural right to state-supported funds are "welfare queens in white coats." If they are, then the average Humanities academic is a hospital attendant keeping many brain-dead ideas of the past alive on life-supporting machines known as tradition. On many it is time to pull the plug; they've been receiving fruitless homage for too long.

With the plug pulled, present-day people might manage to achieve the potential inherent in fluency in communication skills. Toward that end the new concept of literacy just might be the difference between world survival and extinction. It merits the chance to succeed.

Chapter Two

Medicine for Illiteracy

America, we are told constantly, is half-illiterate, a nation lunging toward total illiteracy, with all the known and imagined disasters accompanying such a condition. The situation pushes alarm buttons everywhere. But are they the right buttons with the proper understanding behind the pushing? In our desperate plight we need to examine any suggestions of possible useful means of achieving our goals. Being literate—that is, being fluent in communication—is clearly imperative for the individual and for our whole culture—and the world. The need is indeed pressing: "We are absolutely running out of time," says Ernest Boyer, President of the Carnegie Foundation for the Advancement of Teaching, in a special issue of *Newsweek* devoted exclusively to education. He is voicing a national consensus. "I am convinced that we have perhaps a decade—and I may be optimistic—to make school improvement the universal experience, and to have some confidence in the public mind that the system is working," he warns.

Although all Americans concerned with a problem and trying to energize the populace to action generally threaten doomsday and the on-rush of Armageddon, Boyer clearly recognizes the urgency of the need for literacy. Most of us agree with him. But the question arises whether he is trying to spark the schools to action using outdated stimuli before we realize what the fundamental need is and what adjustments must be made for the radical cure that is required in our day.

If Boyer is merely calling for greater efficiency in the literacy skills of yesteryear, he is inadvertently doing a great disservice to the accomplishments he hopes to achieve. In the light of our admitted failure in trying to reachieve the goals of literacy as they used to be identified, Boyer and all of us need to reexamine the whole concept and our means of achieving it. Times change, the dynamics of culture change. Media of communication change and degrees of needed fluency change, rising drastically in some instances, becoming less stringent in others. People must change also, and regularly reexamine the ways of life they are accustomed to and perhaps hold dear. Not to reexamine tenets is to cut off growth and the ability to cope with the present-day world.

Statistics on the rising tide in functional conventional illiteracy in the United States are staggering. Some reports indicate 13% of Americans are not literate. Other figures state more precise numbers: 20-27 million Americans are "seriously illiterate," some 40 million are "marginally illiterate" and 4 million adults are studying to learn to read and write. On a personal level, illiteracy is crushing. Television commercials aired daily attest to the inconvenience, stunting of career and humiliation of illiteracy. Young people as well as older persons are intimidated by their illiteracy and the fact that the literate condescend to them. Sometimes the reaction is violent. Young people fight and kill when insulted about their illiteracy and the blind alleys it leads them into. British crime-writer Ruth Rendell centered one of her novels, *A Judgement in Stone* (1978), on a housekeeper who was illiterate and flashed out and murdered her employers because when they went to work every morning they kept leaving her notes that she could not read. There are thousands of examples daily from America's ghettos, as frustrated individuals lash out in dozens of ways against a system that keeps them illiterate and then punishes them for their illiteracy. Society, as well as the individual, is deeply and seriously wounded by the illiteracy of its citizenry. Thomas Jefferson quite properly felt that a country cannot have democracy if its citizens are not literate. On a much larger scale, as is dramatically demonstrated to us daily, our world cannot survive with a population of 5-10 billion, most of whom are illiterate. It seems clear that we all must achieve some kind of literacy or the human race—and perhaps planet Earth—will perish.

In a world of such mischief created by illiteracy in conventional terms, it is time for educators on all levels to turn to radical cures for this disease and its fellow-horsemen of a potential apocalypse, school drop-outs, indifference to learning and under-learning, if they can be found. Such a radical cure is available in the educational value to be found in the concept of using the many and varied tongues of our popular culture, instead of elite or institutionalized culture, as the setting for describing and for promoting a literacy that is in keeping with the actual world around us.

Popular culture is generally defined to mean all aspects of the world we inhabit: the way of life we inherit, practice and pass on to our descendants; what we do while we are awake, the dreams we dream while asleep. It is the everyday world around us: the mass media, entertainments, diversions, heroes, icons, rituals, psychology, religion—our total life picture. Although it generally is, it need not necessarily be disseminated by the mass media.

Most important, the popular culture of a country is the voice of the people—their likes and dislikes, the lifeblood of daily existence, their way of life. In America, presumably, popular culture is the voice of democracy—what makes the country what it is. The culture may be manipulated in our day by the media barons—who may react too slowly to the voice of democracy (voiced by the Nielsen ratings)—or by society which may demand too much for the people who create their culture for them. Like it or not, every American owes it to himself and his society to make a great effort, through formal or informal study, to understand the culture around him or her. Often the learner will discover, if he can rid himself or herself of blind training and educated prejudice, that most of the popular culture is to be appreciated—and all must be understood.

So our popular culture—and the drive to understand it—can be used as a tool to assist us in education. It can be utilized in many ways to overcome illiteracy, to keep people in school and to energize our educational system and enrich the materials we teach.

As a necessary preamble it can be utilized to counter the hocus-pocus of academia that presents literacy—and education in general—as a magic that one can acquire only after a long and arduous investment of time and labor. This pretentiousness quite understandably puts many people off. The 1987 celebration the Bicentennial of the U.S. Constitution was an excellent case in point. In one effort, the Commission on the Bicentennial Educational Grant Program had solicited grant applications for "the development of instructional materials on the Constitution and Bill of Rights" for use in elementary and secondary schools because there is "a lack of citizen knowledge about the Constitution and American history." To correct this lack of knowledge, the Commission proposed funding institutes where thirty or more social science teachers would be taught by "two Constitutional scholars" giving a series of lectures and being aided by two "master teachers." Note the language: "two Constitutional scholars" and two "master teachers." Now everybody knows that words and labels are cheap and meaningless. But a great deal of harm can be done when a government agency is so pretentious that it sets about teaching citizens—not to mention public school teachers—about *our* governing document in such phony language. Paternalism does indeed die hard. Apparently the educators in Washington still do not want the people in this country to understand the Constitution on their own. It must be spoon-fed through bureaucracies by Constitutional scholars and Constitutional historians and bureaucrats. Perhaps the bureaucracy thought it might be threatening to have people outside the Beltway understand the Constitution rationally in the light of political events and the language of 1987. Surely the Constitution, like education in general, could profit by a little less pretentiousness, that is in being understood in its popular culture setting, that is the world in which it works.

Popular culture is the everyday lifeblood of the experiences and thinking of all of us; the daily, vernacular, common cultural environment around us all, the culture we inherit from our forebears, use throughout our lives and then pass on to our descendants. Popular culture is the television we watch, the movies we see, the fast food—or slow food— we eat, the clothes we wear, the music we sing and hear. It is the whole society we live in, that which may or may not be distributed by the mass media. It is virtually our whole world.

Though popular culture is to many people the monster that has caused the problems of functional illiteracy and lack of interest in solid education in the first place, it is really—viewed disinterestedly—merely an environment, a force, a background and foreground and a means of communication. It can and should be used as a key to open the possibilities of proficiency in the use of conventional language, especially by those whose use of the language of the media—the main disseminating force of popular culture—is very high but whose utilization of the printed word is generally weak and undeveloped.

The principle I am proposing is that pragmatically one begins with the known and proceeds to the unknown, that one uses what he/she already knows in order to learn something unknown. I propose that educators, recognizing this principle of moving from the known to the unknown, use it in getting people of all degrees of proficiency and unproficiency in the printed word to expand their capabilities.

That the popular culture around us is known, that it occupies most of the time of nearly all of us and that, therefore, properly channelled, it can be the single most powerful force to encourage and drive people toward a goal seems to go without saying. The sticking point will be in getting interested people on all levels of education to accept popular culture as a worthwhile and effective tool in teaching instead of as a distracting and weakening diversion, and in motivating them to act on this knowledge. In education, as elsewhere, we all need scapegoats to lay the blame on for faults we see in society and what we might secretly admit are our own failings to accomplish the jobs we would like to accomplish. If, as a wise man once said, we would make some progress in a task, we must first recognize the means by which the progress might be made and then we should persevere in our goals. I suggest that we know that experience has taught us that in the teaching business we proceed from the known to the unknown, that we use every device we can in that teaching process, that the popular culture around us is well known, and that, therefore, we should use it as educational devices in promoting literacy and love of education and learning.

Popular culture is in fact being used successfully now among pre- and early-schoolers in the highly useful *Sesame Street* and *Mr. Rogers' Neighborhood,* and in numerous computer and non-computer children's games which are teaching children vocabulary and simple sentences. It is also being used in the continued education of senior citizens. What is involved is basically the rudiments of communication. Once the basics have been established, the same principles should be used to build more vocabulary, more complicated sentences and more sophisticated communication. In other words, the popular culture can be used to establish the basics of communication and, as I shall argue later on, in the continued growth of literacy, sophisticated communication and to lure people into a love of learning and education. I am suggesting that popular culture can be a kind of complete textbook for beginners in all fields of learning. It can begin at the beginning, it can develop into all kinds of sophistication, and it can spur interest in every aspect of life and learning known to man and woman.

The beauty of using the popular culture is the motivation it provides if it is treated as a spur to learning instead of an end in itself. Sometimes the tendency is to use the popular culture as its own goal, as entertainment, but it is very easy to switch from entertainment to instruction, from passive acceptance of communication to participatory communication, if educators merely make the effort.

The lure of the popular culture to people is constantly brought to our attention. Children spend more time watching television than they do in the classroom. Add to this all the extra time they spend absorbing popular music, eating, dressing, going to the movies, talking about all these activities, and you have most of every day of most people's lives. That is a constant classroom in which education can take place virtually eighteen hours a day. The trick is to make passing the time of our lives, of entertainment, into an educational exercise. All people are in the business of being entertained. The literate and sophisticated want to be entertained, the illiterate want to be entertained. The entertainment of the literate does not differ in kind from that of the illiterate, only in degree. Both kinds of people want desperately to communicate, and the communication of both does not differ in kind, only in degree. Generally speaking, both have the same experiences of our everyday culture. They go to the same movies, watch the same television, sing the same songs, share eating and dressing experiences. It seems logical, therefore, that the literate and the illiterate use the experiences they share, the motivations they have in common, to bring both groups together in communication and shared American life.

Americans have always prided themselves on being practical people. America has always been the land of the tinkerer, the craftsman, the people who can do things, build tall buildings, develop faster means of communication. People have developed skills because they have seen those skills as being practical and useful. The much-vaunted high literacy rate of the nineteenth century in America developed because people needed to communicate, wanted to develop a sense of community, longed to rise in the social and financial world, and realized that the proper way to accomplish these goals was through the leading communication medium of the time—the printed word.

Despite what may at times seem to be the contrary, Americans still want to communicate; they yearn to develop a sense of community, and they surely lust after social and fiscal upward mobility. Communication among people is more desperately needed today than it has ever been before. In a world which seems forever fragmenting into more and more islands of interests and abilities, people yearn to find the ties that bind them together. Everybody is searching for bonding with other people.

Few people in the United States today are unable to understand and communicate in some of the various media of popular culture. Some cannot handle the printed word but can easily understand and use the various other symbols promulgated by the media. Since literacy is a reference which applies only to an old-fashioned technology, we should expand the term to include the ability to understand and use the vocabularies and structures of other media, the symbols of communication such as television, radio, movies, popular music, rapping, jiving, fashions, vernacular architecture, fast foods, body language, etc. That is, *literacy* should include *mediacy*.

One becomes proficient in the communication symbols because one needs to. So it has always been. In the folk community, people learned to communicate because it was necessary. They learned the visual media— home and community activities, farming, everyday needs—because they realized that the visual media contained elements that they needed to understand in order to get along.

It is likewise easily demonstrable to the populace at large today that they need to understand and be able to communicate the symbols used in everyday communication in media other than those in which the communication occurs. In our compartmentalized world, the media tend to create islands of in-groups which can understand and communicate in a specific language without being able to communicate outside that particular group. Such people are *mediate*—that is, can understand the language of a particular medium—but may not be able to speak in other languages and specifically not in the printed word, the one language common to them all. Thus, several "languages" may be requisite for communication.

The lure to be held out for people learning other languages of communication is entirely pragmatic, selfish and self-serving. One gets along better and more easily in life, one gets farther ahead, one becomes happier if he/she understands and uses the dominant symbols of communication, which at this time happen to be the written word.

An excellent case in point was the ability of Americans to use the dominant means of communication in the middle of the nineteenth century. Although only 60% of adult Britons were literate in 1851, over 90% of America's white population was. There were many forces driving Americans toward literacy—family cohesion, the church, schools, etc.—but the main ones were, of course, private: ambition, loneliness, hunger for knowledge and self-improvement. People did not learn to read and write primarily because they were told to. They learned because it was demonstrated to be for their personal benefit.

But for the past 50 years or so, it has not been demonstrable that the only—even the preferred—way of getting ahead in the world is through the print medium. Technology has invented new means of one's surviving—even flourishing—and has provided people with choices. They could become literate or remain illiterate in the conventional medium.

Many people have chosen illiteracy because the road to literacy in the conventional medium has seemed hard, too difficult to accomplish. The seeming difficulty of achieving literacy in the printed word is, of course, an illusion, often created by people who for one reason or another thought and taught that it was difficult, in other words promulgated by people who themselves had an entirely false notion of what literacy is and does.

Literacy is a democratic tool available to and usable by all. It develops in and is expanded by the latest tools of democracy, that is the latest gadgets of technology. The printed word was, after all, printed by technology. Now there are other technological tools developed which promote different kinds of literacy, in other words, *mediacy*. No longer is the printed word the key to survival. Television, movies, music and all the other manifestations of the culture around us are reestablishing an oral culture in which literacy in the printed word is not absolutely necessary. Naturally the clash is traumatic.

What we have is one technology pushing out another and older technology, with the practitioners of the old clinging to it because they have not worked out a way to manage and manipulate the new. Practitioners of print literacy have reason to recognize the force of the new technology. The cost in emotional and financial terms to change from print technology to electronic technology will be staggering. It is hard to imagine a world that is visually and symbolically oriented, pretty much devoid of conventional printed words, depending on a different kind of mediacy. We can hardly imagine and cope with a world that uses the standard means of communication flashed on the computer screen. How can we even compete in a world that virtually ignores the old form of literacy? The answer is, of course, that the clash is made to seem more dangerous than it really is. There are around us several worlds of communication and all are compatible. Scientists and mathematicians, musicians and medical doctors, operate in the worlds of symbols peculiar to their trade while at the same time living in the world of the printed world. Technicians work in their peculiar worlds of technology yet live among us. But the mutual incomprehensibility among the several jargons creates areas of expertise, and one that suffers most is the area of composition-literacy.

It is a peculiar fallacy that has become almost a truism that says that educators in composition-literacy are the ones who are responsible for developing that competency because effective composition equals literacy, or that literacy comes only with artful composition. So other educational departments that use literacy as a tool in their communication often opt out of the teaching of literacy because they were not formally trained and, therefore, feel themselves not competent to teach and develop composition-literacy. Having installed themselves as sovereign in the teaching of literacy, composition teachers have pretty much shamed members of other literate groups into withholding their assistance. Professors of history, sociology, technology, dance, education, etc. may not be able to write sentences which please their colleagues in the English department, but they communicate. Responsibility for keeping English as the coin of the realm is theirs also. After all, their sons and daughters need to communicate. On Spaceship Earth we all communicate or we fly off course. Now when the English department tries to enlist the assistance of their colleagues in other departments, often they are met with shrugs of the shoulders. It's somebody else's problem.

To a real degree, the English departments have caused their own trouble. Historically, teachers of composition-literacy have worked under the assumption that they are out to train people to craft well-turned, grammatically correct and graceful sentences, paragraphs and essays. This attitude was built on the assumption that in order to recognize and appreciate great literature, you must be able to write "great" compositions. In other words, you write like the "masters," imitating them in style as well as thought.

Such reasoning is flawed from the beginning. In the first place, there may be some correlation between the ability to write the well-crafted sentence and essay and the appreciation of "great" literature, but the relationship is vague and tenuous. The refutation is glaringly and embarrassingly self-evident: most literary scholars, who probe most deeply into the meanings of literature, write anything but the well-crafted and graceful sentence and paragraph. They manage to communicate, but not much more.

Second, it is a misassumption to believe that literacy equals grace and charm in expression. Literacy-communication equals only the ability to string together a group of words that convey meaning. Teachers who do not admit this definition are doing themselves, their students and literacy a great disservice.

The purpose of all media is communication. Electronic media communicate very well. Television is not a "vast wasteland," not a "boob tube," not a "glass teat." Rock music is not pornography. Other manifestations of popular culture are not evil forces trying to destroy civilization merely for the riches of unprincipled people. Like computers, they are merely means of communication, forms of "literacy" that are perhaps more important than, and surely just as natural as, the printed word, and—worse yet to some people—will ultimately replace the printed word. In other words, the mediacy of the new media of communication will eventually replace that of the old. The guardians of old-style "literacy" can go with the flow or be washed over by it.

Washed over by it they will be, provided the keepers of the conventional literacy do not realize the threat and adjust to it. There seem to be two choices: keepers of the conventional literacy can use the communication capabilities of the other media and in so doing maintain literacy for all people in the conventional printed word; or ignore and despise the more advanced electronic media and in so doing guarantee the continued erosion of conventional literacy in the present forms and eventually its disappearance or anachronistic status as a minority practice. It is conceivable that a hundred years from now—or even fifty— conventional literacy in language will have disappeared because it is no longer useful to the general public.

That is not to say, however, that users of the conventional literacy must capitulate to the new, even before it has arrived. On the contrary. But it should be to our interests to realize that the finest tool in the retention of the old form of literacy is in fact the very electronic media that might eventually replace it. That is, the best way to retain the old literacy is to use the popular media and the popular culture they disseminate as a means of teaching it.

People interested in promoting written literacy should understand that experiencing anything gives us a basis for communicating. Communication is analogical. One experiences something in one medium, becomes interested, and wishes to have similar experiences in other media. One "reads" something in television and turns to the medium of print in order to supplement his knowledge, excitement and enjoyment. Unfortunately, of course, one who is excited by television or some other electronic medium frequently is denied access to the treasures of the printed word because he does not understand it.

Here is where the smart promoter of written communication can take advantage of the media. All forms of communication in the modern vernacular world can be springboards for conventional literacy. The key is getting people to realize that the printed word is the common language—the *lingua franca*—that they all need, that will benefit them no matter what "language" they work in.

The electronic media provide access to and enrich the print medium. They open up myriads of opportunities to stimulate the minds and capabilities of students which then can be translated into the print medium. Students respond to the stimuli provided by rock music, by questions of youth behavior as catalogued in the media, by questions of morality, ethics, teenage and adult behavior, by the symbolism in such American phenomena as the fast-food industry, shopping malls, rituals, icons and fetishes. Some of the most exciting and useful courses taught in high school and college level composition courses have been sports-oriented: the literature of sports, sports in American culture, the history of sports. The media fairly bulge every day with subjects that excite and invite the thoughtful student and teacher: the commercialization of Christmas, sex-education in grade-school, abortion, televangelism, the role of the elderly in society, pet therapy, the positive and negative images of such television shows as "Dallas" and "Dynasty." The Popular Culture Department at Bowling Green State University recently ran a successful state-wide writing contest among eleventh-grade high school students on "Should Rock Lyrics be Censored?" The subject was important to the students and stimulated thoughtful essays. The range is boundless, the list endless.

One medium foolishly ignored is the comic book. Everyone knows that in Mexico, Central and South America, the People's Republic of China, and elsewhere, comics are used to teach reading as well as political points of view. In Japan, according to a recent AP article, children, women and business executives read comics all the time. According to one expert, comics exert as much influence over school kids as school itself does. Increasingly comic books are being used to simplify and augment textbooks. How-to comic books are becoming more and more popular, covering all kinds of education and activities. Japan, like America, is a very visually-oriented society. With a claimed 100% literacy rate, does Japan know something about teaching that we refuse to accept? I think so. Let me give you an example.

At Bowling Green State University we have created the Popular Culture Library and are archiving as much of all kinds of popular culture as we can. We have large collections of every sort. One of the largest, one of which we are justly proud, is our comic book collection. Years ago when we were just underway, a man from Toledo called me and said that he would like to contribute his collection of comic books to our archives. He brought down several thousand comics—a station wagon full. Six months later he brought down a thousand, and sometime later another large collection. Being curious about where he was getting the comics, I asked him where he got them and why. He answer was very poignant—very feeling—and very significant. He said that he worked for Toledo Edison as a lineman, and he liked to read. So he bought as many comic books as he could. Now I would suggest that in that man's simple statement lies the whole kernel of an American educational system: a person so desiring to read that he would spend all available cash for the pleasure. There lies the seed for education, and one of the media.

Providing access to learning literacy through these various media does not mean that anybody who teaches composition through the popular culture must undergo a shriveling of his own talents, his own life, if that is the result of such association, though I surely doubt that it is. The teacher should be able to maintain a distance between his private and professional lives. Using the various popular culture media merely means that in a democracy one teaches to the degrees of literacy or illiteracy one finds. Catering to these degrees provides the means of eradicating that illiteracy. Everybody has to begin sometime at the beginning.

All people, no matter how humble, possess the democratic right of access to the valuable and useful experiences of the past and present in order to improve or make more enjoyable their own lives. In our democracy, they cannot properly be denied the tools of access to those experiences.

Which, of course, brings up an informative parallel. Asian-American children are doing so well in American schools and colleges that questions are being raised as to whether they are smarter than American kids. The statistics are impressive: Asian-American kids usually score some 30 points higher than Americans on the Scholastic Aptitude Test, 520 out of a possible 800. Although Asian-Americans constitute only 2.1 percent of the American population, they make up 11 percent of the freshman class at Harvard; 18 percent at M.I.T.; 25 percent at Berkeley. Does that mean that Asian-American kids are smarter than other American kids? Though the jury is still out on that verdict, success seems to hinge on a much simpler and more easily correctable explanation. Asian-American kids work harder.

A University of Michigan psychologist, Harold W. Stevenson, feels that "they work harder largely because they share a greater belief in the efficiency of hard work." Stevenson added: "Japanese mothers gave the strongest rating to the idea that anyone can do well if he studies hard." He might have added that parents know very well that if students do not succeed early they will be condemned to a life in which they never can achieve the highest goals in their society. In Japanese society, success is built from one of the three elite universities and one's capabilities to matriculate in one of these schools are fiercely competitive and established early. Chinese mothers strongly agree with this particular work ethic. A typical Stanford Chinese student's comment was: "In the Chinese family education is very important because parents see it as the way to achieve. With that environment it's natural to study. My friends are that way too. It's not a chore. They know the benefits."

What are we to conclude from these statistics? Not that all other American students are stupider than the Asian-Americans. Not that their parents are stupider. But only that the Asian-Americans work harder. They are "merely entertained" less than other American kids. So what should we do? Being realistic, we may as well confess that television and the other aspects of American popular culture are not going away. One inalienable right that we are prepared to die for is the "American Way" of life—and that "Way" consists of our popular culture. Since we are not going to put technology back into the undeveloped stage, why not use it to further our designs to create and promote literacy? If Asian-American kids learn because their family tradition expects it of them, why don't we get the other American kids to learn because it is so easy and one uses the most enjoyable media to learn from, and because *American society expects it of them*? If the American way of life is so much fun, we should use that way to learn to get even more fun out of it. The American way of life can become even more pleasurable and profitable for many more if we use that means of pleasure and profit to promote literacy.

One of the most incontrovertible but generally ignored media for creating fluency in the standard language is rap music. Rap music is fundamentally music of Blacks. Blacks who are not fluent in standard English have certain characteristics in their spoken English. They change "th" to "d," drop "r" and "d," change the verb "is" to "be." Such a sentence as "The world is dead," becomes "De worl be dea'." This is strikingly different from standard English.

Yet the street fluent Black speaks rap lyrics in Standard English. So the illiterate street Black will sing in rap music the line "The world is dead," while he would speak it as "De worl be dea." Over the last 20 years Rap has become a kind of universal, color-blind music. It is a commercial medium with economic, political and social motivations. Educators in Chicago, New York and Detroit, to name only three cities, recognize the gateway opportunities of Rap music as entries into linguistic fluency. If life can imitate art on an entry level, then art can be powerful enough to motivate a participant once he has entered the gate to continue to imitate the art. Thus, Rap Music can be made a powerful instrument in teaching literacy to illiterate people, if the motivation is recognized and exploited.

Closely allied to the problem of illiteracy is that of drop-outs from the school and educational system. People drop out of the educational track for the same reasons they remain illiterate. One of the main reasons is that they are bored; they do not see any motivation for continuing their education plan or they are not getting anything out of it. Again, the need—as every educator knows—is motivation. One striking statistic bears out this statement. In classes being taught in prisons, the drop-out rate in the average class is 50%; in classes in popular culture, the drop-out rate is zero, without extraordinary circumstances. If people can be lured to stick to learning by the motivation engendered in them, and the media through which it is motivated, it seems logical that if people are interested in the media and the other elements of popular culture in which they live—and which they can understand— these media and that popular culture can be used to keep people interested; all we need to do is use the media as educational tools. We don't even have to tell the students that they are being "educated." They can just still be having fun. The current drop-out rate is desperate; in Detroit, for example, it is fifty percent of the students who begin public schools. Elsewhere the figures are staggering. The need for remedy is clear.

With these purposes in mind, no plane should be too low to begin on and no idea should be assumed to be above the reach of the illiterate or the drop-out or under-achiever until it has been proved to be so. Many Americans may have difficulty with even the simplest words and sentences. But these people are not necessarily stupid or unteachable; they simply have not yet learned the area of language use, and they have not learned because for one reason or another they have not been properly motivated. To teach such people, educators need liberated and active minds looking for ideas of today and tomorrow that will excite and motivate the minds before us. The field of these ideas remains constantly present.

There is no reason for the American educator to think that he will have to stop using the media when he has accomplished literacy in the print medium, that the potentials are short-lived and soon exhausted. Functional literacy through the media is only a beginning. It can be like a person holding a piece of candy just out of the reach of a hungry child. As the child crawls toward the candy, it can be pulled back continuously—until, in theory at least, the child has become an adult. The *bon-bon* of media education can likewise be continually pulled back until the learner is accomplished in advanced degrees of literacy and knowledge, until he is, in fact, what we might call "educated."

Some of my most interesting educational experiments are held in the nursing homes around Bowling Green, Ohio. I go out and talk about such items as the pleasures of people establishing their "roots," of the need and joy of going dancing, of the changing role of Christmas in our lives, that kind of thing. The elderly like to "learn" about such things. One of my friends in a New Jersey college tells me that he teaches a very successful class in Popular Music to a group of senior citizens.

They are delighted when he tells them that he is going to teach the music of the 40s instead of rock and roll. I myself get excited every night at the prospect of my forthcoming learning opportunity. Here I branch out into virtually every learning and teaching opportunity in the popular culture, at least television. The Discovery Channel broadcasts documentaries. Each night I get a step in education by watching documentaries on environment, archeology, arts and crafts, marine biology, climatology, high-finance, glass-blowing, break-throughs in technology, you name it. What I get on this documentary station I could also get on the commercial stations if I worked just a little harder, especially if I had an instructor to tell me what I should be getting. The media are a large loose-leaf notebook which cover every aspect of knowledge and culture. Generally, they cover this knowledge interestingly—or they do not remain on the air. Always, even in the failures, they contain great stores of information, and they present this information entertainingly—which is often more than the instructor does. But not when he is using popular culture materials—stills, live footage, artifacts, examples—to enliven his/her talks. After all, what really could be more interesting than carefully chosen shows of popular entertainment as a teaching device for whole segments of our population? The entertainment is there, the body of knowledge is there, the instructor is there to point out the informational aspects needed and useful. Properly presented, the entertainment of life is an unending source of knowledge and information.

The need is to realize the possibilities and to get to implementing them. Illiteracy, drop-outs and arrested learning are problems that should be attacked directly, not obliquely. Thus, on the matter of effecting education in the United States, William Bennett, when he was Secretary of Education, wasted his time grandstanding by teaching history or philosophy to 8-year-olds in schoolrooms. Instead of feeding his ego and political ambitions by using his office, he should have been out on the streets of Detroit—and Washington and every city in the U.S.— asking drop-outs and fade-outs why they were not in school. He should have been concerned with the very basics of long-range education—that is keeping students in classrooms long enough for them to learn, then teaching them something while they were there. In order to get these students taught print literacy, we must first get them in situations conducive to our purposes and goals, or utilize the situations the students are in for teaching. As everybody knows, the people are learning, but they are not learning what we think is of primary importance. Somebody needs to rethink his position.

Instead, however, people continue to exploit education for their own purposes. Now William Bennett is dedicated to doing more mischief while he advances his own political career. He served as the head of three major department offices in Washington—Chairman of the National Endowment for the Humanities, Secretary of Education and Drug Czar. As Chairman of the NEH he tried to take that department back to the days of Plato, as Secretary of Education he tried to drive students to literacy and as Drug Czar he wanted to frighten addicts out of the habit and dealers off the street. Whatever success he had in any of these endeavors was strictly limited. Now, however, with these failures to his credit, he is contracted to write two books on his experiences. The regrettable thing is that they may well be widely read and greeted as credible. For our safety, we must wean ourselves from the notion that just because somebody is literate, or has had a visible position in life, he has anything to say—or for us to listen to.

Academics are generally uncomfortable in the presence of the multitude of ideas that the media and popular culture provide because they need the feeling of safety and assurance of the old restrictions. That is why they are always searching for new theories with which to approach subjects. Theories and methodologies, no matter how manifestly limiting and excluding, provide comfortable frameworks on which to dry out ideas. Academics prefer the snugness found in the old forms—or variations of them—to the potentials latent in the new and unrestricted thinking possibilities. They prefer knowledge of the theory and methodology to knowledge of the subject. Some even see merit in the frightened and defeatist cliche being circulated in the 80s and 90s by many politicians of going "back to basics."

As David Crowley and Paul Heyer express it, "A new language is rarely welcomed by the old. The oral tradition distrusted writing, manuscript culture was contemptuous of printing, book culture hated the press, that 'slag-heap of hellish passions,' as one 19th-century scholar called it." In this myopic tradition, television will undoubtedly deal harshly with any upstart medium that threatens its preeminence in society.

But society in a technological world moves inexorably forward. The genies of technology do not go back into bottles once they have been released. The practical and sensible thing is, then, for educators to realize the importance and opportunities of the technological society we live in and to utilize its equipment in the teaching of literacy. The opportunities are great—and the penalties for failing are heavy and costly. Too costly, in fact, for us to afford. Either we go with the media or they drown many of us as they move forward. Like a comet with a long tail behind it, technology always drags a stream of kicking and screaming traditionalists behind it.

So popular culture, which on the one hand seems to be destroying conventional literacy, if we will only realize the opportunity and take advantage of it, provides people with the greatest and easiest access to practical functional literacy in the print medium. Never before have so many people had such easy access to so many media of becoming literate and, hence, rising to the top and fulfilling the American Dream. That these media are not utilized to develop mediacy, fluency and love of learning constitutes one of the great and needless shames of our country and time.

Utilization of popular culture in this way would not, of course, cure the whole trouble of print literacy. But if nothing else, the burden of my argument so far would seem to invalidate print literacy as the end-all and be-all in literacy. Literacy in other media would be, in an ideal world, proper literacy; in a biased and imperfect world it will be at least functional literacy, fluency in communication. As such, it centers the human mind and abilities on development of potentials.

Under such a concept there would still be people who would not or could not become fluent, but the number would be reduced by some 90%. Most people want to develop capabilities when they are allowed to enrich their own potentials. Fluency in one medium makes fluency easier in another; generally fluency in one medium does not kill the desire for fluency in another. One feeds on the other. Literacy in one medium breeds love of learning in general; learning in general feeds on more learning.

What I am suggesting may be no panacea, and it would take some time to achieve, though not as much time as would be required to develop near-universal conventional literacy, if that were possible. But it would surely help alleviate the problems caused by a standard of literacy which excludes nearly all kinds of fluency merely because they are not print-literacy. There would be fewer drop-outs and fade-outs from conventional classrooms, and more and more unconventional classrooms feeding students and learning into the general goal of education. A little fluency, contrary to the old saw about knowledge, is a hope, not a dangerous thing. The potential for expanding the small into the large is always great and pregnant with hope.

As we will see, the streams of popular culture water a hundred possible crops of literacy. All we need do is cultivate the potentials and let nature take its course. Most individuals and all of society will reap the harvest. But to begin, we need a broad definition of the humanities.

Chapter Three

Redefining the Humanities

Before we commit ourselves again fully to an all-out war on illiteracy—so fruitlessly conducted many times in the past—we need to define our terms of what illiteracy and its opposite, literacy, are, and what role they play in society. Clearly literacy, though desirable, is not an end in itself. Literacy is the mechanism which supports the culture, which in turn undergirds the humanities, and in so doing leads to the ultimate goal of happiness and usefulness in life. What then are the humanities? The answer to that question and the demonstrated relationship between the humanities and literacy will, as usual, be both controversial and disturbing to defenders of the educational status quo, to the power broker in the business of education. Yet that clarification is squirming for recognition in a world that needs to recognize it.

One of the leading spokespersons for the value of the humanities in society is Lynne Cheney, Chairman of the National Endowment for the Humanities. In her *Humanities in America: A Report to the President, the Congress, and the American People* (1988), Cheney issued a thoughtful, generally well-informed and stimulating statement about the way many people see and read the humanities—and a provoking assertion about the way many others *do not* see and understand the humanities and the role of the NEH in promoting them. As is usual in a report of this kind, though the case is well-made, especially to the already-converted, it leaves sections that should be modified, questioned or enlarged, and reversed.

That there is some problem in the failure of the humanities to fulfill their full potential in the United States is clear. To a large extent that fault lies with the people involved, of course, because individuals seldom live up to all expectations. But to another degree the fault lies in definition, in goals the people want to attain. Ms. Cheney gives the consensus definition in her study—that generally used as a working motto by the National Endowment for the Humanities—in emphasizing the depth of the definition. She reminds us that the Romans gave us the word humanities and generally outlined its meaning to them and to their successors through the ages. To the Romans the humanities were "the

44

good arts." She later reemphasizes this depth by telling us again that "in a democratic society, the humanities—those areas of study that bring us the deeds and thoughts of other times—should be part of every life."

Clearly, those are some of the obligations of the humanities, but by no means all, or even the main ones. The others are more contemporary. The *Report* is viewing the humanities through a telescope turned around backwards. Ms. Cheney follows in the footsteps of her predecessors as Chairman of the NEH in sticking too closely to the definition of the humanities as formulated by the Victorian conservative British poet-essayist Matthew Arnold in asserting that culture is "the best that has been thought and said." Culture and the humanities—by no means the same—are far more than what Arnold thought them to be. His viewpoint was clouded by his seeing reality through his romantic love of the security of the past and his fear of the future. His world was a "darkling plain where ignorant armies clash by night," and his sense of reaching out through the humanities to humanity extended only to his being true to his "love," as he said in his poem *Dover Beach:*

Ah, love, let us be true
To one another! for the world, which seems
To lie before us like a land of dreams,
So various, so beautiful, so new,
Hath really neither joy, nor love, nor light,
Nor certitude, nor peace, nor help for pain;
And we are here as on a darkling plain
Swept with confused alarms of struggle and flight,
Where ignorant armies clash by night.   (*Dover Beach*, Stanza 4)

This is hardly a philosophy to lead a nation into the twenty-first century or to drive an agency of the federal government which is dedicated to furthering democracy. The humanities, to survive, must see beyond this narrow and myopic paranoia.

The humanities must reach beyond the esthetics of the three hand-maidens of conventional venue—literature, philosophy and history. Esthetics—even the "best that has been thought and said"—should be tested mainly or only on the questions of truth and value not only to the individual but beyond that to humanity. Is the literature appropriate? Is the philosophy sensible? Is the history accurate? Validity rests not on whether something is beautiful, imaginative and self-creating but on whether it bears some resemblance to reality and whether it is applicable to humankind as a whole.

Cheney's *Report* quotes one professor's lament: "Students are not taught that there is such a thing as literary excellence as they were twenty years ago. We are throwing out the notion of good and bad, or ignoring it." As usual, the academic is overstating the case and defending her own philosophy and practice. Literary excellence is fine in its place, no doubt, and it helps many a bitter pill go down. But to think that literary excellence validates some statement which under other circumstances—badly stated—would be recognized as nonsense or mischief is simply blindly simple. Life does not work that way. The *Report* glosses the professor's remarks by reminding us that "These are, of course, legitimate questions, but focusing on political issues to the exclusion of all others does not bring students to an understanding of how Milton or Shakespeare speaks to the deepest concerns as we all have as human beings." Again, accurate and perceptive as long as it is not taken too literally. But to understand Milton's statements about our deepest concerns without realizing that his meditations in the divorce tracts were influenced by his unhappy marriage to Mary Powell and that his political thunderings were dictated by his political situation is to simplify complex issues.

So, to many of us the humanities are more than beautiful and "true" statements. The humanities are those aspects of life that make us understand ourselves and our society. They are a philosophical attitude and an approach to thinking and behaving which interpret life in a human context. In other words, the humanities humanize life and living, make it more understandable and bearable and human. In the words of British critic Fred Inglis: "The humanities are the materials with which humanity gains knowledge of itself." There cannot be humanities without some kind of human compassion about the experiences of life, without some kind of "togetherness," or connectedness. If we understand our strengths and weaknesses and our role in the great scheme, then presumably we will have enough intelligence to develop a useful and helpful attitude and action toward our world. If we know the truth— the whole truth—supposedly we will not only be free, but we might also behave sensibly. If we understand the humanities, we might be fully human.

The humanities are without time and limitations. They were important to the Romans, the Greeks before them and the Egyptians before them. But they are not and must not be merely historical statements. Today's humanities are far more important to us than those of the Romans are to us. Nobody should be content to view his or her present-day life through the ignorance, biases and prejudices of the past. One of the goals of education, especially in the humanities, is to develop a healthy— but not reverential—respect for the past while at the same time freeing one from the errors of the past. The old saw these days is that unless one knows the past he will be condemned to reliving it. But the wisdom of the saw should be explicit enough to say that unless we *understand*— not just know—the past we will forever be chained by it. To paraphrase one of our wisest maxims, "Ye shall understand the past and that understanding shall make you free," and presumably wiser.

It is a grave error, as we see it, to believe, as Professor Allan Bloom says in his book *The Closing of the American Mind*, that our role is to fit ourselves into the world of the past. That is the action of an ostrich as he buries his head in the sand and turns his rear to the sun. We don't fit ourselves into Shakespeare's world. Surely if Shakespeare is to live today—should live, deserves to live—his works must be fitted into our world; otherwise he is merely a beautiful heirloom. It is as impossible to go back into history as it is to fit the genie back into the bottle once it has escaped. The humanities are for the living, not the dead.

The *Report* gives a poignant and truthful illustration of this point. Ms. Cheney tells about how a twelve-year old black girl in Stamps, Arkansas, who had been nourished on Shakespeare, Langston Hughes, Edgar Allan Poe and Paul Laurence Dunbar, determined one day to "render a rendition" of Shakespeare's poetry in her church but was prevented by her grandmother because Shakespeare was not black. The girl's justification was sensible. "I found myself and still find myself, whenever I like, stepping back into Shakespeare. Whenever I like, I *pull* him to me. He wrote it for me.... Of course he wrote it ('When in disgrace with fortune and men's eyes' etc.) for me; that is a condition of the black woman. Of course, he was a black woman. I understand that. Nobody else understands it, but I *know* that Shakespeare was a black woman. That is the role of art in life" (15). How can there be a finer statement of the role of the past in our lives!

Increasingly the various media of education—the transmission of facts and attitudes and the development of thinking and reasoning— are broadening the base and raising the levels of understanding and appreciation of the humanities. Presumably, we are becoming more "civilized"—more humane—and maybe to a certain extent this is a result of our deepening understanding of the humanities.

Frequently, however, this deepening understanding comes *despite* and *against* the teaching of the elite humanities scholars. The *Report* quotes a series of questions by philosopher Charles Frankel which end with the forced connection of two irreconcilable elements: "Will [the images of human possibility in American society] speak to them only of success and celebrity and the quick fix that make them happy, or will it find a place for grace, elegance, nobility, and a sense of connection with the Human adventure?" Now common sense tells us that "grace, elegance," at least, have nothing to do with the humanities; those affectations are important only to life style. And as for the taint of "celebrity and the quick fix"—as rottening as it may appear to be to the social body—few graceful and elegant people turn it down in their search for happiness unless they already have it or cannot hope to acquire it. All those paths of life are as much a part of the "human adventure" as any grace and elegance that Professor Frankel can find. We do ourselves and truth a disservice when we force into the bottle of similarities those elements that chemically won't mix.

They also tend to create a hierarchy in the applicability of the humanities that is repugnant. "The humanities," Professor Maynard Mack of Yale University, once said, "are not really something you can democratize. It's like democratizing surgery. Who wants someone picked up off the streets to operate on him? Well, it's the same thing in the humanities." All analogizing is dangerous, and Professor Mack's is particularly mischievous. The humanities are not like surgery. Not every person has the training and the need to practice surgery upon himself or other people. But every citizen has the Constitutional right and the self-given obligation to practice the humanities.

The humanities, if they do anything, erase the gap between the privileged and unprivileged classes in society. Robert Coles, Harvard psychologist and Pulitzer Prize winner, correctly states that the humanities are necessary companions to us all: "The humanities," he says, "belong to no one kind of person; they are part of the lives of ordinary people, who have their own various ways of struggling for coherence, for a compelling faith, for social vision, for an ethical position, for a sense of historical perspective."

Richard Hoggart, one of Britain's leading contemporary social commentators, speaking in a larger context, quite properly said essentially the same thing: "The closer study of mass society may make us have sad hearts at the supermarket, but at the same time it may produce an enhanced and tempered sense of humanity and humility, instead of the sense of superiority and separateness that our traditional training is likely to have encouraged."

Leslie Fiedler, perhaps pushes this reasoning to its logical conclusion, because he believes that the humanities broadly conceived and understood can achieve man's greatest challenge, that of bringing us all together again and united into a community which existed before people became separated by class, education, interests and desires.

The growth of the study and power of the humanities, as the *Report* properly points out, has lagged far behind the development of society. The fault lies not with the humanities but with the academics who profess them. While academics are forming committees—and, I might add, getting large sums of money from the NEH and other Foundations to decide on a proper curriculum and field of study for the enhancement of the humanities—the world is going ahead, as usual far ahead of their academic segments. People, Ms. Cheney reports, "outside the academy are increasingly turning to literary, historical, and philosophical study, are increasingly finding in the 'good arts' a source of enrichment for themselves and their society."

Indeed, they are. And they are reaching far outside those three fields of academic departmentalization of literature, history and philosophy and far beyond the other traditional "good arts." They are reaching out into all aspects of the popular culture for their humanities and finding that all the arts—both "good" and otherwise—have the potential for enriching the lives of us all and, through us, society.

Popular culture is the everyday world around us: the mass media, entertainment, diversions, our heroes, icons, rituals—our total life picture. Although it generally is, it need not be disseminated by the mass media. Most important, the popular culture of a country is the voice of the people—their likes and dislikes, the lifeblood of daily existence, the way of life. In America, presumably, popular culture is the voice of democracy. Like it or not, every American owes it to himself and his society to make a great effort, through formal or informal study, to understand the culture around him or her. He will discover that there are power brokers in elite culture just as in popular culture—most of us have little influence in shaping our culture. Studying the dynamics of culture, often the student will discover, if he can rid himself or herself of blind prejudice, that much of the popular culture is to be appreciated, just as much of the elite is unappreciable.

Actually, of course, there is nothing new in studying popular culture, that is, the culture of the times. As the editors of the *Literary History of the United States* (1955) asserted: "Each generation must define the past in its own terms," as well as the present. And if there is opposition to the new way of looking at the phenomena of life, that is only natural, as John G. Cawelti observed: "Whenever criticism feels the impact of an expanded sensibility it becomes shot through with ideological dispute," and then must be reinterpreted.

Unfortunately, this reinterpretation is often done by specialists instead of by generalists. Ms. Cheney's *Report* quite properly takes up the role of the scholar and his/her specialization in a society which has become so complex and specialized that specialists can no longer communicate outside their own specialization. Medical doctors can no longer understand other doctors outside their areas of specialization. Sociologists can speak only to other specialists in a sub-category. Literary critics who do not understand the jargon of a particular "school" of criticism are deaf and tongue-tied. But the humanities don't flourish in specialties—even among those who specialize in the humanities. The humanities grow in the world of generalities, in syntheses, in questions and answers raised about the purposes and ends—not necessarily in the miles of the road traveled in getting to the ends. But, just as every road consists of the miles separating one point from another, the particulars are ignored at peril

The ends of the humanities are the whole humanities, not Western humanities, not Black humanities, not Eastern humanities or Women's humanities but *total humanities*. It is true that we are in the tradition of Western civilization and humanities; and, undoubtedly, that tradition has many treasures that we should hold dear. But it is myopic and arrogant to assume that the tradition contains all that is needed for us to understand the humanities, no matter how far back we might go. People in the Western tradition are, after all, only a minority of humanity. Individuals throughout the world share in the hopes and aspirations of a common humanity, no matter how widely divergent our ways of living and achieving those goals seem at times to be. On this space-ship Earth we all fly together or we all fall together.

Often we give credit to our ancestors' ways of life and wisdom that they could not possibly have had. Plato, our godfather, flourished in a slave society and despised democracy. To realize his shortcomings does not mean that we toss all of him out with the shortcomings; it merely means that we do not slavishly accept his wrong assumptions and incorrect conclusions. There can be no doubt that the amount of information on virtually all fronts that was available to the "giant humanists" of the past was not sufficient to allow them to come to irrefutable generalizations about everything. It is our duty to question everything they said and invalidate or revalidate their conclusions. If the classics still speak to us, then we should hear them. If their voice is no longer applicable, it should be ignored.

There is no question that it is imperative that the old concepts be tested and modified to incorporate new approaches, new definitions and new areas of subject matter. Otherwise the humanities—in all their ramifications—will prove misguided and generally inadequate to present-day needs and possibilities. Maybe it will be found that the "eternal truths" that the humanities are supposed to reveal have more effective spokespersons in sources that have not been recognized in the past.

T.S. Eliot recognized the need to be mindful of subjects that one might not find compatible with his thinking. He cried out against popular books as his *bete noir*: "I incline to come to the alarming conclusion," he said in *Essays Ancient and Modern*, "that it is just the literature that we read for 'amusement' or 'purely for pleasure' that may have the greatest...least suspected...earliest and most insidious influence upon us. Hence it is that the influence of popular novelists, and of popular plays of contemporary life, require to be scrutinized." Richard Hoggart, one of today's leading English social observers, comments in a typical British understatement, "Literature at all levels has the unique capacity to increase our understanding of a culture."

Neither observer mentions anything about the "aesthetic" beauty of the literature. Using literary "grace and beauty" as criteria for the value of literature, as Jacques Barzun, one of the defenders of old-time attitudes and values, does, seems therefore all the more off-base. The *Report* quotes Barzun in valuing only the "grace and beauty" of any kind of literature: "Excellence is found in many forms," the *Report* quotes, "some of them unassuming and even fugitive. The specifically literary qualities can grace a detective story by Dorothy Sayers or a farce by Courteline, a ghost story by M.R. James or a poem by Ogden Nash."

Barzun seems always concerned that Gresham's law applies to literature as it presumably applies to economics. But "bad" literature does not drive out "good." There are some 50,000 separate titles of books published in the U.S. annually. Never before have so many books been read. In 1985 there were more than two *billion* copies of books printed— 400 percent of the number just forty years before. And that was in a society where ninety-eight of every one hundred homes had television. In total number most of those two *billion* were in popular culture. Which ought to tell the elitists something. If the mountain cannot go the Mohammet, then Mohammet must go to the mountain. And the elite should openly admit what they are actually doing—that is, reading the popular books for pleasure and edification. Just as they are watching television and participating in the other media for pleasure and edification. Sometimes they are bootlegging their enjoyment to themselves. But they fool only themselves, and perhaps the government. There is no need for the elite to dissemble and claim that popular books are the bane of civilization when they read those books and talk about them most of the time. The popular books are, instead, the blessing and the tool of democracy. They spread knowledge and encourage learning.

There can be no doubt that reading stimulates watching television, and that watching television encourages reading. People apparently do not like to live in a quiet, one-dimensional atmosphere. When they pick up a book or magazine to read, many automatically turn on the television set. Likewise, when they turn on the television set many automatically pick up something to read. Further, the television program is likely to stimulate reading in another way: One sees a television show and then gets hold of the book from which the show was made and reads it, just as often one will tune in a television show because the book from which it was made was enjoyable. British crime novelist Ruth Rendell tells how she has seen the television version of her works stimulate people to do all kinds of direct and collateral reading. The media are mutually dependent and supportive. Books, television and movies are only three kinds of media which are mutually helpful one of another.

This means that there should be no sacred domains among the old humanities; they should not be treasured as holy writ and, therefore, be immune to tests of value. They must periodically be asked to revalidate themselves, and if they cannot they must be retired until rejuvenated. Doubtless, many of the old workhorses should be given permanent sabbaticals. They have ceased to have value except as historical markers. The present-day classroom—and research desk—is the one place in society that cannot afford to become a museum of dead ideas and concepts.

Casting out the dead fish from our pond of living ideas is not condemnation of what people have done in the past. It does not invalidate anybody's life's work, anybody's literary or artistic loves, even anybody's evaluation of aesthetically commendable or contemptible materials. Rather, it is a call for intellectuals and other people interested in studying and understanding American life and culture, in its broadest and richest sense, to become broader-minded, more openminded and less exclusive and excluding. Nobody says one has to approve of or like everything that goes on, just as no one has to approve of or like all the "great" works of the arts of the past or the present. Scientists, to our betterment, do not restrict their interests to the "good" things in life. It is foolish for us to pull an ostrich-like hiding of the head and be unaware of the winds that sweep our bodies while the thinking part is in the sand. Such an attitude is dangerous to one's own and the culture's well-being, because in truth American culture continues to grow and develop in its own way pretty much irrespective of the intellectuals' approval or disapproval. Intellectuals may long for the return of the railroad train as a romantic way to travel, but the satellite is flying well and high. It would behoove us to recognize that fact and to bring the humanities into the electronic age. The humanities must prepare us to think our way through the age of instant media. Facts change constantly. "Time dissipates to shining either the solid angularity of facts," Emerson wrote in his essay on history.

It is undoubtedly a flaw of education to assume that the person who knows a lot of facts is educated. Such a person could do well on *Jeopardy* or *Wheel of Fortune*, but so could an encyclopedia that was trained to speak or a voice-motivated computer. The educated person is not the little Bloomlet or Hirschite who has been cloned in the image of the master, but the person who has refused to be cloned, declined to be satisfied working with the lumber of facts that many educators have handed him, but has instead gone on to imagine and build new concepts and constructions.

The academic's tendency is to be rather open-minded while he does not know much and does not have much to defend. But as he gets more and more specialized, he tends more and more to become proprietary and protective over what he knows, apparently in developing such an attitude fulfilling a deep-felt need within himself. Often, we turn off our listening button and switch on our broadcast button too soon. We learn to "profess" exclusively while we should still be learning what to profess. Such a one-way activity is indeed dangerous, for it is self-defeating. But academia persists in being, by and large in the humanities, the old nest of last year's ideas, not the place where new ideas are generated and welcomed in order to be tested and approved or cast out. Academia should generally use the library as the storehouse of old ideas, for there they need not do any harm. Archives are archives, and the classroom of new ideas ought to be something else entirely. We should never assume that we know something that has not been examined and validated. Academia should be the leading, not the trailing, edge of ideas.

We should remember that Josh Billings, one of our insightful humorists of the 19th century reminded us: "It ain't the things we don't know that makes such fools of us, but a whole lot of things that we know that ain't so." We should always keep an open mind about what are the valuable things we know and the worthwhile attitudes we hold. Otherwise, we insult our intelligence and jeopardize the natural and peaceful development of culture and mankind. The humanities, properly studied and understood, enrich immeasurably our journey and assist us in achieving literacy for all. They also assist us in another equally important way.

They help us recognize the false ways that are constantly placed luringly before us, offering cure-alls and quick-fixes that society can ill-afford to tolerate—much less encourage. The humanities are too important to leave in the hands of the charlatans.

Chapter Four

Academic Snake-Oil[1]

In our urgency to make literacy a universal positive force in our society, sometimes we turn to academic snake-oil, and its brewers and salesmen, for cures. Not all merchants of snake-oil, of course, deliberately set out to weaken the body academe with false cures. Like all of us, generally they think their products are panaceas, or at least helpful. Perhaps sometimes they are—as stimulants to thinking, if nothing else. Nevertheless, in their seductive packaging and academic settings, these witches' brews—intentionally or not—often spread a lot of harm, by either claiming false cures or by taking up a lot of valuable time which could be more profitably invested in potentially helpful routes to education.

Two especially mischievous instruments of misguided education which spring instantly to mind are Allan Bloom's bestselling book *The Closing of the American Mind* and E.D. Hirsch Jr.'s *Cultural Literacy: What Every American Needs to Know*, of the same year (1987). Both deserve extended examination because of the harm they generate and perpetuate. With friends like these, education does not need enemies.

Hirsch, to begin with the more mechanical of the two, gives a list of 5000 items that constitute what he considers the foundation of what all Americans must comprehend to be culturally literate and to be functioning members of society. While recognizing that, as he says, "no such compilation can be definitive," Hirsch observes that his list is "intended to illustrate the character and range of knowledge literate Americans tend to share" (146).

The author wants to "establish guideposts that can be of practical use to teachers, students and all others who need to know our literate culture." He, in fact, implies that not to know these guideposts, or others like them, is to be illiterate, ignorant and unable to participate effectively in our culture. The case can be made, and in fact will be made, that instead of offering a useful guide to what people should know in order to be literate, the book really constitutes a mess of fool's gold that misleads society and bears no relationship whatsoever to the needs of society today.

Having a library of cultural references is clearly important, serving the same purposes as any thesaurus or reference book. But having a list of societal references at one's beck and call has nothing to do with literacy—that is fluency in communication—and in fact tends to lull a society to sleep at a time when that society needs to be keen and alert to its real needs. The developed world at the opening of the twenty-first century is no time and place to be asleep at the switch. If one has enough references to serve as coins of society ready at his call—somewhat like punching a few keys on a computer and having the data flash on the monitor—then there is no need to go to the trouble of putting them into the head. Why clutter up the head when there is no need?

Hirsch's argument of having a thesaurus of references handy is seriously flawed because of the specific assumptions upon which it depends. In the first place, being able to make references to certain keystone allusions has nothing to do with how one got the references. Presumably it was by reading, but it could have been orally or visually. For example, there are at least two ways—verbally or by television—one could become acquainted with a reference to Hirsch's "bear market." So one can know Hirsch's references without being able to read print.

Further, his argument about needed cultural references is weakened because of the cases on which it rests. These arguments include the view that there is a center or core to modern culture, and individuals must share the nature of this core if they are to communicate effectively with one another; that this core consists of specific facts and concepts that he has identified or similar ones; that the essential knowledge is to be acquired primarily from the print medium; and that the present design of our educational philosophy and curriculum precludes transmitting the required forms of literacy to our students. These assumptions represent an absolutist point of view, and the policy recommendation flowing from them will do little to facilitate the basic communication outcome, literacy, which most Americans wish to promote.

The guides Hirsch offers to literate culture, and the related guides to literacy—and education in general—tendered by Allan Bloom in *The Closing of the American Mind*, are controlled by a tunnel vision that is both narrowly elitist and terminally conservative. For example, Hirsch observes that 80% of the listed items have been in use for more than a hundred years. Such a listing ignores the knowledge explosion of the 20th century, the importance to individuals of being receptive to the changes that are occurring in the world around us, and the crucial significance of being aware of how life in modern society differs in fundamental ways from that known and understood in the past. In 1987 using knowledge that pre-dates 1900 as a test of "mature" literacy is questionable indeed, particularly in view of the concern with relevant knowledge as a basic communication in the world of here and now.

Although there is some value to the observation attributed to George Santayana that unless we know history we are forced to repeat it, the more sensible fact is that unless we *understand* it, we will be doomed to make the mistakes our predecessors made. Merely knowing the mistakes our elders made is no guarantee of our not making them again.

In fact, history tends to verify the assumption that merely knowing the past is no sign of any wisdom about how to improve the present. Individuals tend to follow in the footsteps of their parents and make the same foolish mistakes their parents made. We know all about family and sexual violence. Yet we seem almost culture-bound to follow in the family ways that we experienced, not able to break the familial chains that bind us. To paraphrase Emerson on history, we might say that the strongest history in any culture is the events of an individual's family.

Furthermore, there is much to be said for the custom of occasionally shaking off the dust of history and being, as Thomas Jefferson observed, interested more in the future than in the past. "Life belongs to the living, not the dead," he once wrote. Life would be far less complicated if it were actually correct that we could solve most of the communication problems we face today by using Hirsch's references of the past, but the fact is we cannot, and there is certainly more danger in facing the past and listening to the songs the sirens sang than in confronting the present and the future and hearing the rhythms of rock 'n' roll.

Literacy has always meant the ability to understand and use the standard form of communication in a particular context and for a specific purpose. In other words, literacy is fluency in a medium of communication and is necessarily a relative concept and dependent upon many forms of communication rather than on the print medium alone. The list of *things that everybody needed to know* prior to the development of the printing press, in ancient civilizations and among prehistoric peoples, would have included items with very little or no overlap with the kind of things that Hirsch and his associates have developed. Indeed, human beings are adaptable animals, and systems of culture are malleable. For these reasons, men and women at all times and in all places have developed media of communication for dealing with the problems of concern to them. So it is with modern culture.

If literacy as defined by elitist standards has declined in recent years, it is because the contents of these standards have lost some of their relevance for the everyday lives of people in general. Ironically, our threatening illiteracy is the direct result of people like Bloom and Hirsch, and to a certain extent the National Endowment for the Humanities, who put credibility in the wrong kind of thinking. Americans, despite their cynicism, are still a heroizing people, who pour all their beliefs into the hands of so-called authorities, especially authorities in education.

We love doomsayers, those who predict Armageddon, because we do not act until on the cutting edge of crisis.

The best example on this point is our authority figure in education, who stares us in the face with his forecasts of doom. Although the authority figures lament that Americans are illiterate because the figures have lost their authority, the fact is that Americans, if they are illiterate, lost their literacy while the conventional educational figures of our day were in authority teaching literacy in their conventional way. It was on their watch that literacy was stolen from us. Now they blame us for their failure, making us responsible for our loss. And they want us to trust the jewel of literacy to their hands again. But those tactics must be denied. Having failed once, they surely do not deserve our trust with such an important element of our culture a second time. We must find other custodians for the light because we realize that the privileged who want another go at the trust really want only to strengthen their own exclusive privilege, not share it.

Arnold's definition of culture is no more applicable today than it was when he first voiced it: "The best that is known and thought in the world." Implicit in this dictum is exclusion. Regrettably in the hands of public and private foundations, present-day funds dedicated ostensibly to promoting literacy tend to discourage rather than promote it because the monies are administered by people who want to revalidate their thinking and perpetuate their privilege, not share it. So they give the monies to people who think like them. They clone themselves intellectually, in precisely the same way adults tend to relive the life patterns of their youth no matter how foolish and disastrous those life patterns were.

In the 19th century, many thoughtful people, like Mark Twain speaking through Huck Finn in his *Adventures*, felt that the best way to get along with the elitists, that is his Duke and King—in the novel, those who pretended to have class—was to humor them. "If I never learnt nothing else out of pap," Huck said, "I learnt that the best way to get along with their kind of people is to let them have their own way." But Huck's—or Pap's—way of thinking disappeared with the mid-twentieth century growth of equal opportunity and challenge of privilege. We are no longer content to humor the self-proclaimed elite; we, too, want a piece of the action. Literacy of one sort or another is the key to the treasure-house of contemporary American opportunities and rewards.

The controversy over levels of literacy in the general population go beyond the consensus on the importance of basic reading, writing and computational skills. The controversy grows out of expanded uses of the concept of literacy. Because America and Western Europe have been shaped and continue to be driven by the evangelical fire of Judeo-

Christian culture, we are biased toward the word as word, not as communication. "In the beginning was the Word, and the Word was with God, and the Word was God," states John's version of the Creation in the King James version of the Bible. "Man's word is God in man," echoed the 19th-century English poet Alfred Tennyson. The weight of this argument seems irresistible. Since the Word and God are one, and this message is transmitted in print, to be opposed to print literacy is almost tantamount to blasphemy. Talk, as we all know, is both easy and cheap. Therefore, we are prejudiced in its use. It is hard to give up our rhetorical customs. "Words guard the shape of man, even when man has fled and is no longer there," comments George Seferis. Yet, a clearer view of Seferis' reverence for the word should have dictated a similar but different statement: words contour the shape of living society. Words, contrary to what Emerson once said, that words are archives, are in fact living entities which dip into the past and soar through the present into the future, deeply influencing culture as they persist. With this realization, changing concepts of the nature of the languages of communications are broadening and having great impact on conventional concepts of "cultural literacy," "mature literacy," "functional literacy," "computer literacy" and dozens of other such terms which direct our understanding of the dogma which dictate "what all Americans need to know."

In fact, words float and control our society. Of words, perhaps the most influential—other than nouns which are the building blocks—are clusters of concepts which we call metaphors, because metaphors are the spirit of language, clusters of concepts that take flat vernacular nouns and pronouns and make them come alive with new zest and meaning. Take for example the metaphor Thought breathes fire. Obviously, the two nouns *thought* and *fire* connected with the powerful verb *breathes* reach new power, for more is achieved by the concept than the sum of its parts. More is achieved through the metaphor than could be accomplished with the simile Thought is like Fire. The simile is language turned into spirit; the metaphor is language come alive. Its effect can be unlimited. It can make a nation out of disparate groups. "We achieve community with metaphor and consensus," correctly observes Robert Fulghum, in the special issue of *Newsweek* devoted to education (92).

Metaphor drives concepts in two directions concurrently, negatively and positively. Communication theorist Donald Schoen, with other theorists, properly believes that metaphor represents a "species of language which needs explaining or explaining away." This is the metaphor that is set in meaning and over-meaning and which serves in somewhat the same way that cliché or stereotype serves in prose-thinking. The metaphor—though charged with the electricity of poetry—controls the line and limit of the particular concept. So the metaphor

Man breathes Fire, which electrifies a concept, gives it extra power and dimensions, but controls its direction and extent of range.

These linguists, however, quite properly see the flip side of metaphor, what Schoen calls the "generative metaphor." This generative metaphor contains the fire of creativity and generates the spark that metaphor plants in the creative mind, the results of which are new thinking or new concepts or new interpretations of old ones. Thus, the metaphor, Man is Fire can generate three new concepts of the three words which spark totally new concepts. Thus, literacy becomes more and more the subject of specialists. The societal context of literacy has become increasingly specialized, and we live at a time in which the total available knowledge and information more than doubles with each passing decade. Collectively we now use an English language containing more than two million separate words. This is a vocabulary that contains more than eight times the number of terms and concepts that existed in the English language at the time of Shakespeare. Our language grows as demands increase.

The knowledge explosion in our society during the course of the 20th century confirms, rather than denies, the success of our educational system. This success is in large measure the result of our emphasis on the discovery and creation of new forms of knowledge, rather than an emphasis on rote memorization of discrete and unrelated facts about our social heritage. Beyond basic skills of reading, writing and math computations, the rewards for literacy primarily stem from a capacity for critical thinking, a capacity to synthesize and integrate information and a capacity for being innovative, which sometimes means mere recognition of the near-obvious. The system revolves around splendid performances and in-depth knowledge of specific topics rather than around superficial facts that are held in common. The parlor game "Trivial Pursuits," in which Hirsch would surely excel, gives explicit recognition to the limited usefulness of the kind of information Hirsch and Bloom wish to promote. But life and society are more complicated than "Trivial Pursuits," their demands and opportunities far more profound and promising.

Both men in different ways are obviously tapping a responsive chord in the public mind, however, or their books would not have been on the bestseller list, merchandising more than two million copies, and in the case of Hirsch garnering from the National Endowment for the Humanities two grants for continued research in the field. Hirsch's work, like much scholarship, had on its surface the semblance of logic and value. Both works draw from the enduring forms of negativism toward the public schools that has persisted since the beginning of compulsory attendance laws and from Americans' love of predictions of doomsday and disaster; in fact, it could be argued that American education thrives on the threat of doom that is ever-present in it. It never lives up to expectations. The recurrent charges against public education through most of the 20th century have included the views that schools are not adequately educating the nation's children, that schools are promoting inappropriate values, that teachers are not adequately qualified to teach, and that formal school attendance is no guarantee of getting or having or beginning an education. The stridency of the criticism might lead an unbiased observer to ask if the doom sayers have a hidden agenda that would not stand up in the bright light of democracy and even-tempered examination.

Hirsch's and Bloom's definitions of "what aspects of culture" and "whose culture" is to be taught are biased. The center of the culture they wish to promote consists of white, male, Eurocentric, middle-class values. In their view, racial and ethnic minorities are, and will continue to be, seriously disadvantaged unless they internalize this core culture of ideas, concepts and faculty information recommended by the authors. Thus, there is "a melting pot" or assimilation model for obliterating the ethnic and social heritages of the many subgroups that comprise the American system. Essentially, Hirsch and Bloom are promoting an ethnocentric view anchored in that past that all marginal or peripheral groups in contemporary society should give up their separate identities and join the American mainstream. Such a view of cultural literacy is promoted as an avenue of upward mobility for the underprivileged. Further, it is argued that the basic priority of public education should be to promote this objective. As commendable as this objective is, it overlooks reality.

The list consists essentially of a Hirsch's Familiar References, similar to our old companion, John Bartlett's *Familiar Quotations*, first published by the Harvard bookseller in 1855 in order to provide answers to students' questions, "Mr. Bartlett, who said...?" Bartlett's purposes, like Hirsch's, were to promote cultural literacy:

"The object of this work is to show, to some extent, the obligations our language owes to various authors for numerous phrases and familiar quotations which have become 'household words,'" he said in his Preface.

Hirsch's work is something of a Bartlett in reverse, "Here's what you should know," rather than "Here's the answer to your question." Hirsch's references, as Bartlett's had been a hundred fifty years earlier, are skewed and biased toward the past Eurocentric culture. Someone from outer space seeing America through glasses constructed of Hirsch's requisites of culture would read a strange world indeed.

There is plenty of Shakespeare in the volume (as there perhaps should be) but no James Baldwin; J.W. Goethe but no Sam Goldwyn; "Finland" but no "Fire next time"; Charles Lindbergh but no Amelia Earhart; Louis Armstrong but no Neil Armstrong; Babe Ruth but no Hank Aaron. The rules for inclusion seem to have been sheer whimsy or worse. Why, for example, one should include "Mary, Mary, Quite Contrary," "strike," "tornado," and "stomach" (without the other parts of the body) is difficult to understand. He includes "ampersand" but not "ellipsis"; one reference seems as erudite as the other. He includes "colon" (punctuation) but not "period" (punctuation), which seems far more important since it is used ten times as frequently. We have John Donne (everybody constantly refers to his poetry) and Sir Francis Drake and the Beatles and Elvis Presley, but no Sam Spade, no Raymond Chandler, no Dashiell Hammett, no Bob Hope or Bing Crosby. We have Huckleberry Finn but no Ahab or Ishamel, no *Moby-Dick*. We have "Orion" but no "Orioles," "bear market" but no "Bear Bryant." The list wanders on and on over hill and dell. Why not, "It ain't over 'til it's over" (guess who said that)? Some entries make sense, some others one finds hard to justify including. At least, however, one could expect the editors not to perpetuate obvious illiteracies and errors, but at least one creeps in. They include the illogical and confusing "holistic" with "wholistic." Well, as the saying goes, that should have been included but was not, "Nobody's perfect."

The truth is that this compilation is merely a list of what several people thought was a good enumeration of 5000 references, expressions and sentences that most people know or probably should know. But at what expense in time and money! Professor Hirsch says that he picked up the idea of the listing from someone in 1978. A talk before the Modern Language Association of America in 1981, a publication of an early draft in *The American Scholar* in 1983 and encouragement from the president of the Exxon Foundation drove him on. He has been supported by grants from The Center for Advanced Study in Behavioral Sciences and at least two from the National Endowment for the Humanities, which currently supports the Center at the University of Virginia. At least three persons have worked on this list, "refining it," for some ten years.

Professor Hirsch announces in the Preface to the book that the listing is not an encyclopedia, which they did not want to compile. Too bad it is not an encyclopedia or annotated listing; then it would be more useful. The listing reminds one of the numerous histories of words and expressions piled up in libraries, now consulted by the antiquarians or the merely curious. One such book is the 1811 *Dictionary of the Vulgar Tongue. A Dictionary of Buckish Slang, University Wit, and Pickpocket Eloquence*, published from the original *A Classical Dictionary of the Vulgar Tongue* (compiled by Frances Grose, an 18th century British antiquarian, and published originally in London, 1785). Such a book is priceless as a picture of vernacular language in early England; the meanings are given long and complete. It is difficult not to see in Hirsch the academic, pretentious equivalent of such late but far more useful books as Jane and Michael Stern's *The Encyclopedia of Bad Taste*, Frank Hoffmann and William G. Bailey's *Science & Science Fads*, or the numerous "Imponderable" books by David Feldman: *Why do Clocks Run Clockwise? When Do Fish Sleep? Who Put the Butter in Butterflies? Why Do Dogs Have Wet Noses?* These books give meanings and explanations. They teach. They do not merely provide a measure against which one can stand and see how fully he/she has remembered 5000 items that a small group of people consider of great importance in society today.

But Hirsch's compilation does not give meanings, and misses where it surely hit. It lists "Vulgate Bible" but no "vulgar tongue." He should obviously expand his list into at least 20,000 references. And that would be a long list to memorize. The regrettable fact is that this listing represents all the weakness in American education at this time. Three intellectuals have spent up to fifteen years "refining" a list of references most people already know, or don't want to know and get along just dandy without knowing. A whole international academic community, the Modern Language Association of America where it was first presented, is called upon as support, vast amounts of money are spent on it, and it convinces many of the American public of the validity of such a list.

Obviously, a computer could do in three minutes the same job that the intellectuals did over a lifetime, and make it much more complete. And if need be, each person could carry around a pocket computer to supply definitions whenever any of these terms are mentioned. Hirsch's listing is a gadget. The fact that American educators and intellectuals take it as anything more reveals why education in the U.S. is in trouble. The listing is a parlor game, perhaps amusing, yes. But the intellectual anatomy of an educated person? A thinking mind? Hardly. Emerson once remarked, "I hate quotations. Tell me what you know" (*Journal*, May 1849). Indeed anybody, even the devil, as we have been taught, can quote without thinking. What we need is more thinking and less quoting, more creative thinking and less remembering.

But it is easy for us to fool ourselves in what we are attempting and accomplishing. George Reedy, Press Secretary under President Lyndon Johnson and lately Nieman Professor of Journalism at Marquette University, in his farewell address in November 1990, argued, perhaps wistfully, that "I am not at all convinced that we professors 'educate' students. What we do is to force them to use their minds." Sadly, he is so wrong. Would that we did nothing but "educate" students! What we do instead is poke facts into students' minds and tell them, at least by example, that they do not need to do anything with the facts—just spout them forth when called upon to do so. It is a charade of human answering machines.

Kirch's arguments fail to recognize the multiplicity and cultural pluralism of the American system. The same realities are not shared by all segments of the population. America is not the same society for the super rich that it is for those caught up in poverty. The experiences with many aspects of American life are not the same for men as for women, nor for racial minorities as for the white, middle-class majority. The perceptions of America are not the same for the aged as for young adults, nor the college trained as for those with only a high school education or less. Differences among subgroups of the population must necessarily be recognized in public education if social life is to proceed in an orderly and workable fashion. By rejecting the pluralism of modern American society, the Bloom-Hirsch school of educational philosophers is promoting simplistic views that gloss over the complexity of the many phases and aspects of contemporary intellectual and social life.

The students scoring high on Hirsch's standards of literacy could at the same time be relatively uninformed about or indifferent to cultural diversity within the United States and dangerously lacking in knowledge and awareness of cultures in the rest of the world, Simonson and Walker correctly argue. To regard the transmission of white, male, middle-class values as the idea for our educational system is both misleading and fraught with negative potentials. It is misleading in the sense of a misplaced concreteness that emphasizes a narrow set of elitist values, esoteric concepts and idiosyncratic events. This is an emphasis that has little relevance for the everyday lives of most Americans today. It is dangerous in the sense that it accentuates a nationalistic and enthnocentric style of thought at the very time that the world, despite the outbreak of militant ethnicity and regionalicity, is becoming more highly interdependent and economically, politically and culturally dependent on one people or another.

Why, for example, should Americans today be culture-bound to give primary importance to culture as that having been defined by the nineteenth century British poet and essayist Matthew Arnold as "man's best thoughts most beautifully expressed" when the task of those people mouthing such elitist dicta comes when they are desperately grubbing for heat, light, housing and food? Surely of more immediate concern, relevance and driving power are the problems of freedom, economic stability and equal rights for women and minorities. Martin Luther King Jr.'s call for passive resistance to injustice may continue to please the white establishment but the voice in the streets shouts quite a different anthem, "Death to injustices." Literacy in Biblical injunctions resonates through the corridors of time, but street literacy is a much more burning and immediate issue. Literacy these days comes with a thousand faces and in a thousand voices, all of which fracture society into dozens of pieces. All make up the democratic constituents of all the society broken into dozens of pieces. All make up the democratic constituents of all the nationalities of this nation. A decade ago a Harvard University survey showed that over 100 nations had contributed, mainly by immigration through Ellis Island in New York Harbor and Angel Island in the San Francisco Bay, to the melting pot that is American society. Now, in 1990, the number has swollen to more than half that many again coming through scores of points of entry. The growing number, if we are to be consistent with our stated political open policy and our history, should be a cause of pride. America's strength has been its representation of a multiplicity of nations. Japan these days likes to make some kind of political statement by bragging of its racial purity and to base its vaunted high literacy rate on that purity. But if that is correct, the final chapter has yet to be written. Classical Chinese exclusion and purity though the centuries did not protect that nation's literacy and national purity from invasion and takeover by an outside people from the north. There are human and political forces far stronger than the standards that form the basis of the implications on which Hirsch's literacy is based.

The major unifying force is, of course, television. Early in its history people were beginning to recognize the universal magic of that medium, with enthusiasm as great as that which greeted the invention of the fast printing presses in the 18th century. "Television means the world in your home and in the homes of all the people of the world," wrote Thomas Hutchinson in 1938 (Madsen 113). "It is the greatest means of communication ever developed by the human mind. It should do more to develop friendly neighbors, and to bring understanding and peace on earth than any other single material force in the world today."

"Television is one of the most powerful forces man has ever unleashed upon himself," observed Nicholas Johnson, Commissioner of the Federal Communication Commission, under President Lyndon Johnson, and author of *How To Talk Back To Your Television Set* (1970). "The quality of human life may depend enormously upon our efforts to comprehend and control that force." Johnson's argument of talking back to the TV is based upon the assumption that the viewer understands the dynamics of television. If that viewer is only a passive, mute couch-potato, all he/she can do is turn the set on/off, remain awake/go to sleep. Passivity is not the dynamic of fluency. Fluency prompts action. To talk to the set, or to talk back to the set, one must understand the language. To control this cool medium, in McLuhan's terminology, one must be a participant.

The global village predicted by Marshall McLuhan three decades ago is driving more and more toward reality, through the learned art of talking back to the television set, and the pressure of 4-5 billion people and growing at the rate of three every second of every day, or a quarter million every twenty-four hours. Most are poor and ignorant, straining for immediate release from bondage and are driving more toward a global ghetto than a global village. Television, contrary to what such Marxists as Raymond Williams believed, is a means of finally de-ghettoizing people, of liberating them. Television does not manipulate and control. Ultimately, the people control television simply by the flip of a switch. People have learned to master the medium. They have come a long way since the small, erratic picture was introduced in the United States in 1939 and developed in the '50s. Now that television is large-screened, almost always reliable technologically and available on scores of channels, people have ceased holding it in awe—as they once did books and always do a newly introduced phenomenon—and treat television as an everyday medium of communication which must satisfy demands or be turned off.

If cats can look at kings in person, as the saying goes, then through television people can level off with lords. Commoners appear on the same program as kings and queens—and tyrants. Television is the greatest democratizer and equalizer yet developed by man. Crime fiction writer Ross Macdonald once said that his detective, Lew Archer, could have access to any house or castle, to anybody, at least once. Television allows access more than once. It is the universal, golden key of admission, the eternal pass. It is the ever-ready and instant movie in the home.

Television does not make us free, but it gives us a leg up on freedom and it brings the semblance of the fruits of freedom. Often semblance is more powerful than reality.

Naturally, the drive is uneven in its results. Research in villages in Japan, for example, reveals that television, instead of homogenizing dissimilar people, tends to keep them, at least for a time, dissimilar. Television advances the differences. In such villages, according to a Japanese researcher, "TV advanced the differences among local villages. It is due not only to differences of the broadcasting situation by areas but also to the differences of cultural background of the community concerned. The differences of natural and ecological environments, types of production and social relations make the difference."

But as its use becomes more saturated, television will undoubtedly tend more and more to make cultures similar. Television communicates through the bonds of commonality in us all. It plays on and develops our similarities. With its instantaneous animation of pictures tied with the spoken language, television is the universal medium, and literacy in it is indispensable if we are going to utilize it, and understand society, fully.

The lure and unifying force of television was dramatically demonstrated in the 1990 World Soccer Games, when an estimated 1.5 billion people all around the world centered their attention on a common subject for a week. Had somebody been able to utilize this common interest for an active goal instead of a pastime, perhaps through a subliminal force, the common movement of so many people would have been irresistible and overwhelming, as have the several rock concerts lately to provide aid to the world poor. On a smaller geographical scale, television actually brought about the end of the Vietnam War by bringing the horror of mass death into the American living room and forcing governmental action. It is just possible that it might have prevented war in the Persian Gulf crisis that began building in August 1990. No people can watch the violence of mass killings and the full body bags being brought home month after month without eventually crying out in protest and effecting changes. For that reason, both peoples confronting one another in a potential war should have open access to free television. Further, television is the ultimate world theater, able to satisfy the most militant ego-maniac in the world. Since after all, television is a one-way theater with minimum audience feedback and stimulation, it is bound, sooner or later, to lose some of its compelling attraction for the person who wants his image always before the eyes and mind of people, and the world will quietly close a theater that has distractions which can be contained.

Clearly then, though there are many forces acting on cultures and people to drive them toward separateness and divisiveness, the common lure of television, which feeds on and reflects the commonality of us all, is bringing people closer together.

Imposing a set of elitist values tends to downplay tolerance for group differences within the United States and in the global community by insisting on uniformity, imposing blinders on the many changes that are occurring and suggesting that our educational system officially endorses the principles of hegemony. To endorse the specific values recommended by Hirsch and Bloom would have the effect of shifting attention away from the emerging concerns of women, ethnic minorities and other excluded and underprivileged groups in our society, of sweeping those issues under the rug in order to deny justice in our society and of inviting corrective explosions in the immediate future. The ghettos of American cities—not to mention those of the rest of the world, especially in the underdeveloped areas—are a powder keg set to blow up the Hirsch-Bloom world.

We see in Hirsch and Bloom none of the themes emphasized that are necessary for transforming the United States into a more humane society, to borrow a term from recent political rhetoric. We see no prescriptions for developing sensitivity to the needs of underprivileged and excluded minorities, to the monumental problems confronted by poor people of all ages, to the injustices of gender discrimination, to the unrecognized needs of an aging population, or to the need for preserving and enhancing the physical environment we will be leaving for future generations.

There is none of Martin Luther King Jr.'s dream of someday there being equality of all people in the U.S. and the world. There is nothing of Jacques Cousteau's cry for eco sensitivity so that the earth can be saved for future generations. There is no drive to find solutions to the problems of AIDS and drug abuse. There is no probe into the problems of warring factions in South Africa, Asia and elsewhere. There is no hint of inquiry into the problem of decreasing energy supplies and a shrinking planet.

Instead, the formula offered is primarily the promise of upward mobility within the business corporation or within governmental bureaucracies. But even there the proposed solutions are misleading. The overriding tasks by the youth of the nation we have brought into our materialistic and consumer-oriented values are not primarily those of developing knowledge about early American history or canonical forms of literature. Rather, the keys to making it within a materialistic framework are those of learning how to cope with bureaucracy, refining the skills of impression management and developing specialized expertise that has marketability. Widespread acceptance of either elitist or instrumental values will promote the individualism of our culture, but will at best make a very small force to drive the United States toward sensitive and humane society.

If the aim of education today is to promote communication and understanding among all segments of our past and present population instead of fragmenting society, an emphasis should be placed on an explicit recognition of the pluralization of life-worlds in modern society. We do not share the realities, and the vocabularies we use are surrounded with connotative meanings that go far beyond dictionary and encyclopedic types of definition. Equality, justice and opportunity cannot mean as much to the ghetto youth as to the white suburban privileged youth. The basic problems in communication are not stemming from the lack of knowledge of the English language or of the social heritage of the American people. These are a part of the shared understandings that grow out of living in a particular society. We may not be able to itemize the particulars, but we know enough of the generalities to be willing to throw ourselves voluntarily into battle situations to defend "the American way of life." We would not so willingly sacrifice ourselves if we did not know what we were dying for.

Instead, all communication necessarily involves interacting individuals taking one another into account and modifying one's behavior accordingly. For this reason, social life is necessarily dynamic, rather than static, and individuals necessarily write their own social scripts as they go along. The notion that mastery of the 5000 items listed by Hirsch and his associates, fulfilling as it were one of the implications of Bloom's theses, would solve basic communication problems in the workplace, in the political battleplace or in interpersonal relations is both an absurdity and an unwarranted assumption about the coherence, stability and simplicity of modern social living. Instead of healing open wounds, Hirsch's medicine would exacerbate them. Instead of uniting society, his philosophy would shift the heart a little and emphasize the polarities.

Rather than saying, "Let us all be socialized into a common mold," the payoffs for society would be much greater if we accepted the old political dictum of Mao T'se Tung to "Let a thousand flowers bloom," or asked for illumination from George Bush's 1988 Presidential campaign talk of a "thousand points of light." We live in a time when a great deal of experimentation is taking place in lifestyles and in people's relationships with one another. The center cannot hold, if there has ever been a center to American culture, against the weight of the experimental attitude. It would be more nearly correct to say that there is very little at the center of modern culture upon which all can agree. Whether we focus on the political, the economic, the scientific or the cultural spheres of contemporary America, the primary changes are occurring at the margin or at the periphery rather than at the center. That center is being chipped away.

We do not have a fully developed or a fully "mature" society, and for that reason we lack a clear cultural definition of what constitutes "mature literacy." We have no concept in our society resembling the notion from ancient China that the edges of the empire constitute the boundaries of the moral universe. With the Chinese this was a given no less unquestionable than that the day was divided into lightness and darkness, and the year into seasons.

Instead, our society remains in a continuous state of flux and development. History is not yet finished with its experiments on forms of communication, kinds of social organization and types of interpersonal relationships. So an educational system that promotes premature closure and denial of complexity—and communicates only in the voice of the past—will be dysfunctional to a nation embedded in a world that places a premium on novelty, innovation and creativity. It writes the last chapter to the book after only the first part has been assumed.

Though the process is generally more painful than pulling a set of molars, increasingly academics are discovering what the public has known since Classical times, and probably back to the dawn of humankind's—as well as animals—awareness of itself and society: that the arts of various kinds and the humanities can have a therapeutic value. "The arts arise from the human need to be healed, to be cured," declared Gregory A. Staley, a classicist who is acting director of the Research Center for Arts and Humanities at the University of Maryland at College Park. Such awareness is the backbone of folklore of all times, of humankind's need for and appreciation of diversion and relief from the pressures of daily existence. Folklore is made up of awareness of these needs.

But canonists in literature generally would be more restrictive. They tend to discover the value of the arts to lie in elite elements or to evaluate to the elite what they discover to be self-servingly valuable. Two examples shed light on the process.

"The ancient Romans," says Marilyn Katz in *The Chronical of Higher Education* (A6, A9), associate professor of Classics at Wesleyan University, "believed that the study of human letters could alleviate pain." Further, George S. Rousseau, a professor of English and 18th century studies at the University of California, Los Angeles, in the same issue of the *Chronical*, points out that a mysterious disease in medieval Italy called tarantism, believed to result from the bite of the tarantula, could be cured by music and especially by performance of the dance now known as the tarantella. Such an observation is hardly new. If poets and playwrights know anything about human nature, we have known since William Congreve's *The Mourning Bride* (1697) that "music hath charms to soothe the savage breast, to soften rocks, or bend a knotted oak." But our academic sages often reinvent the wheel and glory in its discovery rather than ride off into the distance on certain proved assumptions.

As usual, even in our own day, humanists are unable to give an unbiased report on the value of the arts and humanities. Ignorance or willful misinterpretation of facts steals from the popular and gives to the elite, a Robin Hood esthetic grab in reverse. Professor Stanley Jackson, professor of psychiatry and history of medicine at Yale University, observes that as early as the sixteenth century people were writing "about the role of the imagination in both psychological illness and health." Professor Rousseau, cited earlier, talks about 18th century English novelist Laurence Sterne's *Tristram Shandy* (1759-67), which he wrote in the midst of his wife's madness and his own sickness. What has come to be called Sterne's masterpiece was looked upon at the time of publication as eccentricity and bad taste in popular humor, and has been likened in technique, in the words of the authors of *A Literary History of England*, to "comic-strip drawings in present-day newspapers." But now the picture is different and more positive. Often, age and distance in time and space canonize literature and events, especially if the canonization is needed to substantiate a point. It not only makes a difference, in Biblical terms, in whose ox is being gored, but also in whose cattle are being fattened. Often necessity causes changes in bedfellows, and canonists change their texts out of whim, conviction or in order to maintain status. Canonists are not indifferent to self-interests. But they often misread the route to fulfilling those self-interests. They often cut off their face to spite their nose.

It should be mentioned as a reminder that therapy has been needed throughout the ages by the non-elite as well as the elite. The wrath of God has rained on the common people as well as the elite, on the just as well as the unjust. Unfortunately, the common people have not been financially, politically or culturally strong enough to afford relief from their troubles as the elite have. But academics should realize the function of popular culture through the ages. It has been not only a way of life but also entertainment and therapy. It is the poor person's therapy and medium of adjustment to life. Though it has been agonizingly slow in coming, the voice of the people, like that of the turtle, is now, for better or worse, being heard in the land through polls and purchasing power. It only postpones the inevitable, or for their satisfaction seems to delay it, when academics continue to insist that the language of literacy is reserved for the canonists and their canon. Literacy is a constantly growing skill in handling communication that can never be forced into the media that contained it yesterday. Once a new means of communication is recognized, then skill in working in it is established as literacy.

Non-academic groups interested in developing the literacy of our citizens are springing up all around us, and are generally using nontraditional means, canonists and their canon. In postponing change a lot of deviltry is visited upon the heads of all society, as elitists try to maintain their hegemony. In maintaining what appears, if it in fact is not, a no-compromise position in their so-called standards, elitists would willfully or unwittingly keep most of a population out of the enjoyments of literacy. Literacy, perhaps we fail at times to remember, is a blissful state everybody would like to enjoy if all people were allowed to handle in their own ways the keys to the door of admission. This admission, like political equality and presumably free public education, must be in fact guaranteed. In order to guarantee this right, there need not be a destruction of the accomplishment of canonical literacy, and surely not what people will call a weakening of standards. All that is necessary to begin is a realization that literacy is not a state of accomplishment that in order to be valuable must be an exclusionary club not open to everyone. With this new attitude—point of view and philosophy—as driving force, all that is necessary is a new decision that literacy is fluency in communication—nothing arcane or secret, just nuts and bolts fluency in communication.

Non-academic groups interested in developing the literacy of our citizens are springing up all around us, and generally using nontraditional means, or nontraditional media, to promote their goals. Enterprise Village, a non-profit organization situated in Florida, for example, is teaching fifth graders to handle everyday problems through having to cope with them. The Corporate Community School, a Business-

Community partnership with 300,000 members, is achieving striking results from its approach to education for utilitarian or nontraditional media, to promote their goals. Both groups, and many others like them in government and the private sector, realize that the proper end of education is action, not inaction. Education is a hands-on training that teaches through participation, not theorizing, a knowledge as old as the need for someone to instruct someone else in a learning situation.

Ernest L. Boyer, former U.S. Commissioner of Education, now president of Carnegie Foundation for the Advancement of Teaching, and lifetime advocate of proper educational methods, was eloquent when he came down hard on those educationists who speak about "liberal versus vocational" education to the disparagement of the latter. "Education," he said, "has always been a blend of inspiration and utility, but because of tradition, lethargy, ignorance and snobbery, mindless distinctions are made between what is vocationally legitimate and illegitimate." In a reference to what must seem to many a dangerous aspect of Ben Franklinism, Boyer insists that the work ethic should play a strong role in the true meaning of liberal education. His remarks obviously parallel the assumed distinctions between "elite" and popular literacies and advocate the latter. Education is a drive toward literacy, and literacy is the means of serving education. They are an unending wheel of advancement.

Perhaps no better example of the practicality of everyday influence in life-activities can be found than in the experiences of John C. Campbell and his wife, Olive Dame Campbell, and their John C. Campbell Folk School in Brasstown, North Carolina.

The Campbells became convinced that the route to assistance to the poverty and illiteracy in Appalachia lay in educating the people in local needs and in persuading them to stay in Appalachia and develop themselves and their locale, "adapting education to environment." They became convinced of the potential of this philosophy by studying the Danish folk school or "People's Colleges," begun in Denmark in the 19th century when that country was wracked by war and poverty. The students of the Danish "People's Colleges" did not attend to learn grammar and arithmetic, but for the vocational training in agriculture, carpentry and daily subsistence that would educate them to live fruitful lives in their communities. This was not a giving-up of the broader outside life but an enriching development of the life they were leading.

The John C. Campbell Folk School was opened in January 1926, dedicated to teaching a practical fluency in the media of the neighborhood—the everyday activities—and grew into an effective force in the community.

Increasingly, the wisdom of such schooling is permeating our whole concept of education. Americans, who are if anything a practical people, are at times able to recognize needed and practical notions of education and how to promote it. Though some methods need not be applicable across the board, where useful they should be practiced.

Speaking of the challenge of using every means for making learning exciting and possible, world-famous violinist Itzhak Perlman said about teaching music cultures, with equalitarian frankness and reality: "Make them [composers] human, not idols; not objects, but people with feelings and problems...Reading letters of these guys and their music takes on a whole new meaning: (*Newsweek*, Fall/Winter 1990: 49). If people and ideas are made everyday realities and obtainable, people are likely to undertake the task and pleasure of understanding them. The more education is made democratic, the more it is accessed.

The term *literacy* in its initial usage was linked with literature (Latin, *littera*, letter) and referred to ability to write and to read words. Eventually, the linkage with literature implied reading, writing and being able to appreciate works of so-called artistic merit, such as prose, fiction, essays, plays and poetry. Over time the term *literacy* has broadened to include virtually anything written. This broadening was only the forerunner of expanded meanings. Now, literacy means well-educated, having knowledge or learning, and though by implication that knowledge or learning should be extensive, in fact it can be rather limited. So literacy actually means *fluency*, the ability to communicate and understand in some medium of communication. The number of such media is already almost limitless and with many new avenues opening it is growing. It is wise for us to become conversant in them, or at least to recognize their roles in the world, before we all stand with our illiteracy showing while the desperate need for, and benefits of, fluency proliferates.

Chapter Five

Art: The Premier Language Problem

Art, because of its nature, presents an interesting problem in the need for full and open fluency. It is the medium most easily exploited for ulterior purposes by those people who speak the language among those who do not.

Of all forms of elite culture, art is probably the most mysterious and the most easily abused by those who want to make it seem more esoteric than it really is. Art is often attached to the word *genius*, instead of *artisan* or *craftsman*, which would be the words generally used in folk or popular art to designate what artists do. *Genius* is used because the word can be forced, in context, to evoke special tones and meanings. This is especially true if the *genius* is working in a medium that is subject to various subtleties and people are generally not sufficiently sophisticated in its language.

The word *genius*, according to the Romans who coined it, denoted a guardian spirit assigned to a person at birth. Thus *genius* is the essence of the individual, of any individual, and it can be celestial or devilish, heroic or mediocre. Through the centuries it has been especially favorable to the mentally and physically different—a sort of special compensation awarded by a thoughtful and protective God for other deficiencies. So the popular use of the term, as a person especially adept at finding a proper fishing hole, at running footballs, flying a kite, baking a cake— at doing anything that requires special skill—is more nearly proper than the elite effort to make it a barrier by which to keep people unenfranchised and therefore out of the small brotherhood (occasionally sisterhood) of art appreciators and enslaved by their ignorance.

Most people can do most arts with a certain pedestrian skill. Most of us can carry a tune with a certain reasonableness and can improvise both words and music needed to bridge a certain forgotten part, or even hum our own creations. Most of us can drive an automobile, work fairly well on a job, even understand a joke. So music, sports, most of life's experiences are not imbued with the mysterious quality that is attached by its brotherhood to art.

73

Most children, too, can use a pencil or paintbrush to draw reasonable likenesses of the artifacts and experiences of life, even of dreams and nightmares. In fact, such drawings are now being used widely to get children to release part of their pent-up emotions resulting from such traumatic experiences as child abuse, rape, terrorist attacks and fear. Therapists look upon these youthful expressions of feelings as a language speaking about the feelings that conventional words cannot express. Increasingly, also, art schools—both academic and commercial—are telling people that they can become artists if they allow themselves the expense and trouble of becoming fluent in the medium.

But art is not allowed to be merely another expression in a medium of communication. It is elevated into a quasi-religious experience. It is converted into a holdover of magic and necromancy, and a mystery that only a few, those initiated into the rites, can understand. Thus, contrary to all common sense, it is made the premier hoax and hoaxer in life. "If the most brilliant con man had to invent a commodity or trick best suited to hoax," insightfully writes Jon Huer in *The Great Art Hoax*, "it would easily be collectible art."

The reasons for this continued hoaxing are obvious. The interests are too vested, there is too much money, there are too many reputations at stake to allow freedom of speech in this medium. What would happen if art became democratized and broke out all over? What would result if common mortals found that they could in fact paint and draw meaningful pictures? Like an outbreak of democracy, such recognition of reality would be very uncomfortable to live with, since art appreciation is excellent to talk about but painful to share too democratically. Further, and most important of all, the bottom would drop out of the value of art, and the elitists would lose a powerful club with which to demonstrate their superiority over other people.

In the other arts, there is less chance for exclusivity and mystery. In the sister art, music, most musicians play all sorts of music and composers write all sorts. Mozart composed music for children, for "popular" opera. Ralph Vaughn Williams composes all sorts. Leonard Bernstein wrote for Carnegie Hall, for Broadway, for movies. Violinists like Yizchak Rabin enjoy playing Mozart and rock 'n' roll. Arthur Fiedler, capable of leading both classical and popular music, did not despise the latter. One accomplished musician once said that all he had been taught at the Julliard School of Music was how to flex his wrists artistically as he lifted his hands from the piano. Music is not a mystery any more. Among the several kinds—generally recognized as separate but equal— one likes one kind or another—or all—and that is pretty much the end of the business.

But not so with art. There is too much money, prestige and phoniness invested in what one person calls "collectible art" to allow it honestly on an open market. Picasso can have been candid about what art is but his candor does not demystify the product. "What isn't" he answered when asked what art is. But it is difficult not to make even the most obvious statements of "the masters," as we like to call them, oracular when in fact they are only mundane and obvious.

Indeed, we know that art is anything that is called art, is displayed as art, and is set aside as being different—and therefore superior to—other non-art objects. The bottom would drop out of prices of collectible art and those people left holding the pictures and galleries would be thrown back upon private enjoyment as the only fruit of their investments. Elitists would lose a powerful sacrament with which to canonize their superiority over the common people. Thrown back on the exquisite joy of individual art enjoyment as being art's only excuse for being, most people would have to admit the slim pickings of that pleasure, and would have to confess that utility—the serving of some purpose—is art's reason for being. In so doing, art connoisseurs would have to cheapen themselves and admit only common clay as their constituent make-up. This they would find unacceptable.

But such an attitude by the connoisseurs demonstrates one of their many unchanging intractabilities. Historian of art Alan Gowans has demonstrated that the very nature of art, almost without exception, is its utility. Art throughout history, from the paintings on the walls of France, to the rich paintings on the Sistine Chapel, to the various statements of Rauschenberg and Picasso—to the rich workings of Walt Disney—has been created not in a vacuum to serve no purpose but instead for a deliberate purpose—to indicate the presence of game, to convert people from heathenism to Christianity, to entertain, to sell a product.

But the art community subsists in a make-believe world where appearances are kept distant from reality. So inexact is the achievement of art, in fact, that people are unable to substantiate any statement about it, unable to achieve any consensus about the quality of an object. So-called authorities who may have devoted a lifetime to studying art often change their minds about the authenticity or quality of a particular article. The authorities differ among themselves and within themselves. In a world of such inexactitude it is easy willfully or unwillingly to dupe oneself and the unsuspecting and trusting. Deceit of self and public is the order of the day.

Mainly, however, the deceit comes from those people—the camp-followers—who benefit from it. Artists, of course, benefit in fame and sometimes fortune. They enjoy being "creators," driven by some unique genius, and superior to the common herd, though one is hard-put to find a starving artist who would not trade fame for fortune straightaway.

Some do achieve fortune. Salvidor Dali, for example, learned early that there was great money in pretentiousness, and he gave us that pretentiousness in appearance and élan. Picasso early on discovered there was profit in quantity of works produced and created fast, and turned out more than 10,000 works in various media—and everything he turned out was judged if not great then different, innovative, exploratory, "ingenious," and potentially great, despite the fact that his style was so imitative of itself that in effect he copied his own works. Critics and collectors who have trusted their reputations and money in his works—individuals, museums, art galleries, companies—felt the need to develop the myth about Picasso's greatness. Artists, and art, have always lived in and on myth. It is the stuff on which their dreams are built. One is that creative people have such important thoughts that their every doodle is revealing and important. Sometimes it is, of course, as revealing the development of an idea or mind. Sometimes they are just doodles. And everybody doodles.

Artists are generally productive people. They turn out thousands and thousands of artworks of some description, "almost," says Jon Huer in his perceptive and revealing book *The Great Art Hoax*, "like a factory machine." Add to these numbers of finished works all the preliminary sketches and numbers of variants and the number any one artist turns out is doubled or tripled. It would be too demanding to ask that every one of these doodles be valuable. "It would be asking too much of posterity to treat each of their works as a precious artwork of enormous importance," Huer suggests.

Yet that is precisely what the money-changers and reputation-builders do, by canonizing every scrap. In their self-serving religion every thread, every line is a part of the holy garment of the artists and is to be revered—and marketed as such. In the Middle Ages, pigs' bones were marketed as saints' bones. The modern-day equivalent is scraps of art masterpieces sanctified and pushed into the holy canon.

Throughout history artists have held a tenuous place in society. They have always been a "kept" people—serving the same purposes as musicians, courtesans and other diners at the tables of the rich and powerful. With no visible means of support, artists have always been kept at the pleasure and for the amusement of the keeper. And they have had to satisfy their patrons. Michelangelo set out to paint the Sistine Chapel to the order of Pope Julius II, and when the Pope defaulted on his payments, Michelangelo went on strike, not finishing his work until the Pope paid. Mozart was never quite able to please his patrons and he died a pauper. Picasso painted his famous "Guernica" (1937) as what he called "a weapon in the struggle against Fascism" specifically protesting the German and Italian bombing of the Basque town of

Guernica during the Spanish Civil War. Such a work was innovative in subject matter if not in statement.

Artists pride themselves on—and are promoted on the basis of—their innovativeness. Sometimes they do push back the edge of invention and discovery. Jon Huer gives a marvelous—and absurd—example of this nudging of the border. At an art exhibit he was struck by a painting entitled "Grayed Yellow Vertical Rectangle," supplied by an artist named Jo Baer. Huer quoted the official description of the work. "...A flat white (or very pale gray) painted canvas with a narrow black border either intricately broken by fine color lines in the upper, heavier margin, or evenly lined with a narrower inner border of grayed (though often intense) color—a luminescent shadow rather than a direct contrast. This inner border serves as a binding agent for the whole painting. It mediates the encounter of dark edge and light field, while adding an almost imperceptible tension; and it deters the white center from recoiling into space and becoming a window." This detailed and graphic description must have required more mental ingenuity than the painting had, since it was nothing but a white canvas placed in a frame, absolutely blank.

Often, however, artists also sit on tradition and perpetuate it. Historically they have been widely used to paint portraits of their patrons and benefactors, as well as of scenes that perpetuated the past and tradition. Portraits have always been used to demonstrate the strength of past figures, and as such have implied, at least, that the strength of the past is coursing through the bloodstream of the descendants of the bloodline. Portraits of America's great leaders—to wit, Stuart's *George Washington*—reach more toward the past than the present and the future. Just as pictures of great battles of the past demonstrate the greatness of the people who participated. From that greatness we are supposed to gain strength and inspiration for greatness.

Because of the nature of the work and the need for a certain bulk, throughout history artists have generally recognized the value of piece work. In many ways, the artist factory was one of the original production lines and sweat-shops. In these production-lines the artist outlined the form and let his students or associates fill in the details. There was obviously no need for the master to paint background when it consisted only of dabbing paint on canvas, and anybody could do it as well as anybody else. It was journeyman work. With this production-line the artist could turn out a much larger quantity. If people liked a picture of a haystack, say, then all the artist had to do was have his original copied and he could go around and sign these "originals" and authenticate them.

In his work the average artist does not slave for hours at his easel. Once he/she has got the knack of it, and developed his own style, more time is spent in non-painting activities than at the easel. Some people would say that the artist has a better job than working would be.

With the artist's work comes, of course, the problem of authenticity. The work of a Master is a priceless masterpiece. That, although it may seem to be qualitatively just as accomplished, by an unknown name is worthless. With such criteria for value, clearly there always lurks the temptation for the accomplished though unrecognized artist to taste a little of the fortune of the Master by feeding at his table, by creating some of the Master's works. It is estimated that at least half the "masterpieces" owned by individuals and art galleries are forgeries. Art history is full of the stories of individuals who have painted forgeries of the masterpieces with such consummate skill that not only did they get by with hoaxes at the time but the works are still passing as genuine. Some of the forgeries are, in fact, so authentic that the genuine artist himself cannot declare them forgeries.

Tom Keating, in England, "sexton blaked" (as he called forging) many works that he ascribed to Palmer, Blake, Degas, Renoir, Sisley, Feininger, Nolde, Munch, Goya, Rembrandt and thousands of others. Elmyr de Hary, made famous by Clifford Irving in his book *Fake*, himself a forger, with his two partners sold over 2000 forged paintings of Impressionists. In the National Gallery in Washington, six Vermeers were reduced to three in 1989 because of their lack of genuineness, and one of the remaining three is suspected of being a forgery. Throughout the art world, authorities and owners refuse to speculate on the genuineness of their holdings. One of the jokes in the art business, grim but true, goes like: "X (supply your name) painted some 700 (supply your own number) pictures and 1500 of them are in America."

Forgery actually comes easy and natural with our method of training artists. We train and encourage forgery by on-the-job training. All one has to do to see the training ground is to go to a gallery of famous pictures and look around at the men and women who are openly copying the masterpieces. It is a method of training, this copying, as it is in other fields.

During the 50s and 60s, virtually every class in composition in American colleges and universities consisted of trying to teach students to write like Ernest Hemingway. Since the 40s the models for writing American hard-boiled crime fiction have been Dashiell Hammett and Raymond Chandler. Writers have judged their skill and have been judged by the critics on how hard-boiled their fiction was. Critics judged writers on how nearly they approached the skill of their predecessors. Some writers became more Hemingwayesque than Hemingway, more hard-boiled than their masters had been.

Some have become so skilled that their work can hardly be distinguished from that of the masters. Many unfinished literary works— as well as those in other media—have been finished by creators' "disciples" or followers. At his death Raymond Chandler left four chapters of an unfinished novel. This beginning has been completed by crime novelist Robert Parker, published as *Poodle Village* (1990), and critics are proud that the seam between the two authors cannot be identified. So, copying without trying to pass it off as authenticate is a recognized skill in most arts. It is only where there is a kind of artistic plagiarizing, or passing off a Master's idea as one's own, that owners and dealers get their backs up.

In his crime novel, crime novelist George C. Chesbro tells the story of an artist who paints his large canvases in such a way that small squares can be cut out and framed and sold and treasured as complete works of art. Or the whole large canvas can be reassembled as the original and complete work. That is a real piece of art work! Who is being hoaxed? It is like saying that each segment of a novel, each stanza of a poem, each bite of a television program is the whole work. Is there no limit to the foolishness. Apparently the proof of the pudding is the recommendation of the chef, the quality of the wine determined by the label on the bottle.

What fakes these elitists be.

Generally artists do not try to pass their copies off as the work of the original artist. They recognize that they must understand their place in the hierarchy and the art market. It is one thing for an unknown artist to paint a more creative and imaginative work than the master had. But as a masterpiece the superior art is worthless. Quality in art equals reputation and marketability—marketability, with reputation, ownership, history, etc., equals quality. In other words, in art, quality has little to do with verisimilitude to subject, truth of presentation, or quality of feeling on the part of the artist. If there is some coincidence between likeness and the piece itself that is a fortunate coincidence. If there is none, then that can be explained away and made a virtue. The important thing is that elusive ingredient fame. In the art world, once fame is established, an artist does not have to revalidate it with every work. Once it is established it is likely to last longer than the fifteen minutes artist Andy Warhol was inclined to guarantee to everyone. Reputation is like blood-line; once it is established it is likely to last because no one wants to challenge its owner.

The unacceptability of the hoax and the continuation of actual fraud in the art world can be readily seen in the fact that judgment of the quality of art is personal, financial and reputational. The artists are really the least important players in the game of art. They are still being "kept" in the same way they were in earlier days. Except now they are kept by broader forces of society—the powerful, the rich and the "critics"—and are fattened not on money but on reputation and fame. When a "masterpiece" is turned out by the artist, he or she is paid a nominal fee or reward, as creator and owner. But once the artist is no longer around to reap the benefits of his work, the price is likely to skyrocket through artificial stimulation. Intrinsic value plays no part whatsoever with what a work of art sells for and is valued at. Thus, a second-rate rather mediocre picture of flowers by Van Gogh can sell in 1990 for $84 million.

But the artist, were he alive, would get little of the bonanza. He is largely irrelevant. Like a mother, he is needed at birth, but after that the child—the work itself—soon takes on a life of its own, distinct from the parent. As long as they can be exploited—or their work cannot be taken over by electronic devices, say computers—artists will be tolerated. Critics and displayers do not want to amputate the hand that draws the golden egg. But if they ever become unruly and cannot be controlled, they will be replaced. Who will need them? They can easily be replaced by the art factory that will produce pictures of anything on demand. Critics and dealers—and displayers—can use their own devices to make the masterpieces scarce and difficult to get. There is no reason why the Starving Artists' works cannot be manipulated enough to keep the starving artists starving and producing "masterworks" for the benefit of the collector.

Art is big business. Critics' reputations grow big on its back. Museums and galleries achieve international reputation by owning and displaying it. The wealthy use it as the modern equivalent of the ultimate Conspicuous Consumption. After they have their mansions, cars, yachts, hotels, casinos, even philanthropic foundations, they need something else to set them off from other people with the same worldly goods. Taste is the difference. Corporations show their chic status or the taste of the CEO by displaying in the Corporate Office the most expensive art works that the auction houses sell. The Japanese seem especially eager to show their degree of Westernization by investing large sums in Western art. Nelson Rockefeller owned one of the largest collections in the U.S. He said that art had meant so much in enriching his life that he wanted other people to have some of the joy also. Therefore he started a business of duplicating some of his works and selling them at rather stiff prices to persons able to invest money in art, but not cheap enough for all to buy. It is one thing to get democratic and spread pleasure in life around, but one must keep some standards and sell only to those with enough money to demonstrate that they also have taste.

Many collectors are unable to buy and own all they would like. They therefore turn to wealthy colleagues and the public to purchase as much art as possible and display it publicly—claiming it is educational and soul-elevating, especially for the young. Children always have been used by adults for their own purposes. The ultimate manipulation of art and people lies in the huge city, state and federally supported galleries—like the Metropolitan and the National Gallery—which are supported by tax money, not of the wealthy but of the middle class, who are urged to appreciate the Gallery but might not be able to and probably could not care less for its treasures. The rich and powerful always manage to get public support for their own elite enjoyment. For example, in 1990 garbage collectors were enticed to support broadcasts of the Chicago Symphony on National Public Radio. The garbage collectors were called "Waste Management, Inc." but they were garbage collectors, anyway, and probably did precious little listening to the broadcasts. But, undoubtedly, they had been convinced that supporting such a worthy enterprise was to the spiritual, commercial and patriotic advantage of Waste Management, Inc.

Apparently, there is actually no difference between the powerful uplifting quality of the original and that of the copy. The only difference seems to be in the authenticity of the signature—and that only if it is revealed. No picture is advertised in a gallery or exhibit by its owner or its subject, but always by its artist. Thus, a picture of flowers is not advertised as such but as a "Van Gogh." It may or may not have been painted by Van Gogh. The educated guess is that at least half the masterpieces owned by all the collections throughout the world are copies, and therefore hoaxes. Understandably, owners of these "masterpieces," genuine or hoaxed, are not eager to cooperate with efforts to authenticate them. A picture can be worth a hundred million dollars—and deserving of the awe in which we have been trained to hold it—until it is proved a copy. Then it loses all its value financially and is held in contempt by the people who understand those things.

In the so-called collectible art perhaps more than the other arts, because most people can draw lines and daub paint to a certain extent, what is called art "appreciation" must be diligently taught. Virtually all kinds of expression of such art are appreciated by all kinds of people until they are taught that some art is "trash" and some is "masterful." That is, until the viewer is taught that he/she is not supposed to appreciate the painting until he checks the name of the artist, and recognizes a name that is supposed to be thought "great."

The confusion between the two types of art—or dozens of types—comes from the fact, of course, that they are quite similar. The same subjects, colors, paints, attitudes and esthetics are used in all types by all artists, though sometimes the works of less recognized artists might be more realistic and down-to-earth for the average viewer. In test after test under controlled circumstances, it has been demonstrated that the average viewer of art cannot distinguish between what is supposed to be great and respected and what is liked. In fact one psychologist interested in the motivation of appreciation of art discovered that the average viewer is more inclined to appreciate the non-great than the so-called great. In his tests, he said, "There was a consistent tendency across several studies, though, for mass-produced art to be liked slightly more than museum art, a finding that was consistent across two studies." Lindauer concludes from his study that the failure to approve only the "masterworks" results from the fact that the viewers "were relatively young and had little if any experience, education and training in art. Thus, there is no difference between cheap and good art if relatively unsophisticated respondents are polled." He could, in fact, have concluded that if the difference is only one in training, then it is relatively non-existent and worthless.

It seems that in art name means everything. But in the name game, the public are being abused twice. We are abused when we are convinced—often despite all common sense and observation—that the picture of some irises is really a soul-uplifting artifact to gaze upon as long as we can revere the signature. We are doubly abused when, at the art world's pleasure, we are told that the picture of the irises which before we were inspired by is no longer inspiring because it is not authentically by the artist we formerly were told it was by, although the subject, treatment and "spirit" is obviously the same. Now yesterday's treasure is today's trash. What's in a name? Apparently one fraud or two. Confusing? You bet. Deliberate double fraud? You bet. Intolerable? You bet. Preventable? You bet—if we learn the language of the artists and their fellow-travellers so that we know as much about the trade as they do. If one does not speak the language, he or she is easily duped. But if one does speak the language, he is not so easily duped.

The fraud practiced upon the public by the hoax is both amusing and annoying. The public are constantly reminded of the uplifting quality of the picture. We stand in awe of it, breath coming a little short, looking at it and remarking on how the spirit of the haystack has been caught by the artist who painted it. We are taught that such art constitutes the highest spiritual value available in this world. Children, especially, are urged to get the art habit—hence, to support museums and art galleries—because of its uplifting quality. But we discover that the copy is as good at this uplift as the original. In fact, we are never made aware of the hoax. The owner of the gallery will only reluctantly admit inauthenticity. So we are allowed to believe in the genuineness of this secular religious object without being told that, like the religion that commercial evangelist Jim Bakker preached on TV to the fleecing of millions, the picture of the haystack is not genuine.

So the kid stands before the picture with his rapturous face outlining the beauty of the experience. If he were told that he has been a victim of fraud then he might well ask if there is any difference between the original and the copy. He is going to recognize that another kid in Hans Christian Andersen's story recognized that, like the emperor who had no new clothes, there is no difference between the two pictures except in the mouth of the owner. Then he will ask why people pretend there is, and will himself conclude that it hardly seems fair to pretend to qualities and subtitles that apparently do not exist since no one can locate and identify them. If there is no difference between designer clothes and less expensive ones then the only difference must be in the name-calling. Recognizing this, the kid is going to ask why people perpetrate fraud upon the uninformed, and in so doing, upon themselves. He might well ask if that is the proper way to run inspiration industry. The move seems upside down.

Perhaps he will have to be told that in love, war, duping oneself and the public, and in establishing hegemony over others, everything is fair—and generally practiced. Art is a secular religion. The artists make the wine and cook the crackers. The museums and art galleries are the churches, and the owners and auctioneers are the high priests and hierarchy, the critics and theologians. Their whole religion is built on deception and fraud—on keeping people in the dark about the real nature of the ritual. The religion of art thrives on, in other words, not having the sacrament performed in an understandable language—on keeping it in a language understood only by those who benefit from its obscurity. The only defense against this practice is to have everybody become fluent in the language of the service. If people understand the service, they will understand the product, and they will understand the whole ritual. There is little deception in the world of folk art. Grandma Moses did not practice to deceive. She admitted she was just a little old grandma who liked to paint pictures. No mystique about her. There is little deception in popular art. Admittedly, it is used generally for commercial purposes, but it is only art and should be appreciated as such. If elite art comes to be understood by people who are fluent in its language, then its real merits—if any—will be recognized and stand forth honest and fair. Of course, this eliminates most of the hierarchy and theologians and commercial value, but that was only artificial anyway. The privileged, never worry, will find other objects and practices to raise to the icon and ritual status. They have never let themselves down yet.

Of all art popular, commercial art is the most consistently original. Folk artists are generally limited by the paucity of their subject matter and the narrowness of their skill to a narrow range of accomplishments. Elite artists generally stick to a style once they have developed one, so that Van Gogh is always recognizable by both subject matter and style. One recognizes Gauguin immediately by spirit. Elite artists are proud of their style and stick to it. Perhaps, if one investigated too deeply, they are consistent because they cannot change their style.

Popular art, on the contrary, is done to order. You want an illustration for a book about a young boy growing up in Missouri on the Mississippi River, you get one. You want a country scene—the Adirondacks, Atlantic swells, an old house, dusty streets and horses, a schoolyard with children playing—you get it. In the sheer act of innovativeness, a skill in changing styles, in creativity, the popular artist is premier. He/She must be able to deliver whatever is needed, whatever the public wants. So the whole system of values and accomplishments is all askew, upside down. The elite artist is the restricted one, limited by his style and intentions, while the popular artist is the master, his works are masterpieces of imagination and innovation. Historian of art Alan Gowans is absolutely right in saying that all art is basically commercial. We should be honest and admit it.

Popular artists must make sense in their work. They must be in a language that the audience understands. Not so with contemporary elite art. Huer tells the revealing story of how at a 1978 exhibition of nine Pollacks at the Ivan Daugherty Gallery in Sydney, Australia, it was thought that five of the nine were hung upside down. Asked about this apparent confusion, a Mr. Reinhard, Dean of the School of Art at the Alexander Mackie College of Advanced Education, replied: "Five of the nine are either shown upside down in the catalogue or have been mounted upside down in the frames. We hung them according to the way they are framed and left it at that." Such is the crazy, meaningless world of elite art. There is no top, no bottom, no order. If there is no top or bottom to an inspiration work, does one hanging inspire up, the other down? Or is the whole thing a hoax?

As long as they know no better, people apparently like to live in a world where they are told what is superior and what inferior. The code words are *standards* and *quality*, and the definition, like beauty, is in the eye of the definer. Is it that the definers like to keep their public in the same condition as John Milton's sheep in *Lycidas* that "look up, and are not fed," because "the grim wolf with privy paw/ Daily devours apace, and nothing said?"

One can only marvel at such oxymoronic desires in people. We call the virginal the untouched—our Eden to be kept pure. But we also call it, condescendingly, naive, callow and vulnerable. We value the untouched and unlived yet we realize, at the same time, that life must be touched and lived. We all want to remain Peter Pan or Charlie Brown, or Huck Finn forever. But we take advantage of those people who do remain naive. The Vienna Boys Choir have lovely pre-pubescent voices, but luckily, in the minds of most of us, they sooner or later grow whiskers.

All this adds up to the conclusion that mankind was born to be hoaxed and, kept in the state of ignorance, to like it. The strong continue to prey on the weak and gullible. Compared to life in the art world, P.T. Barnum so underestimated his victims that he was himself a sucker to his own philosophy. In the art world you can train a thousand suckers a minute. The weak have only one protection—to understand the language of the hoax and the hoaxer and in so doing explode it. There is a secret language, an underground life being led in the art world. To comprehend the language is to understand the life, and to recognize the hoax. "Never has there been a greater mixture of comedy and insanity in an institution than that displayed in the art Establishment," says Jon Huer, and he might have added, a more self-serving, anti-public, essentially unprincipled fraud.

To understand the hoax is to lift a great cloud of deception from all around our shoulders and to reveal what is going on. To do so is not necessarily to demean true art but to dignify and enrich it through the medium of truth. If art has its hucksters, charlatans, merchants and mafia to market it, it must also have its merits. About it one can surely say, if you know the truth, you will be less duped, and if a dupe you will be your own dupe. You will know the language and the fluency will make you free.

Meanwhile, of course, collectible art is under direct attack by photography. Photography is the great democratizer. It does virtually everything that two-dimensional art can do. And now there are machines that turn out three dimensional holographs which threaten another corner of regular art. Photography is to regular historical art what the development of moveable type was to manuscripts. It will eventually replace it.

One would hope that in the process of replacing canonical art photography would do away with the art Establishment, the theologians and priests and the money changes. But that is not to be. Such people are merely moving from one product to another, establishing their secret cult and practicing their deceit in the new medium. The art Establishment is establishing clear hierarchy between Art Photography and mere pictures, as they have established distinctions between Art Movies and moving pictures. The fight for control of this terrain is more difficult than the earlier one was because people are not as ignorant and gullible as they used to be. But the only protection against this new priesthood is fluency in the language before the art Establishment turns it into an unknown tongue.

The privileged empire of art extends outside the in-group. Like all high-priced marketable materials, art has its mafia—the large auction houses like Christie's and Sotheby's, and scores of lesser ones. Although they do not murder to protect their potential profit, they engage in shady practices to see that the product, as they glibly call the collectible art, is protected and goes at the highest price. Originals sell well. If copies sell well they are sold, apparently without full effort to establish their authenticity. There is a conspiracy to protect investments and the 10% auction fee the house collects. Auction houses, galleries and owners all swear that their holdings are genuine, and they will resist most efforts to establish authenticity. Clearly, reputations and investments are more important than authenticity.

Meanwhile, the public who have been trained to listen to the authorities turn out to be the dupes. We are told that products are genuine masterpieces and therefore culturally and esthetically valuable. Gowans is probably right in saying that every work of art contains in microcosm the age in which it was produced and circulated. If so, we must also be ready to put into the mixture of value the possibility of the hoax. This complicates matters very much.

Art, says Gowans, is created for pragmatic uses, to convert, sell and influence behavior. There is also the ingredient of other items in society which are given value only because they can be given value. As with unused coins. Coins are obviously minted to be used, not to be displayed as works of art. Dealers also sell unused coins. But the U.S. Mint sells unused coins for 25 times their face value with the guarantee that they have not been circulated. The U.S. Post Office also makes a tidy profit in selling uncancelled postage stamps. The intrinsic purpose of the coin and stamp was, of course, as a medium of exchange—to indicate bought services and representative value. Such items appreciate in value through the years as they remain longer untouched by human hands and not utilized for their original purposes. But such value is entirely artificial. Like art, stamps, coins and the thousands of other items which are treasured when "original" have only intrinsic and not relative and practical value. Like them, art is its own excuse for being if it has any intrinsic value. The ploy is to declare value—to put a price on something and hold out until some other person is willing to pay the price.

Experience teaches us that if something can be described in esoteric and exclusionary mystical terms its value can be placed on an artificially high plane. Somebody will eventually be willing to pay the price—and as is the case with all such artificial values, the price will rise as long as somebody is willing to pay what is demanded.

The only protection from such chicanery is knowledge of the real value of objects. To paraphrase the well-known guarantee about the value of truth, "Ye shall be fluent, and the fluency shall make you free."

The greater fluency the greater protection. The lower fluency the greater vulnerability. Only the con artist wants people to remain with no fluency, and only the naive want to remain vulnerable.

Chapter Six

New Worlds in Literature

One expanded meaning drives toward a redefinition of literature. With such a new definition all of society, which presumably benefits from literature, will be advantaged.

Written literature, like oral literature, gives a record of the society in which and about which it is written. It therefore should speak to all people, since all people are interested to one degree or another in the society about which the literature speaks. But for the past hundred years or so, literature with the aid of academics and privileged people has been muscling its way toward a special and privileged place in society and especially in academia.

There are several reasons for this move toward special status. Although the formal teaching of literature in colleges and universities is only a recent phenomenon, many people who believe that literature must be "taught" rather than enjoyed have managed to manipulate their role in establishing and perpetuating the canon of "fine literature" into a special priest-like mission. This role has been to establish the rules by which the canon is established, to protect that canon against those people who do not agree on its "sanctity" and to fight off all efforts to modify the rules by which the canon was established and is perpetuated. In the words of one critic, these canonists teach religion, not literature; more correctly, they teach literature as holy writ.

To a certain extent these priests have grown into power because of the relative newness and lack of universality of literacy. When most people cannot read, it is easy for the priest-class—that is the privileged few—to tell the populace what literature (or religion or proper politics—whatever) is worthy of being appreciated and established as the classics and therefore of being read and perpetuated. It is easy to foist off as literature what is special for the privileged few, who claim to have a sensitive appreciation for canonized literature, in order to build up a mystique about the sanctity of literature, a set of esthetics that literature must conform to, and thereby to exclude those people who are not of the privileged class.

Other literatures serve a more basic and perhaps a more useful function. Take, for example, oral literature, whose original purpose was apparently to instruct (as in how to hunt, how to protect oneself against animals, how to find water and how to win battles) and to pass on history (as in epics and sagas and portions of the Bible).

To achieve these results popular literature, both oral and printed, developed what critic John Cawelti has described as formulas and conventions. These formulas and conventions serve as the backbone of cultural development. Habits and modes of behavior we use today have been used in the past. We do things the way others have done them because that is the way they are done. The continuation of these conventions form the stability of culture. As long as we are familiar with the things done and the attitudes taken, then in the ways of life we lead we are comfortable. This is well represented in academic and intellectual attitudes, as academics and intellectuals like to do things as they have been done, not change sharply. We call sharp changes radical, and people don't like radical changes. On a more mundane level, the success of advertising products, of developing chains of establishments like Holiday Inn, is that people like the familiar. When you stay in a Holiday Inn—or eat at McDonald's, for that matter—anywhere in the world, you know precisely what to expect. You get what you expect, and you are comforted and reassured by the familiar.

But things must change, must "progress." So at McDonald's management market-tests a new food. You try the different food. In eating the new food one is introducing a modification to a line of reasoning on a familiar subject. This is known as invention. It is what drives us forward to new things. Some people resist invention to the death. Others eagerly reach out for it. The point to remember is that this invention eventually becomes convention. Once one has tasted a McDonald chicken sandwich, it becomes part of his regular diet, added to the hamburgers and other already-routine foods. It is no longer invention. Just as man and woman do not live on bread alone, they do not live on invention alone. Convention is like a person's catching up with one's shadow that is preceding him. Invention, no matter how fleeting, is caught up with eventually.

As we catch up with invention we reintroduce it into ourselves, we subsume it into our society. Invention thus becomes convention. That is the progress of society, of human nature, which comes in a series of three steps: convention is developed through invention, which in turn is institutionalized through convention. Life turns in on itself and in so doing, like an amoeba, develops into something different and larger.

Sometimes through inventions—new materials and new uses of materials—conventions develop "esthetic" qualities of skill and verbal virtuosity. Thus, the original purpose of instruction is heightened and intensified through entertainment. Excellent examples are the *Iliad* and the *Odyssey* and the King James version of the Bible. Homer may have taken much less entertaining versions of the troubles between the Greeks and the Trojans and spruced them up into a story that people have found entertaining. There is no way of telling how he departed from the originals. There is no doubt, however, that the King James version of the Bible is the most esthetically satisfying of all versions and that it is the farthest removed from the original and true text. In other words, the original intent of oral and written literature was to instruct. Esthetic side effects generally came later and are tangential, a bonus—or falsification, encrustation and "unnatural" growth, depending on one's point of view.

As written literature develops it may become more esthetically exquisite but also more special and specialized, and farther and farther away from its original intent. Its priest-devotees become more insistent on its exclusive value as the proper and sole voice of the culture in which it is produced, or its voice of the "universals" which are timeless and of sheer "art." In other words, the message is sacrificed for the form, the mechanics and the art. Its devotees insist that Gresham's law of economics is paralleled in literature: bad literature drives out good. But though Gresham's law may be applicable in economics, it does not hold for literature. Bad literature—whatever that is—does not drive out good; it does not even substitute for good. It may supplement, but it does not starve out. Elitists who say that it does are in fact guilty of trying to fix prices, to artificially set and maintain what they call high standards of quality in order to keep their market cornered and themselves in power. They are not in favor of the universal appreciation of the function of literature—around the campfire of original literature everybody got to hear and appreciate. Instead, they want to maintain the priest-class so that they can act as priest-keepers and explainers of the canon by demonstrating their superior role in the intellectual hierarchy. Otherwise their role is diminished and their livelihood disappears.

Just as bad literature does not drive out good, labeling and name-calling—or boycotting—does not create or protect "great" literature. It only creates an artificial barrier that tries to separate the good from the bad, when the two categories do not exist. Some academics think that "great" literature is what they call "serious" literature, and non-elite literature is apparently not-serious. Not only are such distinctions silly, but they are obviously meaningless. Popular literature and elite literature differ in degree, not in kind, not in "seriousness." Robert Benchley's *Jaws* and Herman Melville's *Moby-Dick* are both obviously similar stories. One is more readable and more enjoyable to most people, while the other may stimulate some people to do some troublesome thinking. It is clearly non-productive to say that one book is serious and the other is not. It might even be a superficial reading to say that *Moby-Dick* stimulates more serious thought than *Jaws* does. It might just seem to, and it might stimulate the superficial mind to more activity, whereas *Jaws* provides profound depths for the mind that really searches for reality and meaning. A case can solidly be made, as anthropologist Levi-Strauss has made it, for the belief that popular literature, though less superficially stimulating, provides more indices and clues to profounder universalities than elite literature does. In other words, formulas and conventions are carriers of greater profundities than invention is capable of until it becomes convention. Where popular literature ceases to be non-serious and becomes serious—or serious literature ceases to be serious and becomes non-serious—obviously depends more on the reader than on the author.

Without the artificial laws that elitists create for themselves, written literature would have to compete in the open marketplace for its evaluation and rewards. In such a setting literature would not strive to be exclusive. Authors of popular literature do not insist that people read only their works; they allow for, at times even encourage, readers of other literature. But generally, authors of elite literature insist that theirs is the only literature worth reading. They would, if they could, deny the First Amendment of the U.S. Constitution to popular literature. But it is an open market, and authors of popular literature merely want to be allowed to compete with the elite and let the readers vote by their choice. They do not want an artificial barrier built up which excludes the popular but allows free passage for the elite. The truth is, when all the pretentiousness is washed away, both so-called serious and popular writers are merely trying to pin their names to the bulletin boards of history—and ease their passage through life by some kind of gain through finances, reputation or the pleasure or pain of expression.

It is perfectly clear that given freedom of choice, the public will choose their own "classics," "serious" and "worthwhile" or useful literature. Mark Twain knew that the public would decide between his works and those of Henry James, and he was perfectly willing to depend on their judgment. He knew, to paraphrase Lincoln's political comment, that some people would choose James some of the time, but not all people would choose James all the time. Twain was willing to take his chances in the competitive market of free literature. He would let James write for the thousands while he wrote for the millions. There lay his power.

As Raymond Chandler would say fifty years later about the need to take crime fiction from the parlor and country estates and put it on the mean streets where crimes are committed, Twain was determined to write of his own experiences in the vernacular for the vernacular market. To the genteel age such writing could hardly be called literature. Literature was Longfellow, William Dean Howells and Henry James.

James, Twain's *bete noir*, was trying to elevate literature into the heights of refined society. Twain was trying to write everyday literature for everyday people. As he wrote later to his friend Andrew Lang:

> Indeed I have been misjudged, from the first. I have never tried in even one single instance, to help cultivate the cultivated classes. I was not equipped for it, either by native gifts or training. And I never had any ambition in that direct, but always hunted for bigger game—the masses. I have seldom deliberately tried to instruct them, but have done my best to entertain them...Yes, you see, I have always catered for the Belly and the Members."

Thus, Twain was writing his own Declaration of Literary and Cultural Independence, slowly and methodically working it out and spreading it to the masses so that they would have it as a part of their culture, to confirm and amend as they pleased. In so doing Twain was separating himself from the European conventional influence and thumbing his nose at Europe and at American intellectuals who still bow to Europe and its misplaced standards. "All kings is mostly rapscallions, as fur as I can make out," (ch. 23) Huck Finn explains to Jim. Emerson in his own way had said pretty much the same: "God said, I am tired of kings, I suffer them no more." Both Emerson and Twain were declaring for popular literature and popular democracy.

It is one of the more amusing yet aggravating paradoxes of modern academia that even those academics who rail loudest against the dangers of popular literature are avid readers of such literature; but they read on the sly, often ashamed to admit their practices.

Contrary to what many elitists believe and continually assert, popular literature, though perhaps conservative in sticking to the formulas and conventions, is subversive and revolutionary. It liberates a population. Some elite literature is experimental in more than form, but it is in form in which elite literature excels. New approaches are made to point of view, to philosophy, to development, to control and to subject matter.

But popular literature experiments in pushing back the boundaries of subject matter; it constantly flirts with invention growing out of the convention, and constantly pushes back the boundaries of subject matter. Take, for example, romance fiction, one of the most vilified forms of popular literature today. There is considerable experimentation in the introduction of new materials in the genre—not so much in individual books but in the total output. And in its mere existence it gives women a forum for their developing political, cultural and individual freedom. Crime fiction is currently undergoing a metamorphosis from detective fiction into a broad type that will eventually challenge the general approach of best-selling popular fiction. General best-selling literature considers questions of utmost importance to society. Irving Wallace, for example, has written about a Black man who became president of the

United States, a televangelist who fell considerably before the Bakkers' disaster and a movie queen who was able to conquer four rapists who kidnapped and tried to destroy her. James Mitchener in virtually every one of his books writes of the world since creation.

Most obviously popular literature in the form of pornography continually tests the restrictions of the First Amendment of the U.S. Constitution, forcing legal minds and society to reexamine its definitions of acceptable human expression and behavior. Popular literature in its many forms is constantly pushing into new subject areas and new freedom of expression. In a commercial metaphor, popular literature is a cash crop that must be profitably sold on the open market. Elite literature, on the contrary, has created for itself and perpetuates a subsidy that makes it state supported, in such agencies as the NEH, NEA, Ford, Rockefeller and thousands of other foundations, and because of occupying a privileged place in the arts is able to develop into esoteric and excluding forms without really satisfying its original purpose. About it one can say without too gross an exaggeration, to paraphrase the inscription beneath Mark Twain's bust in the Hall of Fame: "Loyalty [to elite literature] never broke a chain or freed a human soul." It may have enriched the freed soul, but it probably had precious little effort in freeing it.

Scholars of literature may not be in the business of generally breaking chains or freeing human souls; that may be felt to be a political process. But they surely should not be in the business of deliberately using literature to keep the human soul enslaved, of creating a privileged class separated from an enslaved class—one able to create and perpetuate so-called "fine" things in life and then to exclude a majority of the population from enjoying them. The elite should be happy and eager to modify their definitions of what literature is and should be, to embrace the popular written literature of all times for its value and to use it as part of their courses in enriching and instructing themselves and their students in the riches and uses of written literature.

There is another move that should be made in the redefinition of literature. Students of all fields of learning and endeavor in life have their "literature" also. Anthropologists have their particular fields of their "literature." Egyptologists study holdovers of ancient life as their literature. Throughout the arts, humanities and sciences each group has its own literature which is used to reveal the essences of life.

If in fact students of written literature are interested in milking from this record the ultimate possibilities of what it will reveal, instead of just "enjoying" it, they must take as their field of study, their literature, all the "literatures" that the other fields provide and meld into one general and specific approach. Alan Gowans, one of the leading scholars and theorists in the world of the history of art, insists that if one can read any artifact properly and completely he can understand the world; in other words, every artifact is a microcosm. Assuming that this observation is accurate, then the proper avenue of approach to this full reading of any artifact seems to be all the "literatures" that are provided by all the fields.

The literature of a nation, a time, a period, perhaps even of an individual, should be all the statements made by the culture of the time. The purpose of the student of literature—the necessity and obligation of the student of written literature—is to read all these "literatures" and see how one casts light upon all the others by contributing to the total *literature* of the peoples of the time. This study should include antecedents and successors—thus it is timeless. It is also a literature without borders and limitations—so it is comparative and international. It includes the readers—thus is humanistic and sociological. It includes impact—thus is consequential. It includes all the cultural contents and implications. Thus it is ecusymbiotic—it includes everything.

Consequently, for example, for a proper study of Herman Melville's *Moby-Dick* one needs to know all there is to know about the whaling industry of the middle of the 19th century, all about candles, about corsets, about art and architecture of the time, ship-building, recruiting and living conditions of whalers, marriage customs and strains, child training and development, economics of Wall Street—all that Melville read when he was actually writing the book, all that he had read and heard before he started writing the book and everything that all the people he talked with had read. One needs to become a citizen of the eastern U.S. of the 19th century and be able to read and fully understand every object that might be found in a time capsule buried in 1850. Then having learned as many facts and concepts and philosophies as possible, one should use an ecosymbiotic approach in trying to put all these strands of life together into a large "literature" that can be properly read and understood.

With Melville perhaps more than with most other writers, this approach has been attempted. Everyone remembers Howard Vincent's pioneering effort (1940) in *The Trying-Out of Moby-Dick* for which he read every book that demonstrably had been consulted by Melville before writing his book. Vincent's effort has recently been carried on in David S. Reynolds' *Beneath the American Renaissance: The Subversive Imagination in the Age of Emerson and Melville*. In this monumental book, Reynolds seems to have consulted every printed source of all kinds of literature available in the period. Never mind that he gave it a prejudiced and biased reading. He did present it and make it available for the unprejudiced reader to mine and understand.

So now the printed conventional literature of the world in which *Moby-Dick* was written is pretty much available. But before one gives the "final" reading to *Moby-Dick*, he or she must learn to read all the other "literatures" of the time the book was written: the texts of anthropology, archeology, art, music, geography, sociology, transportation, economics, domestic affairs, sex, birth-control, religion, Indian-lore, feelings about the Portuguese, etc. All these elements of the life of the time are symbols, words, sentences and "literatures" of the culture of the time. All are strands in the same skein contributing to the full meaning of a piece of written literature.

The literature of the student of the humanities includes all the statements made by a diverse and at times seemingly chaotic world. It may not be vital that the student learn all the literatures before he starts trying to understand literature, but it is necessary that he develop a proper attitude toward and respect for the realization that all are important. All this "literature" comprises a very thick and fine-printed book that needs to be handled and appreciated. Again, it is not so important that one read it all at one sitting, even in one professional lifetime. But it is important that the student of the humanities and written conventional literature take the trouble to buy the book, learn the languages in which it is written, and determine to keep dipping into it throughout his career, with the proper attitude. Any other approach is selling the subject of literature, civilization and oneself short.

Popular fiction is not the voice of a privileged few who arrogate unto themselves the direction of a society but the reflection of a total culture. Given a choice, who would not opt to take the larger rather than the smaller prize?

Chapter Seven

Literacy Through Popular Fiction

All artifacts and aspects of life, whether inherited or created, whether consciously or unconsciously used, are laden with culture, and are therefore excellent texts from which to read the culture of the people using them. People whose life is centered around the wooden plow and stoop labor have shaped their lives around that artifact and practice. In America during the Depression, the mule and plow became intrinsic to the American way of life. At a considerably later time, the washing machine on the front porch of many poor homes indicated a way of looking at the world. The one-room schoolhouse and the bible-pounding preacher are aspects of life which have controlled and shaped the American way of life in many parts of the country.

Experts in various fields of culture-study believe that their own medium is the most revealing. Alan Gowans, for example, one of the half dozen leading art historians in North America, believes that an art object if properly understood and read is the most revealing specimen of a culture. Many people, however, because they are more familiar with it and because it can be interpreted in varying degrees of skill, think that the printed word is the most important medium in a developed culture.

Of the printed word, the fictive—including fiction and poetry—has generally been considered the most intellectually penetrating because it allows the imagination to create from the actual world and the desired world. It allows the free flow of imagination to create the world and picture of the world as the creator wishes. So, though it is at times made out of the tissue of very little reality, it is a wish-book for what might be and of what the author sees of the world around him. Elite fiction is the land of head's desire. Or at least such is the conventional thinking.

In fiction there have been through the ages works which have been called the "serious" and the "popular." That which has been called serious has supposedly been created by the so-called thoughtful persons who have tried to observe, analyze and perhaps recreate reality in their own image. But to the degree that such creators have remade reality and society into the image they desired they have intensified and falsified it. Their worlds simply are not real. No one, for example, has ever seen a person as intense as Hamlet, or anyone as false in portraying reality as Sir Laurence Olivier playing Hamlet. No one has ever known characters as intense as those created by William Faulkner. No one has ever played with so marvelous a child as Huckleberry Finn—or even Tom Sawyer. To the degree, then, that the "serious" person recreates reality, he creates artificiality.

A far more faithful picture of reality can be found in the fiction of persons who are less intense (perhaps even less "thoughtful") and who are more intent on telling a story than in creating unforgettable characters. Since the dawn of time the story in general has been more important than the characters. So it was with Aesop, with Homer. Thus we have stories which recount marvelous and important events but whose characters are only named and are not developed into any kind of unforgettable character. The story, not the characters, is the thing of importance. Such authors are marvelous story tellers, and in their stories they float many important aspects of culture. But the reader must be very careful in reading and understanding the assertions and hints in such stories since they float by swiftly and often without any emphasis. For example, if a story teller mentions that somebody got on the elevator in the building, pressed the 40th-floor button and pushed aside the other people as he rushed out, then we must know that in his society there were skyscrapers, elevators that were crowded, and that some people were in a hurry and perhaps rude, etc. So the popular writer, the one who writes for the general public—not the elite artist—is the person who reveals in his works more reality than make-believe.

There is, of course, a great question as to what "popular" writing is, and whether it is the most revealing of the arts. Probably not. Popular writing is not really the art of most of the people. In America there is an estimated 13% of functionally illiterate persons, in other words people who can't read well enough to be self-sufficient in society. Further, even the most widely selling book reaches between one-half and one percent of the population. In fact, only about two percent of Americans, apparently, buy most of the books. The same people read books all the time, and apparently few new readers are brought in in large numbers. Of the readers of books, by far the large majority read the popular books. They read these popular books because such books are the ones they can understand and enjoy, and they are the ones that constitute their only reading. If there were no books of this kind that the readers wanted to read, they would resort to other means of entertainment—television, radio, walking, movies, talking, etc. In fact, a case could be made that the so-called elite authors promote illiteracy because they write books that are so far above the interests or styles of the average reader that they cannot be read. This unreadability is of course in many instances deliberate. Generally, however, to a certain extent the old snobbish impenetrability has disappeared from much elite writing as the nation has become more subject to desire for democracy and lust for riches. The elite author today wants to make money. He is therefore inclined to write books that will sell. This is a different attitude from that of old, and reveals not only creeping democratization of "standards" but also of galloping capitalism. People, even the elite, will sacrifice recognizably false principles for money.

It must be recognized that America, despite being one of the most reading of societies, follows, as it must, reading demand. In the U.S., according to the New York *Times,* every year there are some 39,000 books written that never get published, while there are some 40,000 published. These are mostly sold in large corporate-owned bookstores where books must move in order to be accorded any shelf space. The average shelf-life of a book is 6 weeks. The U.S. Government no longer allows tax write-offs for book inventories, so publishers do not take chances on long-range sellers and remainder the books as soon as they slow down in their sales. Commercial publishers won't touch titles that promise to sell fewer than 20,000 titles—and soon. As a result most authors, despite the mega-bucks earned by specific authors, earn something less than $8000 per year. No wonder they curse those authors who know how to write for large and profitable audiences!

Nevertheless, the stream of books, new and reprints, continues to flow across the shelves in the bookstores, and book publishers continue to earn enough to pay large amounts for selected titles. In this flow there are elements of American culture to be read and understood. Any day's best-selling list is very revealing.

What do those books tell us? They show us ourselves. They are mirrors that show three-dimensional culture and our place in it. Just as there are all kinds of readers reading the books, there are all kinds of authors writing them. The themes revealed are numerous.

One of the most important themes is that of the hero. America is a land of male and female heroes. Sophisticated and technological, urbanized and fast-paced as Americans' lives are, they always keep in sight the anthropological need for heroes, and sometimes the need brings them close, as with a zoom-lens camera. Especially in times of stress and unsureness with one's present, heroes are brought in to serve their anthropological role in civilization and culture.

In popular literature today, these heroes serve particularly useful purposes. In many ways the most important book about a hero today is not fiction at all, but autobiography: Lee Iacocca's autobiography. This book so much parallels the American dream and the American experience that had the author not already been larger than life, this book would have made him a giant. But being a giant, he made the book larger than life. The net result is a book that should be wrapped in red, white and blue and dangled from the light held aloft by the Statue of Liberty. Iacocca tells of his modest beginning in Pennsylvania, how his parents came to this country from Italy, passed through Ellis Island and began to envision the dream of liberty and prosperity. He recounts how he suffered from being a minority kid in the neighborhood (as many foreign kids have always suffered at the hands of the majority) but how he overcame those setbacks. More important, however, he tells how he, an ex-poor foreign kid, took on the giant Henry Ford, Jr. and would not be intimidated by or kowtow to such arrogant wealth and power. Fired by Ford simply because Ford didn't like him, Iacocca signed on with Chrysler Corporation and through articulating the American dream rescued Chrysler from disaster, paid back the money he had borrowed from the U.S. government, and proved again that in America pluck and luck and hard work count. But the story of the man's courageous life doesn't end there. After having licked every monster in the world, Iacocca ends his autobiography by admitting that his has been a great and happy life but that his great love has really been America. And he takes on the project of raising money for the cleaning and restoration of the Statue of Liberty. No greater love and appreciation for America can be shown. Iacocca is really a demonstration that every American could have become great if he or she had really wanted to, and is vindication of the American dream. With a virtuous performance such as his life has been, he could have run for President at any time, though he disavows any interest in political office. And his chips have been sharply enriched by the fact that the Secretary of the Interior fired Iacocca from one of his Commission jobs, citing conflict of interest as the cause, because somebody in the White House, apparently, felt that Iacocca was getting too large for his tuxedo and was making political hay that he would later feed to politics.

Iacocca is unabashedly pro-American. He has the touch that endears him to America. Let me give you a portion of the chapter with which he ends his book.

He began his work with the Statue of Liberty-Ellis Island Centennial Commission as

a labor of love for my mother and father, who used to tell me about Ellis Island. My parents were greenhorns. They didn't know the language. They didn't know what to do when they came here. They were poor, and they had nothing. The island was part of my being—not the place itself, but what it stood for and how tough an experience it was.

But my getting involved in the restoration of these two great symbols is more than just a memorial to my parents. I, too, can identify with their experience. And now that I'm involved, I've found that almost every other American I meet feels the same way...

And those are the values that the Statue of Liberty represents. The Statue of Liberty is just that—a beautiful symbol of what it means to be free. The reality is Ellis Island. Freedom is just the ticket of admission, but if you want to survive and prosper, there's a price to pay...

I go back to what my parents taught me. Apply yourself. Get all the education you can, but then, by God, *do* something! Don't just stand there, make something happen. It isn't easy, but if you keep your nose to the grindstone and work at it, it's amazing how in a free society you can become as great as you want to be. And, of course, also be grateful for whatever blessings God bestows on you.

But heroes must have a keen sense of timing and must recognize when their page in history must be closed, when it is time to fade away. Iacocca has out-lived his image and has tarnished it lately, in at least two ways: in being unable to stem the tide of automobiles flowing in from Japan and overwhelming the Chrysler Corporation; and, more important, through his immense yearly salary as Chairman and CEO of Chrysler of over seventeen million for 1991. To many people he now represents professional failure and personal greed.

But heroes come with a thousand faces. Another one on the best-seller list of fiction was *A Creed for the Third Millennium*, by Colleen McCullough, an author widely known in the U.S. especially for her smash hit *The Thorn Birds*. *The Thorn Birds* was epical. It overwhelmed the American reader (and watcher of television) with the grandeur and pathos of its sweep. It was life. *A Creed for the Third Millennium* attempts a broad sweep in another direction. It attempts to philosophize about the need of the present world to attempt to save itself from destruction and the turn to religion so prevalent in the U.S. for the last two decades.

This book attempts to be philosophical and to a certain extent opens itself to both praise and criticism for its attempt. Elite critics and authors don't like for popular writers to appear to have any brains. They are not supposed to think. Years ago, for example, popular novelist Irving Wallace was consumed with the idea that he ought to address the question of how might and what would be the result of a black man becoming president of the United States. So he wrote the novel *The Man*, the story of a black man who was elected vice president of the United States and succeeds to the Presidency upon the death of the President. Black elite author James Baldwin criticized Wallace for his effrontery in writing about a Black man. Wallace responded that he felt that the problem he wrote about was sufficiently important to be aired and discussed and if he wrote the story millions of people would read it, whereas if Baldwin wrote it, though it might be more personally genuine, the story would be read by a very few.

McCullough's message in this story *A Creed for the Third Millennium* covers a subject discussed by philosophers, political scientists, science fiction writers, religious people—and all of us. That is, isn't it time that we began thinking again for the umpteenth time about how mankind can be saved from mankind? Her message is nothing new—love will do the trick—but her symbolism and development of the story are somewhat fresh. A smart and dedicated person from a small town in Connecticut fights against corrupt and self-interested bureaucracy in Washington. Finally appointed to the bureaucracy, though working as much outside it as inside it, the man becomes convinced of his own mission and nearness to God, and when it becomes clear that he can't save the world, even in the third millennium, he commits suicide on a cross, in a manner embarassingly close to that of former holy people. He crucified himself. What is the newness of this novel? Well, it is not so new as it is a fresh way of stating the old. In his make-believe book, *God in Cursing: A New Approach to Menial Neurosis*, (published in 2032) the hero believes that God, in chasing Adam and Eve out of the Garden of Eden, cut us off from Himself and in so doing did mankind a favor; He forced man to become self-reliant, to depend upon humanity. This is a simple restatement of the humanism that in the first decade of the 20th century bothered many religious people. But Dr. Christian in his book feels that having been forced to become self-reliant rather than God-reliant, man now can seek God in a new and honorable way, with dignity. As he says, "Every one of us needs a bulwark against the loneliness of life. For life is lonely. Sometimes intolerably so." And he urges that we not abandon God but "Turn to God. There is your bulwark against loneliness!" Thus McCullough's book within a book.

What would a stranger from a strange land understand after reading this book? America is a nation that has many anxieties, with many people seeking ways out of loneliness, and many people prepared to write books (and appear on television) to satisfy that demand. Americans do want love and will pay about any price to get it or the semblance of it. But, according to McCullough, will the third millennium have the answer? Apparently not. Christian, as prophetically named as the chief pilgrim in the old best seller of centuries ago, *Pilgrim's Progress*, crucifies himself because he recognizes that he is not the answer. It is hard to tell whether this story is a satire, a condemnation or an affirmation. But it is revealing. It shows that concern with religion is rife in the U.S. today.

Perhaps the most popular novels on the best-selling list however, are the straight love stories. Of this group there are millions sold every year of the erotic historical romance—the so-called "bodice-ripper" or "virtuous virginals." These are sold in the supermarkets, drugstores and bookstores to lower-middle class and blue-bodice readers. Written to a formula which requires so many sex scenes of such intensity each hundred pages, these books have through the years developed along with the growth and along the lines of the power of women's liberation. In the early days, the women in these books were virginal, submissive vessels who catered to every whim of the macho man and trailed him through life happy just to be a "woman." But these books have developed in parallel lines with the growth of women's liberation. Now they center around independent, career-minded women who are tough, have their own minds, are beautiful, sexually experienced and have a role in life. Yet in the end they submit to the handsome man. If they cannot pursue their careers with the man in charge, they are willing to give them up—they have completed their ambitions in life of being successful in their own careers.

These books are highly romantic, of course, but they are also very educational. One of the requirements for each book is that they be factually authentic. They travel all over the world, situate in all historical periods, and describe in great detail the surroundings. They are mini-educations in exotic countries and times. Readers know that when they are traveling through the pages of these books, they are taking well-informed tours. If the travel guides use florid language or unrealistic plots, the trip is still worthwhile.

Somewhat more wide-selling are the unstereotyped romances, such as the 1990 best-selling novels *Illusions of Love* (by Cynthia Freeman), *The Glory Game* (by Janet Dailey) and *If Tomorrow Comes* (by Sidney Sheldon). All three of these are by novelists who sell in the millions in paperback. *Illusions of Love* does not picture a new situation. It tells the story of two young lovers who were forced by circumstances to part but who by chance run across each other again after 25 years and discover that their love is unquenched. *The Glory Game*, by the fantastically wideselling Janet Dailey, is an old story dressed up for new readers. It involves a happy wife and family whose husband and father leaves them for a beautiful young woman. The older wife then flings herself into a new behavior and eventually, after all kinds of international glamorous adventures and travel, discovers a new life and dignity. Sidney Sheldon's *If Tomorrow Comes* is a new twist of a fertile mind who writes almost exclusively of wealth, power and beautiful people. This time he departs from them, at least on the route to a return. A lovely, idealistic poor girl is about to marry into the world of wealth, privilege and snobbishness. Circumstances force her instead to murder a mobster who has destroyed her family. Because of corrupt politicians and law enforcers in New Orleans she is sentenced to prison for 15 years, where she is raped, beaten and almost destroyed, until she discovers how to beat the system, gets released and goes on a foray of revenge of her own. She destroys each of the peoples who victimized her in her naive youth. At the end the next page of her life seems to resemble all too much the first page. So the wheel of life has turned full circle and has its closed circumference.

These are straight middle-of-the-road Best-selling American fiction of the day. What do they tell us? What could a non-native American read into and out of these novels?

First of all, it is immediately obvious that American readers are very interested in sex. The Romances are illustrated on the cover by scantily clad women who are physically beautiful, aware of sex, determined to enjoy it and not ashamed. The pages fairly sizzle with sexually-steamy scenes. They are more than suggestive; often they are explicit. But they are not pornographic, at least not hard-core pornography. Most authors go just as far as they can in their suggestiveness and explicitness but stop short of pornography, at least as they see it. Often they have outside readers who stop them short of indecency. Irving Wallace's novels, for example, were read in manuscript by his novelist wife who blue-penciled all passages that were abridged propriety. Andrew Greeley, a best-selling novelist priest in Chicago who writes some sexually explicit scenes, has his manuscripts read by a dozen outsiders, religious and lay, to make sure that he does not go too far. But the presence of so much sex indicates that American readers, maybe because of the current immense importance of evangelists and other professional religionists, enjoy trips of fancy into the erotic. It seems to be at the same time an awareness and enjoyment of new-found sexual freedom laced with the pleasure of the forbidden. Sex sells, as we say, and dalliance is delightful.

In addition, these novels indicate a new freedom on the part of women in society. In the Romances they are no longer tied to the bedpost, their lives circumscribed by a lot of staying home and tending the husband and children. They travel, they are professional, they develop their potential and they are liberated. If sometimes they in the end revert to the traditional role of women, it is after a fling that showed there may be more in the future. They have, to paraphrase the cigarette commercials, come a long way.

They have come an even longer way in the novels of such writers as Sheldon, Freeman and Dailey. They are their own heroes. They are just as powerful as the men—maybe a little more devious—but they get their way. Their ways to success are sometimes not socially approved, at least among the square set, but they demonstrate to readers that they stand on their own feet and are masters of their own crafts and lives.

Sometimes, in fact frequently, most of the writers—some more than others—are severely criticized for the society they picture. Father Andrew Greeley, for example, in picturing the liberated female in her "natural" role in life, is taken to task by the Church and by many critics. The world he pictures, they assert, is hardly seemly enough for a man of God to be picturing in novels. Greeley's response is fascinating. And he has the data to demonstrate his conclusions. As a priest his main role, he says, is to preach, to bring the wayward back to God. His best route is the kinds of novels he writes. Frequently he polls his million readers as to why they read his novels and what their conclusions are after they have finished one. Eight out of ten of his readers tell him that they are better persons after reading one of his books, that his novels are in fact sermons. His conclusions are, therefore, that in picturing real-life situations he is effective in getting people to turn from their sinful ways and to return to religion and worship of the female God.

Another fabulously famous author on the best-selling list, as he has been for at least a decade, is Louis L'Amour, author of numerous Westerns. The western novel has had an interesting history in the U.S. Beginning with Owen Wister's *The Virginian*, (1902), the Western has pictured a macho world of men, backed by two kinds of women, the schoolmarm and the whore. There were no in-betweens. The stereotype was broken, however, with the introduction in the 1970s of the so-called "Adult Western," which pictured on the covers of the books buxom females who were neither school-marms nor whores, but just women. They had moved from the schoolhouse or the whorehouse to an address on main street. They knew the power of their spirit, their glands and their guns. They would tussle with a man sexually, grapple with him in a wrestling match and shoot it out with him at the OK Corral. Although these were obviously designed to cash in on the contemporary interest in women's liberation and freedom in sexual behavior, they actually broke forever the stereotype of the old western. Thereafter, perhaps inevitably, the Western would be much more realistic and life-like. In other words, the "adult westerns" were a corrective.

Even more of a corrective, perhaps, has been the work of Louis L'Amour, whose works are now published in some 70 languages with sales running well over 100 million, and which constitute a kind of revisionist noveling of the whole history of the American West. L'Amour was offended by the "lies" told about the development of the West, about the treatment of the American Indians, and set out to revise the whole version. In a series of books whose heroes are the Sackett family, L'Amour covered the development of the West in general, the Southwest in particular and California especially. Obviously they meet and satisfy a need for hundreds of thousands of Americans. People read these books because as they say, they tell about life as it really was in the West. Many readers, not all of whom are men, remember the history of the west as told to them by their parents and their grandparents, and they feel that L'Amour tells it like it was. So at a time in American culture when the Western which used to virtually monopolize the TV and movie screen has virtually disappeared, it has a very vital and growing life in the printed page. This is a paradox which seems to suggest that the American public is hungry for information and "correct" history. This conclusion is borne out by the mountain high flow of books that give documentaries, facts and genuine evidence of virtually every kind of American life.

As the Western has disappeared from the TV and movie screen, the detective story, roughly speaking a kind of urban western, has come virtually to saturate it. And as it plays frequently on the screen, it sells rapidly in the bookstore. Of the current best-selling writers, the British author Agatha Christie is still the all-time best seller, and numerous other British authors fill the shelves alongside her works, writers like P.D. James, Ruth Rendell and others. But Christie's position has given way to other types. One of the most astonishing recent productions was Umberto Eco's *The Name of the Rose*, a *Moby-Dick* kind of deep and rich detective and Gothic book about 14th- century Italian Franciscans. And Christie has given way permanently it seems to the perennial best-seller John D. MacDonald, who always has a couple of books on the best-selling list. MacDonald has several reasons for being popular. He is always writing about contemporary social and cultural topics. He writes about the drug trade, about the urbanization of rural areas, about mobsters and about corruption. In addition, he develops characters, especially women, who are at least partially fulfilled and lead lives up to the fullness of their potential. Further, MacDonald's hero detective, Travis McGee, though a super-stud on the surface, is a sensitive, moralistic throw-back to the days when one's word was his bond, when old-fashioned ways of life obtained before the computer, crime, greed and lust destroyed the American way of life. McGee, whom MacDonald calls a "tattered knight on a spavined steed," in other words is an anachronism who fights for the conventional virtues. In the 60-plus novels he has written, with McGee and without McGee, MacDonald has stood firm for what he thinks is right. The number of his sales would indicate that a large number of the public stand behind him.

Not all, to be sure. The total sales of the so-called British type detective novel, in which the puzzle is the whole point—the reader is concerned with who killed whom, how he or she did it, with, in other words, the resolution of the crime—still outsells the American counterpart—American readers turn to other concerns. They are more concerned with the social and cultural aspects of the crime and the criminal. In British fiction it is really unimportant what happens to the criminal once the crime has been solved. American detective fiction, on the other hand, is more concerned that justice be done, that the criminal pay. Sometimes this is done through the process of the law, sometimes it is done by the individual taking the law into his own hands as a vigilante. In other words, with a kind of lawless violence that has been endemic in American culture from the very beginning.

American culture has always been deeply concerned with this violence. Frontier fiction, mountain fiction, historical fiction, Western stories, detective stories—and numerous other genres—have demonstrated that the world is fraught with evil and violence, that it needs to be purged, and that violence seems to cleanse the body and regenerate the spirit. Undoubtedly this spirit was engendered and fertilized by the frontier experience in America, with the violence associated with settling a new land, especially when this settling was strengthened by a religious spirit which preached that the settler was superior to the aborigines on the land and to the land itself. Now that the frontier has been squeezed into cities, in many ways the violence is more compressed, more intense and more explosive, especially since the aboriginal has changed to ourselves. Often now he is "foreign," that is a member of an ethnic group which is a new intruder, a group who has always borne the scorn of the dominant group, or someone engaged in anti-social activities. The need to purge—to exorcise—demons is still very much a part of America's present and future life.

But not all American best-selling fiction looks to the present and the future. There is indeed a very strong current of nostalgia pulling American culture into a backward fixation of glance which, though enjoyable and perhaps therapeutic, may also be dangerous if overindulged in. Such an attitude is of course taught by the televangelists like Billy Graham, Pat Robertson, Jerry Farwell who use the thunder and lightning of the Bible to turn us around to the presumed virtues of the past. Educationally, also, we are trying to "go back" to the three Rs of Reading, Writing and Reproachment. Further, a people when scared and feeling insecure with the present always turn to the past for comfort. These conditions, and others, pulse through the body of society today in the United States, with a corresponding pile of books spilling from the press all the time.

Of these still a best-seller is Garrison Keillor's *Lake Wobegon Days* (1985). Keillor is a humorist who performed for years every Saturday night on the radio show "A Prairie Home Companion" from Saint Paul before moving his show to New York City. A kind of Lum and Abner, old-fashioned cracker barrel show of gentle humor, with jokes about life on the farm and in the small town, this show exploits a gentler, freer, safer, more relaxed and humorous world of yesteryear. Keillor has a kind of Mark Twain-Will Rogers attitude toward the world around him and his kind of people. They are all good people, and life is amusing and sunny. But like Mark Twain and Will Rogers before him, Keillor sees the cracks in the good facade and jokes about them. His people are quaint and grotesque, to be sure, but they are good people and nice to be around. We may not all want to live in Lake Wobegon, but we would surely not destroy it. It is an excellent place to escape to when the world is too much with us, an amusing place to visit every Saturday night. Let me give you an example of a Fourth of July celebration in Lake Wobegon.

The Flame (of the gunpowder celebration) flickered briefly on the Fourth of July. Major arms shipments came in from the Dakotas in May and June, fireworks being illegal in Minnesota; ammo was stored up, heavy artillery and bombs and rockets were moved to the front, and on the eve of the Fourth, light skirmishes broke out between the town constables, Gary and LeRoy, and the insurgent forces, who competed to see how close to the old Chevy cruiser they could set off the charges. After dark, the law cruised down the alley at about four knots, its long white beam sweeping the backyards, Gary and LeRoy peering out the open windows—*Did they see us?* Yes! Run! *No, wait.* Now, good old Larry, the one who can play Taps with his armpit, darts into the alley and fires a colossal rocket that arcs gracefully over the cruiser, where it explodes a few feet in front of the hood ornament with a shower of purple sparks and a blast that rattles garage doors, and the Chevy's taillights burn bright red as Gary hits the brakes and throws it in reverse, burning rubber, and you and four boys run like rabbits through Mrs. Mueller's yard—*Unnnhhhhh!* What happened? *I ran into the birdbath.* Come on, get up! *No, you guys go on, I'll just lie here and die.*

'I saw you!' the law yells. 'I know who you are!' It yelled that at us for years, meanwhile more and more trash barrels got bent out of shape from cherry bombs dropped in them to see the cloud of ash come up and hear that big boom. Watching the Volunteer Fire Department set off the official fireworks was not the same, even when the Roman candles exploded horizontally into the old people's section and the lame leaped out of their lawn chairs and ran.

What does this parallel to the deviltry of Tom Sawyer, and the popular fiction of America in general tell us about the U.S. reading public? Are these people all sub-literates who should read "better" stuff or nothing at all?

The answers are resounding No's to all those questions. This kind of literature is that preferred and read by many millions of people. If we believe in literacy, then we should promote this kind of literature. Are these readers sex-starved and sex-obsessed stereotypes who are a drag on society? Perhaps, but unfortunately they are only copies of their fellow-Americans in the elite, jet set. We poor middle-class people can't afford the saturnalia the privileged engage in all the time. It would behoove those people to clean up their acts before asking us to whitewash ours. Is this kind of literature really "inferior" to the elite, or are we being hoisted on a set of phony issues? Obviously we are. So what should be done about the whole business?

The question of the esthetics of popular fiction is tied in with many complex drives, most of which reflect man's apparent necessity to arrive at and maintain some kind of pecking order that places him above somebody else. Although snobbery, the feeling of superiority and inferiority—like death and the exploitation of the poor—has always been with us, it probably received its most famous and long-lasting boost

in the person of the nineteenth-century British poet and essayist Matthew
Arnold, and present-day disciples who having learned his views insisted
that culture was something only a few fortunate individuals were born
with or could ever achieve; some people had it while others did not.
In definition, culture was the best thoughts of mankind most beautifully
expressed.

But such antiquated thinking is no longer tenable. A new set of
aesthetic criteria should be set up for this kind of book, or, more desirable,
the old set should be made more flexible because we realize that the
set of elite criteria currently being used by many critics and academics
is inappropriate, prejudiced and out of date. Literary realization has
finally caught up with reality.

British crime novelist P.D. James perhaps illustrates this
development as fully as any other author or critic. James, whose favorite
author long has been Jane Austen, began writing crime fiction as a
stepping stone for more "serious" writing. But when she had learned
the craft she realized that she had also discovered the medium. She had
no need to try to write other kinds of fiction in order to express herself
philosophically and artistically: "I saw the writing of detective fiction
with its challenging disciplines, its inner tensions between plot, character,
and atmosphere, and its necessary reliance on structure and form, as
the best possible apprenticeship for a serious novelist..." And as she
maintained that respect for her form, each book has been, in her words,
"a landmark in [her] gradual realization that, despite the constraints
of this fascinating genre, a mystery writer can hope to call herself a
serious novelist."

If we all could develop as James, and countless others, did, we could
more correctly and openly evaluate these books and weigh them on their
own terms. Then all of us could read and enjoy them without doing
it clandestinely with the guilty feeling that we often suffer from. We
would recognize that the old criteria no longer hold, if they ever did,
and that those of us who claim to be scholars interested in the social
and cultural milieu around us must read the popular books
indisciminately if we are to understand the motivations, psychology,
forms of entertainment—in short, the culture—of the people around us,
and therefore of ourselves.

This observation is nothing new. Well over a hundred years ago
someone writing in Blackwood's *Edinburgh Magazine* recognized what
is only becoming more and more obvious:

Popular literature is a reflection of the period in which it flourishes—its active as well
as its meditative life—its politics and its romance, and we rest assured that there is not
a movement in it, not a force, not an atom of life which has not its counterpart in
contemporary history...Literature, in fact, now implies far more than it did before. It
is now a complete representation of society...It is to the historian what the dial-plate

is to the time piece; it is a perfect index of the innumerable processes at work throughout the whole frame of society.

Except in details, perhaps, the statement could not be more directly on the mark and speaking directly to us today.

In the world of fiction if we reduced everything to a kind of creative Fowl Farm, there would be some swans bedazzling us with their charm but, undoubtedly, there would be a much larger gaggle of geese. Perhaps they all, in their way, lay golden eggs of varying karat. These eggs provide coins of the realm for virtually everyone and for everything—for the promotion of democracy, of literacy, of the development of esthetic tastes and of enriching culture. The only ones who do not pass these coins openly are the elite, and they do not because in general on the surface they seem content with their place in life. But they do buy on the black market and they do exchange coinage illegally. They seem generally content to behave thusly. They do not want to come up from elitism. As a result they inhibit its flow and growth and thereby engender the elitism they enjoy and want to perpetuate. Obviously then, the richness of the popular culture study is too important to leave in the hands of the elite. Literacy means far more than they understand or care to admit.

A case study—that of the works of Ross MacDonald—presents a painful example of the waywardness of American academics and intellectuals and holds an important lesson for us all.

Chapter Eight

Ross Macdonald:
Or The Need for the Oath of Macdonald[1]

The shock of recognition among literary scholars other than those who read "pure" literature for enjoyment only is forcing a general reevaluation of the purposes and accomplishments of so-called popular fiction and demanding that all of us reexamine the stances—our training, biases and prejudices—from which we view this form of literature. This new viewing will demonstrate that popular fiction, because it is written in and of everyday life for people in everyday life, tells us much about life and culture. Popular fiction is literally everybody's fiction and as such carries powerful statements and revelations pertinent to everyone. As such it is a powerful stimulator of print literacy.

Richard Hoggart, one of today's more perceptive social observers, was correct when he said, "Literature of all levels has the unique capacity to increase our understanding of a culture." In what is now a generally accepted thesis, Leslie Fiedler insisted that popular literature is "subversive" in that it breaks down the feeling of separateness that elite literature encourages and in so doing can perhaps achieve man's greatest social challenge, that of bringing us all together again and uniting peoples into the kind of community which existed before people became separated by class, education and interests. Popular literature, and popular culture in general, is the cutting edge of democracy, relentlessly freeing people from class distinction.

Popular fiction is also subversive in undermining existing attitudes about canons and in forcing us to reconsider fiction's ultimate purpose. Years ago A.O. Lovejoy correctly observed in his book *The Great Chain of Being* (1936) that many academics are interested in ideas only when they come dressed in full warpaint, recognized and sanctified by traditional authority. But literary criticism and literacy recognition mature, as everyone knows, by rewriting credos and points of view. John Cawelti, one of the leading popular culture scholars of today, has pointed out, "Whenever criticism feels the impact of an expanded sensitivity it becomes shot through with ideological dispute," and changes in definitions and canons to Democracy and ultra-speed printing presses in our day are having a particularly heavy influence on fiction and definitions of standards of quality, causing many of us to reexamine the way we read fiction. Ross Macdonald, who through the years both suffered from old biases and joined in the fight against them, serves as an excellent touchstone for an examination of the validity of some of the old attitudes and offers suggestions for what might be more useful approaches.

One of our biases is the assumption that the fiction we individually and collectively—often without examination—appreciate is "good" and superior. Such an attitude reveals a band-wagon, follow-the-leader mentality, which denies and rules out independent, individual and fresh examination and forces many of us to overlook—or *under*look—much of the value of fiction. The band-wagon effect results largely from our centering on the newest literary theory which we feel is bound to *at last* provide the "true" approach to the study and understanding of fiction. But the history of literary criticism is sufficiently filled with the discarded relics of "true" theories to convince the observant critic that although sharp and trendy theories may cut deep and cause much blood to spurt, they miss most of the muscle of meaning.

The stories which have had the most nearly universal appeal and effect through the ages have been fairytales, myths and folktales. "Once upon a time," is the introduction to a fiction with universal and timeless appeal. Next in order of timelessness are the stories crafted by individual authors from the folktales around them into single works but molded without bedazzling out of them the simplicity of the folk approach. The *Iliad, Odyssey, Gilgamesh, Moby-Dick*—which in Melville's words was "a romance of adventure founded upon certain wild legends in the Southern Sperm whale fisheries"—and *Huckleberry Finn* are only a half dozen examples out of a countless number that could be cited.

Such stories utilize motifs, formulas, stereotypes and cliches which float the obvious, taken-for-granted expressions of life. These age-old methods of working out stories are the stuff of life which we experience daily, and the stories' ultimate strength and universality rest on familiarity and assumption taken in those motifs and stereotypes.

The role of motifs, stereotypes, formulas, conventions and inventions has been thoroughly studied by John Cawelti. He quite properly states that conventions "help maintain a culture's stability," and "if the individual does not encounter a large number of conventionalized experiences and situations the strain on his sense of continuity and identity will lead to great tensions and even to neurotic breakdowns." Cawelti also says quite correctly that inventions "confront us with a new perception of meaning" and without new approaches to life's seeming new situations "the individual will be increasingly unable to cope" with this world. The key word in Cawelti's quote is *coping*, and the ability to cope with the world remains fairly constant; the world changes but the coping remains pretty much the same. The most obvious kind of fiction which accomplishes this goal is so-called popular fiction. What then is this popular fiction?

Printed popular fiction is, of course, the modern version of the fairytale/folktale. This fairytale/folktale was used to entertain and instruct people in pre-literate societies. In increasingly literate societies, oral and printed folktales flourished side by side. In a predominantly illiterate society the popular fiction is oral. In a literate society the popular fiction exists in various forms of print. In a relatively simple illiterate/literate society the popular fiction is unsophisticated. In a modern-day complicated, complex, dynamic literate society the popular fiction comes in many forms, with many faces and purposes. All to one degree or another consciously or unconsciously incorporate new elements of contemporary life and culture. All introduce some new elements, and all depend in one way or another on the formulas and conventions of old for their appeal, their "truth" and their lasting quality. Sometimes the lasting quality seems to reside in the dazzling individual way—say in *The Maltese Falcon*—or sometimes in the accumulated works of an author—say A. Conan Doyle—or sometimes in a genre—say crime fiction. Sam Spade and Sherlock Holmes seem unforgettable, while Hercule Poirot may—just *may*—fade, though at the moment no hero of crime fiction stands higher in readers' minds. In the 1980s crime fiction is reaching out to become more nearly mainstream popular fiction, and its ultimate value as a major statement of mankind may reflect society's interest in and need to come to terms with violence. Popular fiction, clearly, is the bedrock and mainstream story of a society.

This conclusion drives one reluctantly to another painful deduction. Though popular fiction often seems stereotypical, repetitious and unimaginative, generally it is rather the reader who is formulaic and stereotypical in her/his thinking and understanding. Intellectuals have associative and analogical minds. As they read fiction they like to pick out echoes and references to other works they know. They like to make themselves superior to their reading material by finding these references and hearing these echoes. But academics have short spans of tolerance. As soon as references and echoes become obvious—so that others can recognize them—then an academic begins to resent the associations and finds them offensive. But such reading is macroscopic and general. It deals only with the gross and general. Physics, economics, all physical and social sciences recognize the indispensability of closer, more detailed, inside, microscopic studies. Literary critics too are happy to engage in microscopic readings of "elite" fiction because it seems to merit such detailed study, but they want to deny detailed analysis to popular fiction because on the surface it sometimes seems not to merit or demand microscopic analysis.

Nothing could be farther from the truth. Elite fiction is obviously demanding. It has its difficult concepts, arcane words, abstruse constructions. These are obvious and external, like coconut husks which must be cracked before one gets to the meat. Popular fiction, on the contrary, *appears* to be easy. It has no coconut shell surrounding it, no *obvious* impediments that demand attention. But popular fiction is more than it seems. It is the white meat inside the shell of the coconut. It is the life-sustaining, the life-carrying food. It will be zesty or not, depending on the reader's taste. But it contains far more than it appears to contain. A microscopic micromotifing study of the fiber and liquid reveals that popular fiction consists of a complex and complicated world below its surface woven into the formulas and stereotypes and conventions little dreamed of in its general appearance. In fact, elite fiction allows a superficial reading—which may appear profound—while popular fiction, though it can be treated in a superficial reading, to be properly understood demands deep and understanding analysis. So the apparent fault in the value of popular fiction lies not in the stars but in the star-gazers, not in the fiction but in its readers.

Nobody has felt this more deeply or stated it more clearly than Ross Macdonald. In printed and oral statements over the years, and throughout his fiction, Macdonald made it perfectly clear that in his mind at least the valuable and true fiction is that which develops the popular themes and motifs and directs them back to the people. With a Ph.D. in English from the University of Michigan and a dissertation on Samuel Taylor Coleridge, Macdonald should have had at least a nodding acquaintance with all kinds of literature and its ultimate purposes.

Although Macdonald saw some superficial difference between the writings of the "masters" and popular authors, he saw their interdependence and their extensions. Popular authors learn what they can from the "masters," he felt. But these "masters" also "depend on the rather sophisticated audience and vocabulary of shapes and symbols which popular fiction provides...' if they are to ring with universality and veracity. "A functioning popular literature appears to be very useful if not essential to the growth of a higher literature," he observed. And there is a "two-way connection between the very greatest works and the anonymous imaginings of a people." Popular fiction, popular art in general, was, to Macdonald, "the very air civilization breathes...Popular art is the form in which a culture comes to be known by most of its members. It is the carrier and guardian of the spoken language. A book which can be read by everyone, a convention which is widely used and understood in all its variations, holds a civilization together as nothing else can," Popular fiction, to Macdonald, "reaffirms our values as they change, and dramatizes the conflicts of those values. It absorbs and domesticates the spoken language, placing it in meaningful context with traditional language...."

Macdonald's purpose in writing fiction was to bring some order to chaos, to "give a true sense of human life," as he saw it. He said he wrote "about now, the relationship between the various parts of society," in order to make understandable a complex structure.

Macdonald's subject was "human error." His interest was "the explanation of lives." In answer to the question why detective story writers devote their talents "to working in a mere popular convention," he said "there may be more to our use of the convention than meets the eyes." The literary detective has from the beginning provided a "kind of welder's mask" which enables him/her to handle "dangerously hot material." Sometimes Macdonald has indirect but devastating consequences in achieving his purpose. In *The Drowning Pool* (1950), for example, he used the snob's concept of formula writing to point out the silliness of elite concepts. Lew Archer is told that a play "is not written to a formula." Yet Archer, obviously speaking for Macdonald, thinks the play is silly and meaningless, written by a phony for a group of "wonder people" who simper about "Existentialism...Henry Miller and Truman Capote and Henry Moore, Andre Gide and Anais Nin and Dkuna Barnes...and Albert Schweitzer and the dignity of everything that lives" (43). They make no worthwhile contribution to society or to the literature they endorse.

Macdonald turned to crime fiction because of its comprehensiveness. It presents life as dangerous and flawed. It "recreates at some distance the fall of man, his death, and his survival." To Macdonald "the real interest and potentiality of the mystery resides in its use for symbolic and psychological and social purposes..." (98). To him the mystery novel "carries the theme of private and public evil to a mass audience." Significantly to those of us who may wonder about the value of popular fiction, Macdonald felt that crime fiction's "value lies first in its style and strength as a story—then in its evolution of the shapes and meanings of life in all their subtlety and surprise" (96).

To Macdonald the detective is an "underground man," "who reflects a lack of interest in—even an impatience with—special privilege," who sees a sense of "interdependence among men," and has "a certain modesty" in his attitude and behavior. The detective is a universal man in the Emersonian sense of the word, a "representative figure," a "model for life." The detective moves easily among all classes. In *The Drowning Pool*, for example, Archer derides a woman for being a snob but she still invites him to her party.

Detective fiction levels society, mainly through its vernacular and everyday language. "Democracy," to Macdonald, "is as much a language as a place," or political condition. "If a man has suffered...under a society of privilege, the American vernacular can serve him as a kind of passport to freedom and equality," Macdonald said. To have a democratic society, he continued, "You have to have a classless language." In his effort to bring about this classless society, Lew Archer speaks for the underdog, the poor and the disadvantaged. Throughout his books, to one degree or another, Macdonald pictures Archer or his other leading characters as the people's hero.

Macdonald was always interested in the dynamics of social and psychological behavior, especially when people have been crowded into space too small for their natural inclinations. He first chose California as the setting for his stories because it seemed that a brave new world was being born there, on the last frontier. As time progressed Macdonald stuck with the state because on this "last frontier" people were being pressed with their backs to the sea, unable to move farther west and consequently bringing about pressures and tensions not existing elsewhere in the U.S. In *The Way Some People Die* Macdonald called California a "hellish place" (128) filled with "thieves and murderers and confidence men." It is a "suburban wilderness" filled with "the human animal" (112, 120).

Concepts of animals, wilderness and the frontier permeate most of Macdonald's works. All are held together by the author's reaching back into time and using implied or developed myths and traditions. All of his books are a search of a father for his son or a child for his father. But there are many other thrusts also. *The Galton Case* is a modernized variation of the Oedipus story. In *The Drowning Pool*, Archer stresses his "ancestral memory." But Macdonald Americanizes his myths with "old American traditions" which affect Archer, that is the tradition of James Fenimore Cooper's Natty Bumppo. In *The Drowning Pool*, Archer identifies himself as "Leatherstocking." In *The Zebra Striped Hearse* Archer calls himself "Bumppo."

Through linguistic references Macdonald constantly links his stories with a broader literary context, as one would expect a Ph.D. in literature to do. But his references are more fundamental than casual and mere name-dropping. In *The Way Some People Die*, he bases his development on references to Achilles and Hector, Jacob and the Angel. In *The Drowning Pool* Macdonald refers to Oedipus and Electra complexes, to Babel, to Adam and Eve. *The Underground Man* strengthens its messages with references to Abraham and Isaac, to Diogenes and Oedipus, to Lazarus. There are of course other clear or very subtle literary allusions. "Abandon hope all ye who enter here," with which he begins *The Zebra Striped Hearse* is obvious. Others are more subtle. In the same novel, six bathers on the beach constitute a Greek chorus on the drama of youthful America, and in stating the tragedy that will unravel. In *The Drowning Pool*, in three short paragraphs, Macdonald parallels for his purposes literature's story of the murder of Thomas A. Becket.

All stories are developed in a language that is always apt, descriptive and very much alive. His figures of speech are so graphic they are almost palpable: "His eyes were small and dirty like the eyes of a potato" (*Barbarous Coast*) and "His chippie was just an animal he used—a little forked-legged animal." In one story Archer points a shotgun up "toward the unoffending sky." Elsewhere he looks at a dark picture which seemed "that its darkness was the ultimate darkness of death."

Macdonald was one of the early crime fiction authors who saw the full ramifications of his kind of story. He felt that like all popular art it exists to be enjoyed, but that it reveals the shapes and meanings of life in all their subtlety and surprises, and that its real strength resides in its "use of symbolic and psychological and social purposes." Its real value rests in the fact that it carries the theme of private and public evil "to a mass audience." Macdonald's main purpose was to return mystery fiction to mainstream literature, "where it began." He tried to put into his novels "a whole version of life in our society and in our time." Many critics of crime fiction generally are against such aims. Jacques Barzun, for example, insists that as soon as a crime fiction author tries to write something beyond the mere formulaic story, he has ceased to write crime fiction. The reviewer for *The New York Times* took Macdonald to task upon publication of *Sleeping Beauty* for trying to write something other than crime fiction. Such is the wisdom of the learned.

Scholarly study of Macdonald reveals one of the paradoxes of scholars/critics and the work they do. It is a theme all too familiar— the unwillingness of some scholars/critics to see beyond their training and biases. There are scores of such persons. Jacques Barzun, quoted above, is one. Matthew Bruccoli can be used as another example. After talking for many hours with Macdonald, presumably reading his books, and in fact writing two books on him, Bruccoli opined: "There may be no such thing as a democratic literature, because literature requires an aristocracy of equipped readers. The crowd has its own crowd-pleasers. Even when Ross Macdonald was being read by both the common reader and the uncommon reader, he was appealing to overlapping—but separate—constituencies. Perhaps that is what democratic literature really means." Thus creak the fossils of the past as they bend in the wind of modernity.

Readers with other points of view more sympathetic to Macdonald's might well suggest that scholarship/criticism on literature and fiction that requires "an aristocracy of equipped readers" is missing the point and purpose. Democratic literature demands democratic critics, and democratic criticism and scholarship could profitably be one and the same, extended as needed but always developing parallel and jointly.

A discussion of such a valuable author should probably end on the words of the author, Ross Macdonald, rather than of the critics. There is obviously much to be learned from this humble man who took all of mankind and society as his field and tried to communicate his observations about life to us. His main attributes were sincerity and humility. They are not bad attributes, even for academics. All scholars/ critics, of both popular and elite fiction, interested in the novelist as society's teacher and critic, might remember the Hippocratic oath required of all medical doctors when they begin to practice their trade. It would be beneficial if we scholars/critics, whether we lived up to the expectations or not, took a kind of Macdonaldite oath, which might read: "I will be humble in my approach to the purposes and values of literature. I will hear it all. I will let an author's words speak for themselves, and I will always try to be true to those words when I represent them." Macdonald felt that the true criticism of crime fiction is vitiated by the anti-intellectualism of intellectuals. Their pose prevents their full development. We could all benefit by keeping in mind Macdonald's variant of the reassuring words and the smug and superior, "There but for the grace of God go I," and read instead, "There go I, in spite of the grace of God."

In the world of literature, blind snobbery is now rampant, the latest, though undoubtedly not the last, refuge of privilege fighting to maintain its position.

Chapter Nine

The Phony Issue of TV Esthetics

Though television has been with us for forty years, it is still a medium that confuses and frightens the intellectuals, who by and large still refuse to see it as a natural development in the media of communication. In the last two decades there has, however, been much useful development in the study of television—what it is, how it works, its impact upon and interrelationship with culture in its broadest sense. We clearly understand that television is a unique medium, different from movies and radio in both forms of communication and entertainment. It is a small, intimate form which must be understood in its own technology, on its own terms, as an all-pervasive medium that occupies an important role in up to 99% of American homes—and increasingly in growing numbers of homes world-wide. Therefore it is imperative that we become fluent in its language.

In the last 20 years a lot of condescension and resulting nonsense has disappeared from television viewing and critics' vocabulary. But there is still more than enough around.

Although we may still get aggravated by the sameness and repetition of programs and by the overwhelming saturation of commercials, and although we may secretly half agree with the old remark by Newton Minow that television can at times be a limited wasteland, most responsible critics nowadays do not think the desert covers even half the land and should therefore be abandoned in our thinking. The desert, with a little irrigation of common sense, can be reclaimed. Television, like the two media closest to it, talking and seeing, is too important and pervasive a part of our daily lives to be abandoned. Increasingly, we recognize that television—like conversation, sights, books, movies and all forms of communication and entertainment—can have its high spots but that many examples—perhaps most—will be mediocre—run-of-the-mill. But there is nothing unusual in such an observation. Most of life, most entertainment, is dull—at best mediocre. The Pasadena Rose Parade gets boring long before it ends at noon. Imagine how dull it would become as everyday diet. The football Superbowl can be borne once a year, but no more! The Boston Symphony performs for the same customers only once a week and changes its program all the time. *War and Peace* can be read only every few years. Perhaps this is unfortunate. As all researchers know, the more one experiences some work of art or entertainment, the more rewarding it becomes. But it is reality.

We have learned how to accept and appreciate most of our art forms and means of communication. We can stay with them or walk away. But, as usual with the introduction of a new form of communication, we have expected too much from television. We have demanded that it be as exciting and entertaining as *Gone With the Wind* for 18 hours a day 7 days a week. We have also expected it to be educational—the best of all media, both entertaining and educational at the same time, like the rare stand-up comedian or exciting slide-lecture, or production of *Hamlet*. We have mistakenly assumed that television should somehow be an animated book—that as we flipped the pages the pictures and print would come alive beautifully and soul satisfyingly.

But we have learned that television must be viewed as a small-screen box which gives us an intimate view in the privacy of our homes of material that can be instantly communicated and is likely, for various reasons, to be designed for the largest possible viewing audience; that except for news programs, certain documentaries and certain series, the programs are going to be designed largely to be self-contained units, fairly indifferent to antecedent and following materials (such shows as MASH and MTM were exceptions); and that therefore, in this failure to tie into real life the shows are to that extent "artificial." But all art is artificial. Not many of us know any Hamlets, or Shanes or even Hawkeyes. We know people of much less complexity and heroic stature.

We also know that television must be accepted on its own terms. Television programs may be enjoyed for their own development, laughed at for their incidental humor, valued for what they teach (directly or indirectly) or prized for their own form and esthetic achievement. TV is essentially entertainment, and as Michael Eisner, President of Paramount Pictures, said at a Academy Forum Luncheon, "It is still entertainment, and all still needs the basic values on story and plot and interpersonal relationships" (JPC, 15:2, Fall, 81 157-63).

Sometimes we forget, however, that although television may be appreciated for any one or several of these aspects, it should be viewed for *all* at the same time and *more*. Just as TV is obviously in its infancy as far as technology and content are concerned, we viewers are hardly more than toddlers in our appreciation of the full potential of TV—for tomorrow, and even for today. It is a medium that is so new and complex we need to experience it more on a comparative and understanding basis, especially before we draw any negative inferences. In order to understand more of its potentialities, we need to know more about what is going on in Canadian, European and Asiatic television.

Before we condemn American TV and praise English, for example, we should see enough of the latter to realize that Masterpiece Theater's imports are the top of a heap of a British diet that would drive most Americans to our game shows and soaps with wild appreciation. Before we are stunned by critic George Gerbner's Violence Profile and think that violence on TV is the cause of our national and social troubles, we should realize that there are nearly half a hundred acts of violence occurring daily on Japanese television. Before we decide to burn pornography and pornographers, we should understand the role of pornography in the lives of the placid Japanese. Before we reach our conclusions about educational TV, we should see what is happening in China, where the TV set has almost just been switched on and yet where new "Television Universities" enroll some 324,000 students—not many in so populous a nation, but an indication of an attitude of things to come.

In television a little watching is a dangerous thing because it may lead one to erroneous inferences. Unconsciously one may fail to realize the newness of TV and will therefore base one's conclusions too much on similar media—books, movies, etc. Before we arrive at the final and true means of evaluating TV, we need to develop new vocabularies, new attitudes, new methods, new insights and a new fluency. Otherwise one may be led to faulty evaluations.

One may also be led to superficial conclusions. We are all by now familiar with John Cawelti's concept of invention and convention in the arts—of formula, of his notion that the popular arts depend more on convention than the elite arts which are more inventive and more different one from another. Popular entertainments use more sameness in their development, follow clear and obvious lines of development, are more formulaic, that is predictable. But we realize that such a description is not necessarily a condemnation, just as its opposite—the inventive—is not necessarily praise. In America we have made a great to-do over the fresh, the unique, the different. We do not want to read a book or a story if we have read one like it before, we do not want to see a movie if we have seen a similar one. One of our favorite ways of dismissing something as worthless is saying "It's just like..." when in fact it may merely seem to be like something else. We have made a fetish out of newness, and that is a superficial and self-depriving attitude. Nothing is without precedent, as Francis Bacon observed three hundred years ago. All ideas, all art, all developments stand on the shoulders of antecedents. In so doing each lengthens its range of vision. All of us must know more mediocre people than brilliant uniques. Life is that way. So is the formula. *On the surface* formulaic art may seem all the same, but that is really no reason for us to despise it. Underneath the surface everything is different. In fact, formula has a double-barreled effect. On the one hand it seems to blunt probing into newness, to homogenize into a sameness. But actually it is freeing and liberating in the same way that the short story, the sonnet and the limerick can be. There is a strict formulaic form about the popular 32 bar song, but apparently the variations are infinite. Not having to invent a new form, the authors who work in the accepted and proved forms can devote their time to subtleties that often—especially on TV—escape the viewer. That is why the formulaic show is appreciated in reruns. It's like instant replays in sports. The viewer sees and appreciates more the more often he sees the event, for he sees beyond the obvious and the surface generalities.

The subtlety and complexity of the formulaic development is sometimes more apparent in some shows than in others. In the larger TV show it is at times well camouflaged. The old *Hill Street Blues* of NBC, for example, was so densely peopled, so richly orchestrated and fast moving that it had up to a dozen formulas working at any given time (philosopher cop, divorced but loving couple, nosy but public spirited newswoman, father figure head cop, dedicated cops on the streets, misfits but comradely patrolmen, etc.). Thus by the time a viewer sorted out all these movements, he thought he liked the show. It was a kind of *Gone with the Wind* of television cop shows. *Nero Wolfe*, on the other hand, was not successful in attracting a large audience because it was so narrowly developed and orchestrated that the general viewer failed to appreciate it. It was like a jazz quartet. Obviously the authors and producers assumed that a large audience would be familiar with Rex Stout's rather narrow formulaic development in his books, and if they had, the TV formula would have been rewarding—despite the fact that out of sheer necessity Nero Wolfe had been miscast. In this case lack of familiarity was doubly unfortunate. More familiarity with the books would have made the TV show more familiar, and pleasure with the books (tens of thousands) would have made the TV series, which was cancelled after a year, more widely pleasurable.

Despite some possible variations in approach and degree of participation, the liberal and open-minded viewers and critics of TV in general realize that it is the most powerful and most thoroughly democratizing medium ever developed, and they appreciate it for that reason.

Nevertheless, here is an apparent and incomprehensible narrow-visioned, short-sighted, troublesome attitude abroad in the land, nurtured by some professional and academic critics and harbored by many people who do not bother to examine and understand television, the world around them or even themselves.

They like to say that television should be taken seriously. So do we all. How can any thoughtful person think that any medium that touches virtually every life in the United States should be taken any way but seriously. Occasionally, however, there *is* the hold-out, to the puzzlement of us all. For example, the Director of Opera at Wolftrap, the arts center just outside Washington, boasts that he does not own a TV set, will never own one, has never and will never watch television; yet, paradoxically, some years ago he used government money and three days of time to attend a conference on how opera can most effectively use television. My advice to him, had he asked, would have been to watch Nashville: Grand Opera can learn a great deal from Grand Ole Opry, which demonstrates that the message should *use* the medium, not fuss around endlessly about *how* it should be used.

Often "serious" critics draw the analogy of TV with literature, with education, rather than with entertainment. Although we like to analogize, and although we like to associate one form of art with another, we should realize that TV is not literature. It is a medium of communication more nearly like talk or gossip than anything else. Literature, despite its serious advocates, is also primarily designed for entertainment rather than education—but through use of another medium.

To take TV seriously, one does not have to equate it with another form. And if we do we should not misassign roles to both. Although we have properly assigned the role of education to books, as at least a part of their possible use, and although the transmission of knowledge was an early role of books, they are not even *primarily* for education. Books are a medium of communication—to be used any and every way communication can be used—and primarily as a means of amusement and entertainment; so are theater, drama, ballet, opera, etc. In education, we should not forget that Socrates, Jesus and other noted teachers used word of mouth and dialogue rather than books in their effective teaching.

There is every reason we should take our entertainment seriously. But not too seriously. It took Americans 150 years to learn to play; it may take us another 100 to learn to enjoy play, or to get the critics to allow us to enjoy it. A Roper public opinion poll of June 18, 1981 indicated that TV is second only to the family as a source of enjoyment. Such an attitude is bound to excite cries of social and educational apocalypse among critics. But Armageddon is not near.

Our inability to enjoy play perhaps parallels our short-sighted understanding of television. Horace Newcomb, one of our insightful critics, thinks that "our fears about television, no matter how healthy or well founded, have restricted the development of a critical climate for television." He is surely correct. And this fear is aided and abetted by a more fundamental and deep seated academic-elitist complex which has inhibited our appreciation of and development in TV as in all other esthetics, which I see as an inhibiting force.

Lawrence Laurent, in "Wanted: The Complete Television Critic," calls for the critic who will "Stand above the boiling turmoil while he plunges into every controversy as a social critic and guardian of standards." Such a watchdog attitude and such language, although half liberated, is also half culture-bound. Before one can guard standards, he should know what they are, and one who is inclined to want to *guard* standards rather than *promote* them (whatever they are) may be a half-dangerous person. Often, to paraphrase the learned 18th-century lexicographer Samuel Johnson, the cry of guarding standards is the last refuge of an elitist.

In effect the fight for standards is fundamentally a fight for privilege and power, a defensive position of the haves against the have-nots, so they won't have to share the goodies. It is the defensive posture of the blue-bloods, the blue-stockings, the FFV, the DAR and others against sharing with the masses or with the *nouveau riche* or rich media barons. Obviously it pays to be alert, for everybody to a certain extent is a fox in the henhouse, but the position and motivation of the elitists should be understood for what it is, no matter how subtle, so that it can be more efficiently countered. Their aim is to protect in every way their privileges.

The elitists have justified and defended their position in the Western world since at least the days of Plato. It is interesting that Graecophiles have long insisted that the Athenian populace of Plato's day was so sophisticated that one could go down on the street and pick up a group of citizens at any time and have them march to the theater and perform any play by Aeschylus or Euripides. But paradoxically they also agree with Plato when he called these people "oxen of the world." Plato, we should not forget, like most elitists, had a position to protect.

This *guarding standard* against the Canaille, as they were called in the French Revolution, the "Swinish Multitude," as Edmund Burke called them during the American Revolution, and the "mass," as people call them today, has strengthened many protagonists throughout Western history. In 17th-century England, for example, when the illiterate asked to be taught to read and write, the privileged tried to deny them both skills because they felt that the ability to read and write would ruin these people as servants. They were, finally, at first allowed to learn to read because it was felt that as long as they could not write they could be kept as servants. Then, as now, it was felt that the pen was mightier than the eye. Being permitted to learn to write came slowly.

The importance of entertainment as a means of subjugation could be illustrated a thousand times. One from Britain in the 18th century can serve for them all. In 1760, there was presented a play named *High Life Below Stairs*, which was something like the contemporary TV drama *Upstairs, Downstairs*. The purpose of the earlier play was to demonstrate the threat of giving common people the right to lead their own lives. "The whole play was a moralizing satire, showing servants extravagantly entertaining when their master was away, stealing from him while aping the manners of high society." And in the theater, "The whole race of domestic gentry... were in a rage at what they conceived would be their ruin." But most unfortunately entertainment tends to democratize. The servants in the gallery at this presentation hissed and groaned, bitterly resented the play and threw handfuls of half-pence onto the stage. When this play was presented in Edinburgh, 70 footmen threatened to burn down the theater if the play went on:

Soon after it began, a great noise was heard from the footmen's gallery. The gentlemen in the pit called out to them to be silent; or that otherwise they should be turned out, and never permitted to enter the playhouse again. The footmen were granted free access to the gallery while their employers sat in the pit. The disturbance still continuing the footmen were all turned out, and the managers were desired not to admit any footmen into the gallery for the future. (43)

At a subsequent meeting the gentlemen decided that "The spirit of independence had to be crushed by making servants more dependent on their masters" (43).

Through the years this proprietary and snobbish attitude has been modified somewhat through necessity, but the reasons for its existence have lain under a thin soil of democracy, never giving up, never abnegating its claim to the control of society, allowing the "popular" aspects of entertainment—letting the mob have their circuses and hippodromes—but always insisting that the elitists with their superior tastes are protecting the mass from themselves.

The 19th-century British poet and essayist Matthew Arnold, who dreamed of a golden era when culture was considered to be the best thoughts of mankind most beautifully expressed, has had his latter day followers in America. Perhaps one of the most blatant was the high priest Englishman F.R. Leavis who wrote in a small pamphlet, *Mass Civilization and Minority Culture* (1930) that the small minority of proper critics in the world "Constitute the consciousness of the race," and must save the world from "popular fiction" and other damning influences. "Art," he insisted, is "the storehouse of recorded values and in consequence there is a relationship between the quality of the individual's response to art and his general fitness for a humane existence." T.S. Eliot, who feared that "popular literature" was the most powerful, pernicious and long-lasting influence of all must surely have discovered that television was infinitely more pervasive and powerful.

It is hard to imagine that such anachronistic and unreal attitudes still prevail among intelligent people, but they do—and widely. For example, Harvard college, after floundering around for several years trying to discover its purpose in present day America, finally proposed a new "core curriculum" which had "six basic characteristics of educated men and women." One of them is "Good manners and high aesthetic and moral standards."

The cry of standards tends to restrain us all, undoubtedly inhibiting or preventing the production of much powerful and enjoyable art. The otherwise perceptive critic Robert Warshow, in dealing with the question, was hoisted upon his own petard. In talking about the movies he led himself up an unfortunate garden path: "I have not brought Henry James to the movies or the movies to Henry James, but I hope that I have shown that the man who goes to the movies is the same as the man who reads Henry James." Warshow was wrong; they are not the same man or woman, and never will be. To think that they are or to wish that they were is in fact granting an importance to James that he never had and insulting the people in telling them that they should strive to rise to Henry James. Most viewers of movies and television would agree with Mark Twain that James was writing for the few and deserved to be read by no more.

Most of the people who watch TV did not care for the recent PBS production, or rerun, of James' books. In such a work as *The Golden Bowl* they found so little life that the producer had to introduce a Greek Chorus to interpret the inactivity. H.L. Mencken was certainly correct in believing that James suffered from looking to the Old World instead of the west, the Frontier, for models of life. James belongs not to commercial television or the Public Broadcasting System, where the privileged are still getting the "servants," that is the public, to support their way of life, their standards, but to a self-supporting Private Interests Company. Television, like the arts in general, should support itself without subsidy. The James mentality, if it got around too widely, could kill all popular art, especially television!

TV is obviously the most powerful distributor of entertainment-education developed so far. It is the greatest democratizer of the arts. It is not leveling down or up. It is instead mixing all the arts and showing that virtually all can be enjoyed by virtually everybody. All can be popular. Any standard of esthetics must be broad and democratic. Roger Rollin, a critic of real perception, insists that the only real authority about aesthetics is not the critic but the people. In popular arts, he insists the rule is "one person-one vote."

TV is not raising or lowering standards. Standards are being broadened and enriched. To a certain extent this is because the critics are becoming more humane and human in their understanding and evaluation of the popular arts, especially television. But it is also because we the viewing public have less and less to do with the critics. We do our own thinking, and allow the critics to talk only to one another.

They do not represent our point of view. Their island of influence is being eroded away.

Still, there is a legitimate place for the critic if he or she can locate it and find it comfortable and habitable. Everyone his own critic is not a bad rule of thumb. But we need a word to substitute for *critic*, which unfortunately still has negative overtones. *Evaluator* might be a more useful term. If we need any TV esthetic we will insist that it not be the phony ones imposed on us from the outside, by people who have selfish purposes to serve. We will insist that the esthetics be natural, human, and that it be for culture in the large, the *popular* sense. Perhaps the words of Robert Coles, psychologist and Pulitizer Prize winning author, should be engraved on the TV set and typewriter of every critic: "The humanities belong to no one kind of person; they are part of the lives of ordinary people, who have their own various ways of struggling for coherence, for a compelling faith, for social vision, for an ethical position, for a sense of historical perspective."

As television becomes more and more a natural and accepted medium of communication in our lives and culture, it will have stronger and silent effects and controls. As we are directed and influenced by other generally accepted and ignored standards of communication in our society, for example—cliches, stereotypes, biases and prejudices—so will we by television. But television, because of its very nature, is more powerful than many other media. This strength makes it imperative that we all become fluent in the language of the medium so that we can take advantage of its strengths and minimize its dangers. Perhaps in no other medium in our culture today is it more necessary that we develop a high level of fluency.

Chapter Ten

Illiteracy About the "Illiterate"

The so-called "folk" of any population, though generally less well-educated than the elite and less pretentious about their literacy, are an integral segment of the society. Designations of their culture, *folklore* and *folk cultures*, have generally taken on new connotations during the last three decades. During the mid-1900s, in at least one way, they stood for protest against the establishment. In the 60s, for example, the radical chic New York set, like Leonard Bernstein and Norman Mailer, found folksongs and folksingers like Pete Seeger and Joan Baez and their political protests especially meaningful. They wined and dined the entertainers and proudly acted as their sponsors.

But there is much more to folk culture than entertainers and protests and their impact on the jet set. Folk culture represents a whole way of life. Generally it is conservative and clings to the status quo and may represent a kind of mystery (even aggravating hostility to modernity) to people in other areas of culture. Folk cultures may not always hold models for industrialized and democratic societies to follow. But folk cultures have managed to survive for thousands of years, and perhaps in that survival alone there are lessons for modern societies to learn from. Further, the folk vote and have a voice in the workings of society, and therefore constitute an important segment, which should be understood.

Despite the spread of democracy and the rise of the working classes in America, the elite among us often are so indifferent to and illiterate about the folklore or folk cultures that the folk world represents the equivalent of a low-frequency communication that seldom or never reaches their ears. Many elite, especially now that the active protests of the 60s are a thing of the past, are indifferent to the folk cultures. The poor who cannot afford bread are not invited to eat cake, and at best the privileged use folk culture as a kind of 2nd language, therefore only half-learned and used only when necessary.

Yet folk culture represents what has been the dominant world culture since humankind began. If we liken the existence of the earth to a 24-hour clock, mankind has been on the earth only the last minute, and

128   The Many Tongues of Literacy

the non-folk for only the last few seconds. Cro-Magnon man 45,000 years ago and the branches of the hominid tree that preceded him had some kind of animal-folk culture. Most works of communication—except the electronic—including so-called works of art—were brought into being in folk societies. Homer, and thousands of Homers now lost in history, was a folk poet working in a folk society.

In Europe the decline of dominance of folk culture came between the 15th and 16th centuries. In America folk cultures were certainly important during the 18th century, and with the rise of regionalism and ethnicity currently becoming very important, folk cultures are again strongly influential. For example, in 1952 I recorded the folk singer Drucilla Hall, of Vernon, Alabama, whose repertory consisted of nearly 300 songs, both long and short. The daughter of a tenant farmer, she was only marginally literate, but a mistress of folksong. My mother, Nola (Trull) Browne, a graduate of Montevallo College, was a folk singer whose repertory included over 350 songs ready at her command placed her among the most prolific singers in America. Folk societies in this country are filled with thousands of such individuals. Certainly in all the Third World today, and in many pockets in most countries in the developed world, folk cultures are still the voices of most of the people.

Among the sophisticated of the Developed Countries, many people very literate in the conventional sense of the word remain illiterate of the folk cultures which exist around them. Many academics, in fact, pride themselves on this illiteracy and look upon their mark of literacy as being the degree to which they have progressed away from folk cultures. To such people the folk are print-illiterate despite the fact that the folk are obviously quite fluent in the media of their cultures.

Folk cultures are important to us. Clearly many aspects of folk cultures—like many qualities of elite cultures—represent less than desirable qualities. But they are here; they exist. They have been the guiding principles and lasting qualities for many peoples through thousands of centuries. They therefore contain many lessons of great value to us today. Folk cultures constitute various media of communication that the elite should become fluent in if they are to understand the world in which they live and if they are to take from the folk cultures any of the obvious treasures and resources that certainly exist there. Like the rain forests or species of flora and fauna that exist and contain vital treasures that the world should come to know, folk cultures cannot be ignored. To remain illiterate about this segment of culture constitutes a painful and wilful disregard of a major segment of our world.

Sensitivity about the interconnectedness is gaining momentum around the world. "The loss of cultures, or of traditional knowledge within cultures undergoing rapid change, is a problem which is at least as serious for humanity as is the loss of species," says Jeffrey McNelly, Chief Conservation Officer, International Union for the Conservation of Nature and Natural Resources, Gland, Switzerland. He points out the indispensability of knowledge of environment. "Crucial knowledge about how the environment might be used to provide benefits on a sustainable basis may be lost forever, along with the species that have supported human welfare for thousands of years," he warns.

In some sections of the world, records of medicinal herbs found in the wild are old. In China the *Huainanzi* (a Han Dynasty classic, 206 B.C.—220 A.D.) states that Shen Nong "tasted hundreds of herbs himself and drank the water from many springs and wells so that people might know which were sweet and which were bitter. On some days Shen Nong tasted as many as seventy poisonous herbs." In the First century, Tacitus, the Roman historian, visited the Germanic people to record, in his *Germania*, the beliefs and practices, especially folk medicines vital in their lives. Some areas of the world, because of the combination of soil, climate and rainfall, are particularly rich in medicinal herbs. The three rain forests of South and Central America and Africa are especially fruitful. In Hubei Province, China, the flora are so rich that the bees produce medicinal honey.

The pervasiveness and lasting quality of home remedies—as these medicines direct from nature are called—is astonishing. Throughout Alabama, in 1950, for example, one collection showed 4340 beliefs and practices in use to one degree or another. Some were wholeheartedly accepted. For instance, "For swelling use a poultice made from mullein leaves" (Browne 106). Others were, perhaps, less widely used. For example, "Stew pine tops in water, make a tea and sweeten; give for colds" (Browne 51). The effectiveness of these medicines is validated pragmatically by direct evidence, coincidence or imperfect observation, or psychology. But they seem to work, and we know from the scientific lab that they do or can be made to be effective. One collection of frontier medicine was *The Indian Doctor: Dr. Jone Williams' Legacy A Useful Family Herbal* (1827), a compilation of 87 cures for various ailments, such as "inveterate old sore legs," "phthisic" and "stiff joints and shrunk sinews." Pharmacological analysis of the cures for such diseases demonstrates that generally one-third to one-half were in fact effective to one degree or another, and in this particular collection by Dr. Williams only one was found detrimental. In our own day it is well known that plants and herbs—and animals—from the rain forests and other generally unexplored sections of the globe provide most cures for our diseases.

Elite illiteracy about folk cultures is not the inability to understand at least partially the folk's language—English or another—but indifference to and illiteracy in all the other forms of communication that constitute the folk cultures. This illiteracy creates tensions and omissions of cooperation between strengths—and weaknesses—of folk and non-folk cultures. Efforts must be made to establish links, at least through common languages. Literacy means more than a dip—a raid—into folk culture, to retrieve such things as folksongs, some artifact on which to base a fad. It means fluency in the languages; not folk cultures as a second language, but fluency in the media of communication of folk cultures as a first language. These media of communication constitute folkspeech at its fullest. In an effort to become literate in folk cultures, much can be learned from professional folklore scholars. The ultimate goal is fluency in the language of the humanities, the elements common to us all, elite, popular and folk. Once the fluency is achieved, then other results follow. What are those results and what are the means of achieving them?

Most folklorists try to be comprehensive in their studies, including all aspects of folk life. According to one leading scholar, Jan Brunvard, "Modern folkloristics embraces oral, customary, and material aspects of tradition equally, and it makes eclectic use of theoretical and methodological approaches from anthropology, linguistics, communications, psychology and other relevant areas. The hope is to develop a viable approach to studying the whole phenomenon that is known as 'folklore' (behavior, texts, performances, effects, etc.) whenever and wherever it occurs and from a point of view that is uniquely 'folkloristic'."

But toward what end are folk cultures to be studied? What is to be gained of value to humanity and the humanities from a study of "the whole phenomenon" that is known as "folklore"? What is to be gained of value to humanity from the isolating and the studying of phenomena associated with particular, distinguishable sets of people as isolated by academics and intellectuals? The subject is not settled. But, clearly, there is more to be gained from the study of folk cultures than is generally included in the conventional approach to the field. Folk culture studies are too important to leave to the conventional approach, just as the study of the humanities in general is far too vital to human society to leave in the hands of the so-called humanists—especially elite humanists—alone.

Some folklorists are interested in the broader outreach of their studies. Alan Dundes, for example, one of today's leading theoreticians and innovators in folk culture studies, looks toward the broader and more humanistically useful study of his field. He thinks that folklorists by analyzing folklore "can discover general patterns of culture." In his eyes, "Folklore as a mirror of culture provides unique raw materials for those eager to better understand themselves and others." But Dundes unfortunately stops short of the full thrust of his implications. Folk cultures may be raw materials to outsiders but to the folk community its culture is smooth, finished and comprehensive and provides answers to the problems that society faces.

True, folklorists and we can better comprehend the subject by more fully understanding a portion of society, and these understandings can lead to generalizations of patterns of culture that benefit people interested in the results of literacy. But the folklorist who is content to stop without these benefits to the humanities to be gained from the study of folk cultures leaves two areas insufficiently explored which would benefit from folk studies. One might be the people themselves. Alan Dundes makes a jab at evaluating this. "Folk should be put back into folklore," he says. "Folklore represents a people's image of themselves," he asserts. "The image may be distorted but at least the distortion comes from the people, not from some outside observer armed with a range of a priori premises."

Folklorists and general students of culture should realize that though the immediate reason for studying folk cultures might well be so that we can better understand a portion of society in its context, this is not the ultimate purpose of knowledge of the subject, nor of knowledge of the folk. The real reason for the scholar, especially the student in the humanities and social sciences, to study folk cultures should be in order to tie them in with the world cultures that have existed through the ages and continue to live today.

In other words, the study of folk cultures offers a range of the universality and depth of those cultures which unite them with cultures around the world. This tie-in with elite, popular and other folk cultures gives a dignity, truth and importance to folk cultures which they have not been accorded so far. It is a serious mistake to restrict the significance of folk cultures short of the general humanities and even to the folk humanities themselves, though this is an extension ordinarily denied to folk cultures. This needed extension is achieved through the study of the humanities *and* folk cultures and the humanities *in* folk cultures. Such inclusion requires considerable effort on the part of the student. These humanities, or the knowledge of them, cannot necessarily be achieved though the individual approaches to the study of folk cultures though literature, history, anthropology, sociology, linguistics, communications, psychology, architecture, entertainments—but far more effectively through the study of the humanities *in* and *of* folk cultures. In other words, the study of folk cultures through literature, anthropology and the other disciplines provides the scripts of the humanities but they are not the humanities. Their humanities are far more than the individual parts. Like elite and popular culture, folk cultures are more than the sum of their parts. And far more significant.

To a large extent the proposal here is that the study of folk culture be restored to what it was before academics began separating it from the generalities in which it properly belongs. Throughout history folk cultures have had a symbiotic relationship with other cultures and participated in whatever larger or smaller cultures existed around them and have been recognized as integral aspects of the cultures people lived in and close to. Peter Burke, in his splendid study, *Popular Culture in Early Modern Europe*, demonstrated how Europeans of the 15th-16th centuries were essentially folk civilizations moving toward becoming urban—that is, less folk-communities. In England, Shakespeare's world was essentially a folk world, no matter if many individuals like himself, Ben Jonson, Queen Elizabeth, the Earl of Oxford and their associates were hardly exemplifications of the folk. England, with its uniquely English determination to remain a country of isolated villages and linguistic enclaves, was perhaps in many ways more of a folk nation than others in Europe. But what was true of England and Europe has been paralleled throughout the world to one degree or another at one time or another, and in most countries is still evolving.

As cultures throughout the world have tended to move beyond conventional folk societies, scholarship on folk cultures has moved into the process of separating the study of folklore into a discreet discipline, for political, fiscal and perhaps scholarly needs. Though these moves may have assisted in the short run, and may be proper on a narrow continuing basis, in the development of the humanities in folk cultures—surely one of the ultimate goals of folklorists and presumably one of the goals of humanities scholars in general—it is time that at least one branch of folk culture and humanities scholars start generalizing again and searching out the humanities *in* and *of* folk cultures.

In order to do that it is imperative that we recognize that folk cultures are a medium of communication which transmits the essence of the humanities, whether or not those humanities are always recognized and extracted. It is imprecise, of course, to equate the humanities with folk culture, for the humanities are much more comprehensive and inclusive, but the overlay is sufficiently close, at least in outline, to make the equation useful, as I have tried to do in the following pages. The perceptive reader will see when the variation is significant and will modify my remarks to fit the changed constituents.

Great effort should be made, if not by folk culture specialists then by humanities generalists, to place the study of folk cultures back in the humanistic tradition and to associate the folk humanities with the elite and popular traditions. To do so is to extend and enrich concurrently the folk, the popular and elite humanities as general humanities. These folk humanities feed a wisdom and universality that exceeds the individual folk communities. For the observer they shed a great deal of light on the human condition and on ways best to deal with it. It is therefore time to put the humanities back into folk cultures and the folk back into the humanities.

The folk humanities are an integral part of the total humanities of the world. They fit into a larger unit. They constitute a culture that is worldwide and will continue to live, as it has for countless ages, at least into the foreseeable future. Perhaps no better key to the time and geography span of folk culture can be found than Stith Thompson's *Motif Index*, as it shows how certain motifs—which are the smallest units in a setting which generate action—are worldwide. The stick-fast motif, found in Joel Chandler Harris' lovely and informative story of the Tar Baby and Br'er Rabbit, in which Br'er Rabbit smacks the Tar Baby with his four paws because the Tar Baby is rude and won't answer Br'er Rabbit's inquiries, for example, is found in 17 counties throughout the world, even in countries that have no tar or resin and, thus, apparently would be unable to understand the story.

But there are far more important elements of the humanities represented by local folk cultures that are tied into the universal. For example, service and benefit to humanity, traditionally associated with the culture hero, can be seen in, among hundreds of other examples, the legend of Johnny Appleseed. Appleseed roamed throughout the Midwest U.S. during the last half of the 19th century distributing knowledge in the forms of book chapters and other publications he carried from one person to another, and practical assistance in the form of appleseeds that people planted and benefited from, and through both activities gave a knowledge of the value of empathy, sympathy and community assistance on the American frontier—and by implication on any exposed flank of society. Davy Crockett, through the legends of his life and death, gave clear evidence of the value of selflessness in a growing nation. He/she who loves a nation enough to die for it, as Crockett did, demonstrates one of the more heroic and valuable elements of the humanities.

Animal tales always speak to the human condition, as this one from Alabama demonstrates. But in order to understand it, one must be literate in the folk storyteller's idiom.

The Frog that wanted to be Big

Dis on I always tells to de little chillun in Sunday School.—
De mother frog want her children to think dey was de biggest people in de worl'. And dey did. One day dey was walkin' down de road and saw uh turkle. Dey saw tat de turkle was biggern dey was. So dey rushed home and ask dere ma if de turkle was biggern dey was. Ma frog started swellin' and swellin' and swellin', tryin' to show dat she was biggern de turkle, and she swell up till she busted. An' de moral of dat story is: Don't go 'roun' tryin' to be biggern other people.

After I tole em dat story de little chillun go 'roun' playin' like dey is swellin' up bigger 'n' bigger and shoutin' "Boom!" (Browne 95)

Folk stories also demonstrate how country people deal with the shortage of food (and the therapeutic value of a sense of humor), as this blending of two Alabama folktales shows:

Mountain folks is the best folks in the world. They don't often have much, but they are awful free with what they do have. One time a stranger came up to a mountain cabin about dinner time. Well, the father of the house asked the stranger to come and have dinner. All they had to eat was boiled taters served on bark. The man was rather shy about taking many taters when he saw that that was all they had. So he just took a couple of little ones. The husband said: 'Go ahead, take some more taters.' The man took one more. The husband said: 'Take some more taters. Just take a damn lot of taters.'

Another time another stranger came to this same mountain family and asked to spend the night. All they had to eat that night was taters. Taters fried; boiled taters; baked taters. Cause he was hungry, the stranger ate a pretty good bait of taters. Well, later on that night, he woke up sick at his stomach. He went outside the house and vomited. While he was out there the woman of the house heard him and came out to see what she could do. When she found out that he was sick at his stomach she said: 'Well, we ain't got no medicine in the house, but I'll be glad to make you some tater tea.' (Browne, 108)

Humor does help to grease the sledding of life. But folk humor has its own subtleties, which is different from the cultural milieu of the elite. In order to comprehend it, one must be literate in the medium and in those subtleties.

The humanities in action in the folk community can be seen in the numerous ballads and folksongs which permeate nearly all folk communities. Songs are in many ways extremely useful carriers of the cultures in which they thrive because being basic they are therefore an "art," and as such they allow a certain impersonal impunity to the singer, so that nearly any subject can be covered, especially if it can be disguised, and because people tend to pour a lot of sentiment and conviction into the freedom and license given them in song. "Give me the making of the songs of a nation, and I care not who makes its laws," said Britisher Andrew Fletcher of Saltoun (1655-1716).

It is, of course, dangerous for people to impose cultural and political standards and interpretations on moments in history, because to avoid anachronistic misinterpretation one needs to understand completely the cultural milieu surrounding an event—or a song—in order not to pervert and misinterpret the artifact. But songs undoubtedly float certain universal and timeless aspects of humanity. With caution in interpretation they can be useful today in helping us understand the cultures of past singers as well as our own culture.

There are thousands of ballads and folksong that would be usefully illustrative. "Lord Randall," famous from the 17th century on and still widely sung under several names gives us a picture of a man poisoned by his lady-love by putting the potion in eels or eel-broth (a common device in 13th century Italy). His hatred for her deed and the curse he placed upon her apparently was favored by society. In this version, called "Lord Donald," the concluding stanza voices the curse the victim places on his murderess:

'What will ye leave to your true-love, Lord Donald, my son?
What will ye leave to your true-love, my jollie young man?
The tow and the halter, for to hang on yon tree,
And lat her hang there for the poysoning o me.'

Another poignant ballad, "Barbara Allen," has through the centuries pictured a hard-hearted woman who, having been slighted for some reason by her lover, when summoned to his dying bedside refused to go, leaving him dying unconsoled and apparently without love. When she learned of his death, however, she was stricken with remorse and immediately died of a broken heart. They were buried side by side. From their adjacent graves grew flowers which intertwined symbolize their eternal love.

This ballad has long been a favorite. Samuel Pepys commented on its magic in the 17th century: "In perfect pleasure I was to hear her [Mrs. Knipp, the actress] sing, and especially her little Scotch song of Barbary Allen." Oliver Goldsmith said of it: "The music of the finest singer is dissonance to what I felt when our old dairy-maid sung me to tears with 'Johny Arstrong's Last Goodnight,' or 'The Cruelty of Barbara Allen'." Though there are many versions, the cruelty of an unforgiving heart is common to almost all. The sentiments and symbols are of the folk, and must be understood in that medium. The entire song demonstrates the development of those symbols.

The power of this ballad, as it protests hard-hearted cruelty of one human being for another, even with persons who cannot possibly have any connection with such behavior except through the long line of human compassion, is great today. Singers, especially women and audiences, still shed tears and lament the indifference, the lack of compassion of one human being for another, of "hard-hearted Barbara Allen," who refused love and attention at life's final act, the man's dying.

Among folk culture's many artifacts—and visual representations of artifacts—there are many which indicate the folks' reactions to the challenges and problems of life. Architecture, for example, reveals how men and women have tried to design their structures and living space to make them less uncomfortable, less subject to the vagaries of outside weather, and to ease the physical discomfort of living under potentially restricting and hostile conditions. Painted and photo representations of these aspects of life demonstrate how people have shaped their art according to their attitudes and reactions to life.

All these efforts to face up to and stare down the various aspects of life have the essence of the humanities just as much as do the utterances of the popular and elite stages of culture. 19th-century British poet and essayist Matthew Arnold's dictum about the definition of culture— "Culture, the acquainting ourselves with the best that has been known and said in the world"—is easily translated into the folk idioms: "The most useful aspects of life most helpfully said." "Everybody has their problems. We don't know where we came from or where we're going, so all we can do is hope." Out of sheer necessity hope springs eternal in the folk breast and flows in the folk idioms from the individual to the collective heart.

Media sage Marshall McLuhan felt that the popular languages as transmitted through television are creating a global village, in which, as Leslie Fiedler sees it, there can be a real sense of community similar to that which existed in folk communities before people were separated by class, interests, goals and ambitions. Undoubtedly, both are substantially correct. But in some instances the drive is in the opposite direction. In some folk cultures—Japan, for example—television is perpetuating regional and village cultures at least temporarily, by creating communities of interest around television sets, to the exclusion of the outside world. But the barrier of regionality can be easily breached electronically and silently. Television is the quiet visitor, who having been welcomed into the house, stays on and dramatically influences attitudes and behavior. Television is the visitor, instead of the literary man, who came to dinner and was not allowed to leave.

Folk cultures, despite temporary aberrations, tend to drive, at least verbally, toward brotherhood and sisterhood. Those are the traits of the humanities.

Often it takes intellectuals, driven astray by their misguiding intellects, many decades to relearn what their predecessors knew and took for granted. For example, historian of art Alan Gowans believes that in order to understand art one must know what purpose it was created for and serves, in other words, how it fits into the communication system. "In order to know art, one must know why it was created," he feels. Folk wisdom has always known that the primary question one asks about art is, "Why did you do it?" Gowans feels that every artifact if properly understood can mirror the culture in which it was created and circulated. In the folk mind the question might well be, "I wonder why he did that. What's he going to do with it?"

Frank Lloyd Wright's philosophy about the imperatives of architects which "enlightened" the architectural world—that architecture needs to grow out of the land on which it rests—was before his time the working necessity of people for thousands of years in their folk housebuilding, as evidenced in the form of caves, log houses, igloos, grass sheds, sod shanties, rain forest pygmy leaf huts, bungalows, lean-tos, all of which had to utilize the building materials available and modify the structure to suit the terrain on which it was built. What is so new about that which is thousands of years old? Only the short-sightedness of the people doing the looking. Folk communication had long stated the obvious: You build with materials at hand and in a manner best suited to the environment.

In fact all elite culture, as nearly everybody knows and some will acknowledge, stands neck deep in popular and folk cultures. Elite culture is like a classical mythological animal, with folk feet, popular culture body and elite eyes and nose. The three are equal and inseparable. The same nutrients feed all. The head cannot exist without the body, the body without the feet, though among intellectuals the talking head is also an important part of popular and folk cultures. But in folk culture, actions speak louder than words and results are more important than hypotheses. The finished act or product is more significant than the plan or blueprint. That is not to say that folk cultures are not filled with dreams. In fact dreams are the very spirit of folk cultures—as mythologies, marchen, animal stories, horror stories and witches tales testify. Nearly all the dreams and fantasies of elite cultures today have been at one time or another a part of folk cultures, have pulsated through popular culture idioms and, despite the feeling among elitists that their culture is the origin of all that is good and which trickles down, the folk-popular culture idioms have moved over from their spheres to energize and vivify elite culture.

It is indeed time to put the folk back into folklore, as Alan Dundes says, and into the broader culture also, and to learn the languages they speak. To examine a folksong, tale, practice, or artifact without realizing that it is an important aspect of folk life, idiom and culture is to under-evaluate and under-appreciate folk cultures and to deprive cultures of important ingredients. The folk humanities are the very heart of folk cultures and the foundation of all cultures and humanities. Folk humanities, like popular and elite humanities, drive toward generalizations that are needed in a world that for too long has been pushed towards specializations, separations into castes based on origins, finances, education and accomplishments. The humanities address the commonality in us all in languages that all citizens need to be fluent in.

Nowadays when elitists speak of the humanities, they seldom mention the folk humanities. Lynne Cheney, Chairman of the National Endowment for the Humanities, in her NEH Report *Humanities in America* (1988) mentions all the buzz words for the conventional evaluations of the humanities. She talks about Western civilization and even hints that there might be room for the intellectual study of popular culture properly elevated to elite planes. But not once does she name or even hint at folk culture as being within the realm of the humanities. Bloom, in his best-selling study *The Closing of the American Mind*, already had his own mind closed against folk cultures; it was not gentlemanly enough for his taste. E.M. Hirsch, in his book *Cultural Literacy*, includes the word "folklore" in his 5000 items needed to allow one to call himself/herself literate, but he uses the old-fashioned term "folklore" when "folk cultures" is the more appropriate term. Cheney, Bloom, and to a certain extent Hirsch, are canon-conscious and folk-blind, when folk literature in all the media pulsates all round them. These days everybody is familiar with Johnny Appleseed, Daniel Boone, Davy Crockett, George Custer, the Erie Canal, the great song "Shenandoah," jump-rope rhymes, how to build a boat and a fishing net and how to choose the proper mate for marriage—all speak with the voice of the humanities. These subjects address themselves to the practical problems of living—of being human.

In writing about them the various forms of folk literature are perhaps more vitally a part of the humanities than other forms of literature are. They do not use Matthew Arnold's precious literary phraseology, nor Lynne Cheney's; but they do use Abraham Lincoln's, Carl Sandburg's, the cowboy's, the workman's, Emma Lazarus's, the working woman's and Martin Luther King Jr.'s. Like the canonized humanities among other people, the folk humanities include every aspect of life from the domestic to the spiritual, from the physical to the imaginary and from reality to fantasy. Though written in a different idiom for a differently educated group, the folk humanities reflect Robert Cole's listing of everybody's dreams of survival and happiness.

They are obviously comprehensive and all-permeating. To paraphrase Lincoln's remark about God surely loving the poor because He made so many of them, Jehovah must approve of the folk humanities because He made so many of them. Presumably when they inherit the earth, as promised by the Bible, the poor's folk humanities will prevail. Meanwhile, like old leather they wear long and well.

They are not like the ever-changing theories of life of the intelligentsia, which are truly writ in water, like Keats' name, or, more properly, writ in academic publications. Peruse the list of intellectual theoretical fads which has flowed past us lately: premodernism, postmodernism, structuralism, destructuralism, constructionism, Marxism, Stalinism, perhaps Gorbyism and post-Gorbyism, ethnicism, regionacism, etc. So far they have not been concerned with such precious arguments as the great scientific disagreement in the late 1980s, published in various media, over whether coffee is beneficial or detrimental to drinkers' health. But give us time. Perhaps in imitation of the 18th-century controversy, as outlined in Jonathan Swift's *Gulliver's Travels*, over whether people should break their eggs at the big-end or the small-end, we will have heated debates between the Big-Cupists and the Little Cupists—perhaps even the post-Cupists—when the conflict has run its course.

To the intellectual, theory and methodology is, like teaching methods in a College of Education, an end in itself, a passing fad, not a means to anything.

There is simply no pretentious intellectual fad that is too silly for the intellectual, especially if it has been discredited, as for example the continuing notion of Marxism as a viable theory of criticism in the 1990s in the face of the total collapse of the Marxist theories in action in the Soviet Union. Former Secretary of State Henry Kissinger—with years of experience on the faculty at Harvard—was surely on target when he observed that the reason academics are so petty is that they have nothing important to occupy their minds. Either that or the intellectual's mind is not capable of handling anything more complicated than the trivial. It pettyizes every idea it touches. The life of the mind that many intellectuals want to lead may well be only a very simple pin-ball machine that they like to play with while the real game of life goes on about them. *Voila. C'est la vie dans academie.*

Academics like to sail their yachts down the gentle current of so-called intellectuality, caressed by their own medium of communication, and come to anchor at some small island which represents the latest fad in theory-making. But the flotsam soon passes, the theory fades, and it is time to weigh anchor and drift to the next island. The thin, one-crop, unproductive soil of these islands is revealed if one looks back upstream at the long line of now-abandoned stopovers with their pathetic shredded flags limp and listless in the breeze. But the academic yachts have too small intellectual motors to drive toward new ideas or to create new thoughts. So scholarship in the elite humanities essentially consists of drifting from one seemingly promising theory-fad to the next, with no rich soil in the offing. Ponce de Leon could not find a fountain of youth in the swamps of Florida. Intellectuals cannot find rich soil for their cultivation because their plows are too shallow. Lincoln's observation about not being able to fool all the people all the time apparently does not hold for intellectuals. Throughout academia people are dedicated to fooling most of themselves most of the time. *Plus ca change, plus c'est la meme chose.* The more things change, the more they stay the same.

But the folk humanities do not pass with every yearly change in rhetoric. They were here yesterday, are here today and will be here tomorrow. The folk wisdom of the American humorist Josh billings perhaps hits closest to home in connection with the folk and their humanities vis-a-vis the canonical humanities: "It ain't the things that we know that makes such fools of us, but a whole lot of things that we know that ain't so," he said. That the folk humanities may be closer to the mark of truth than the elite humanities is demonstrated by the fact that the folk don't have to change theirs as often as the elite do. The folk humanities endure. With the folk humanities, the question "What's new?" is almost certain to be answered with, "Not much," whereas the same question to a conventional elite canonical humanist is likely to elicit the naming of the latest intellectual fad that buys great mileage today on the elite superhighway but will be discredited tomorrow. Folk wisdom has always had its versions of Shakespeare's observation, "What fools [academics] be," and a large portion of those versions is laced with four and three letter words. *Plus c'est la meme chose, plus ca change.*

The change now as we look toward a needed rejuvenation and revitalization of the humanities should be the assurance that there is much to be learned from the realization that the folk humanities should be, *must be,* a vital part of our search for the value of the full potential of those humanities. An old universal riddle supposedly asked by the Sphinx of all passersby is germane to us today: "What walks on four feet in the morning, two at noon, and three at night?" Humankind, the answer, needs to include the realization that we need the folk, the popular and the elite humanities to help us struggle along.

Without all three our picture cannot be complete. This total picture cannot be communicated or understood without fluency by all in the languages of all three media. Folkspeech may at times suffer from many of the same limitations of popular and elite languages. Nevertheless it is vital to the communication of cultures.

Chapter Eleven

Literacy in Interdisciplinary
Academic Organizations

American revolutionists are almost always short-sighted and short-winded. They lack staying power. Whether political, social or academic, most revolutionists see a problem that needs to be solved, a wrong that should be righted, a government that needs to be overthrown; and once those changes have been effected, the revolution seems to have been achieved, and the drive peters out for want of any further cause for continuance. Then the people who yesterday were beating down doors become bureaucrats and theorists and rationalizers; those who rooted out one system become entrenched in their own system, and that system usually stays around, eating its own creation and gradually going to seed, until the next short-sighted revolution overthrows it.

Such has been the revolution in the last half century in American academia against single-discipline studies. Many academics have seen value in interdisciplinary or cross-disciplinary approaches to learning and teaching, and have made efforts to bring about change. Although these efforts are continuing in various fields, in most, especially those that have been around even for a few years, there are strong efforts to kill the revolutionary spirit, have the new innovative drive revert, at least in spirit, to the conservative approach, and in so doing to stunt or kill the drive that tried to bring about the change in the first place.

"Narrow your approach and specialize," is the constant wail for American academics if they are to succeed. Originality in research and consequent publication demands specificity in interests. A glance at the *Publications of the Modern Language Association* over the past few years, or an individual number, or the many sessions of the yearly meeting, shows how hair-splitting the researchers are. We used to worry about how many angels could dance on the head of a pin; now, to bring about fruitful research, we have utilized some Marxist or post-modern theory to investigate the origins of the dance they are performing. The Modern Language Association is not supposed to be any hotbed of innovation, but one could expect that among such widely read communities as are

141

to be found in literature departments there might be some people interested in generalities.

But there is simply no mileage in synthesis these days, in trying to see what all the research and assumed thinking adds up to. The point is to find or create one's own little sink-hole and stir up the mud and water hoping for new insights. Lynne Cheney states in her latest official publication on the state of the National Endowment for the Humanities that "twenty years ago one out of six college graduates majored in the humanities. Today the figure is one out of sixteen" (33), and the number is surely dropping. Perhaps, unless drastic measures are taken, humanities majors will disappear altogether. The cause is of course conceptual, but it might also be definitional, an argument made throughout this book. If we can rejuvenate the concept of the need for the humanities among people and then modernize the definition, making it less exclusionary, then perhaps we can save the humanities real and genuine and make them viable again.

Through the years there has been a constant effort on the part of many good-willed people to blunt the cutting edge of efforts to keep the humanities alive and well. The thrust has been the devaluation of the humanities themselves in academic training and subsequent life. The humanities have weakened through the years with the advent and development of scientific and technological wonders which seemed to be of greater importance. The scientific humanities, which nudged aside the old, were based on new concepts, new urgencies and new needs. Such an attitude was short-sighted and perhaps a little misguided. Now with the realization that the humanities are not to be replaced by scientific and technological developments and with the influx of billions of dollars (from foundations and the government), possibly the rush toward the elimination of the concept of the humanities can be reversed and they can be made real and enjoyable and livable again by tying the humanities in with literacy. That is, to make literacy in the humanities the goal, not the treasures which for themselves should be acquired and hoarded. The humanities should be viewed as valuable enrichments of life that make the holder double wealthy. In other words, the humanities can be properly identified as being like financial capital and coin of the realm—something to enrich the individual and something he can use in the marketplace. Perhaps it is time for the people interested in the humanities to hire their Madison Avenue advertising agency and develop a marketable image. After all, that is what America is all about.

Three academic groups, among others, have for the last half century worked to develop in the humanities two sorts of literacy. The first is the old concept of literacy as fluency in communication—communication among the various interdisciplinary fields in the humanities and where there is no communication to develop it. Second, a concept of literacy is found in the workings of academic organizations, their organization, purposes, goals and means of maintaining direction and achieving goals. The three academic organizations are the American Folklore Society, the American Studies Association and the Popular Culture Association. Though by no means the largest of the academic groups that profess interest in the humanities and perhaps no more worthy, these three groups nevertheless represent common goals, common interests and common problems. Perhaps demonstrated literacy in one or all might serve as some kind of model for literacy in the others and to outside groups trying to achieve similar goals.

Of these three groups, the American Folklore Society, founded in 1889, is the oldest. It was born as a realization that there are many aspects of culture that are ignored or despised by academia and should not be. So a group of individuals in such fields as anthropology, English, religion, etc., started collecting and studying beliefs and practices of society and researching and teaching the materials. At first the efforts were amateurish and dilettantish, but they began a trend. Through the years the AFS has suffered some precarious times of existence, but interested students have held on. They have felt that there are folk cultures that one must become literate in if one wants to understand a large segment of society— a segment that is changing but not disappearing, and which is so complex and important that it demands its own literacy in order to be understood.

Through the years certain "schools" of thought and certain geographical schools have tried to insinuate themselves into dominance and control and have succeeded to a certain extent. But members of the AFS are a fractious and headstrong group. Never quite accepted into academia as bona fide, quality people, they have always had to knock on the doors for admission. As a consequence, and this is really the most important point I want to make in contrasting the two associations, the members of the AFS have kept open minds. They would not be mind-controlled by their leading academic schools or leading academicians, though many of them did tend, naturally, to tilt toward the schools in which they had been trained. Folklorists have been interested in the subject more than in the methodology of studying it even more than in the "quality" of the material they produced. They have spent less of their time and energy in testing and proving the quality of their work than in doing the work. They have been pioneers instead of settlers. They have left the settling and the methodologizing of the surroundings to the lesser folk—who were content to come along and put up the fences—and to the bureaucracy.

The American Studies Association was born with a questioning and a challenging—not rebellious and certainly not revolutionary, but more than skeptical—attitude of the status quo. As we all know, a group of pretty conventional academics, surely with the exception of Carl Bode, from conventional departments (English, History and Philosophy, essentially) got together and said—in what was then perhaps challenging but which we now think of as in pretty tame terms—that students and faculty could learn more about civilization and life and literature if an interdisciplinary approach is taken to researching and teaching in these areas. In other words, the conclusion was that people could teach better if they knew more and could see the connection and interrelationships among thoughts, and it would then follow that the students could benefit from this new approach.

The idea grew as long as it was new and creative and will continue to grow as long as it contains those pulses. But the concept did have trouble getting established on many campuses simply because it was not an easy task to make headway against conventional disciplines in conventional schools among conventional scholars and teachers.

The reasons are simple. Academics generally are interested in learning facts, not in opening and exciting minds. We are interested in developing ways to progress in the areas and methods that we have learned. Therefore we tend to want to perpetuate our own kind, to clone ourselves and our mentors over and over. If one studied at the feet of Leon Howard, for example, as I did, one is likely to feel that nobody knew more about American literature in general and Herman Melville in particular than he did. After all, he had written three or four books on the subject, had lectured for years in this country and abroad and was a fine person and a great friend. Just to be like and as strong as Leon was the goal of his many students. But in this attitude, we failed to learn and understand everything that was *implicit* in what Leon taught though not always *explicit*; that is that he was just a laborer in the vineyard working his own particular materials his own particular way, and that we should learn facts from him, observe his methods, and then by building on what we had learned from him, go on and do our own things. By standing on his shoulders, as Francis Bacon had observed 350 years earlier, we could see further. He was inviting us not to stop with him but to use our own minds and go on to open up new vistas. Such an attitude is easier for a giant to articulate than for his students to implement. We get caught in a trap such people often unwittingly set.

We tend to believe that our mentors are more heroic than they are— or at best we fail to see that heroes are self-acknowledging individuals whose most heroic accomplishment is creating greater heroes than themselves. Thus instead of making our own footsteps, we tend to walk in those of the mentors, and we feel content with this stride.

On a larger scale we tend to clone the schools we came from because we were told while there, and perhaps by the world also, that such and such is simply the finest school—in the South, in California, in the U.S. or the World. Schools like to circulate and perpetuate such myths, of course, because they are self-serving. Sometimes they are right—but meaningless and very negative to a graduate's growth. For as long as we try to translate Harvard or Yale or Princeton or Michigan or Florida or Bowling Green to the Boonies, unexamined and unimproved, we merely take a shadow-clone, a watered-down version which loses a great deal in the translation. Always wrong-headed, at times this transportation becomes ridiculous. For example, at the University of California at Los Angeles, years ago the English Department hired a linguist from the University of Michigan who came out to the deserts of tinsel town to bring the learning of the great school of Michigan, which Warner Rice, chairman of the department, was rumoring to be one of the best in the world. Because he had had the finest instruction in Old English possible, this instructor simply read his U. of M. notes to his UCLA class and knew very little else. The result was disastrous. Luckily the students knew more than the instructor, complained to the Department and got the young man fired. I assume having failed among the west coast heathen, this person went on with his U. of M. notes to enlighten another campus.

So the people who remain always Harvard-people, Penn-People, Yalies, Leslie Fiedler-students or Leon Howard-clones are caught in a skin which ought to become increasingly too tight but which they often do not want to shed, and they therefore remain stunted in their growth.

Let me give you another example. A leading Herman Melville scholar, Howard Vincent, did a herculean task during the last three decades in searching out materials that Melville read and obviously used in his writing of his classics *Moby-Dick* and *White-Jacket.* Vincent read all the books that Melville read and demonstrated how Melville used these materials in writing his two books. Some fifteen years ago I was talking with some graduate students at the University of Southern California about the use of popular culture in supplementing and amplifying conventional scholarship. I began my talk by stating explicitly how valuable I thought Vincent's two books are. Then I went on to say that unfortunately Vincent had stopped short, or that much work remains to be done if one is going to understand completely, or more fully, the mind that created *Moby-Dick* and *White-Jacket.* I suggested that the full background of those books would include not only the books that we know Melville read, but all the others that were around and that he *might* have read—all the books that were read by the people Melville talked to, his friends and acquaintances—and all the other information that people in Melville's day knew: folklore, pseudo-folklore, geography, pseudo-geography, history and pseudo-history—everything. In other words, in order to understand fully Melville's mind when he wrote those books, a person would have to be a compendium of 19th-century America. That made sense to me, and I saw no malice or negative criticism in the remarks. But as soon as I had finished my statements, a hand went up from a young assistant professor, who told me in no uncertain words that he had studied with Howard Vincent, that he thought those two books are perfect, and he resented my mentioning any way that scholarship might go on building on Vincent's two studies. But other persons have seen the job as unfinished. Another scholar, David S. Reynolds, in his book *Beneath the American Renaissance*, added immensely to a comprehensive study of the world in which Melville lived and worked. More work is still needed.

On a larger scale this restriction of schools and heroes is expanded into another restrictive attitude: that of "schools" of approach, or methodologies, and even the notion of the need for these approaches. Again, I would like to use the ASA as an example.

As long as the ASA was trying to revolutionize and change the study of the Humanities, it had muscle and momentum. Often this was against the strongest wishes of many members of the ASA. I know many people, especially in English, who wanted to bring in the tried English approaches to the ASA immediately and hide-bind it in those methodologies. Generally, the feeling was that those methodologies guaranteed quality and standards—a grave concern with the ASA scholars. Now as far as I am concerned, the cry of standards, to paraphrase Dr. Johnson's famous remark about the cry of self-serving patriots, is a red-herring which cloaks other considerations—philosophical, political, social, personal and pathological—and is only relatively consonant with actual quality of work.

The ASA had a high ground from which to wave the flag of those attitudes. But I would contend that in such an attitude there are the seeds of defeat, or lack of development and stunted growth simply because the goals are visible and the mind is set.

I would suggest that the ASA has needed through the years and needs now especially a new attitude toward its mission. This year, for example, at the biennial meeting there were 500 presentations. The subject was limited to "Boundaries of American Culture." The ASA was working on its methodology, with its quality and standards, its thematic approach to its field (though the subjects ranged widely), and the result was 500 presentations fewer than one-fourth the number we have here at the Popular Culture Association, which meets yearly.

Now those statistics tell me something and raise a series of questions. The main question is, Is the ASA treating itself properly? Is the ASA being fair to its potential?

This is the question that the ASA people frequently ask themselves; generally the answers leave a great deal to be desired. For example, Princeton University got a grant to hold a conference on its campus on "Reconsidering American Studies in the Eighties: A Core Course Proposal," asking 9 leading ASA people to ponder the question about the proper approach to teaching American Studies. The scholars examined and dismissed William Goetzmann's suggestion for "modules of methodology," meaning, I assume, samples of different approaches; they recognized and sort of approved the method used at the University of Pennsylvania and the University of California at Santa Cruz, which is the autobiographical approach. After two days, the scholars' conclusion was twofold: "that a core course should definitely be required at Princeton and that it would consist of no prescribed texts or approach." Finally, the conference ended with the feeling that the "proper role" of American Studies, at least at Princeton, is "ever encouraging the possibilities of multidisciplinary analysis." The consensus of the conference, in other words, was that the American Studies should not strive for consensus.

This was a quaint conclusion for the investment of 9 leading American Studies scholars and thousands of dollars plus possibly 800 hours of deep thinking and continuous talking. This two-fold conclusion was published in the same newsletter which states that the ASA is setting out to raise $100,000 of desperately needed cash. The thinking here may be a bit muddled.

There may be a lesson to be learned from observations recently made by Arthur Levine, President of Bradford College, about the similarity between problems of higher education and those of the auto industry. One of his conclusions is that members of the auto industry contributed to their own fall by living in the past instead of the present. "There was a tendency to live in the past," he said. "Major social and economic changes were not recognized. Declining public confidence and satisfaction were not perceived. Tomorrow was projected on the basis of yesterday." One of the lessons learned should be that "the historical record shows clearly that in hard times the most successful institutions have been those that responded best to the educational needs of their day. They attracted students, finances and national reputations when other institutions failed. This is the challenge facing higher education today" (*Education and National Affairs*, 9/20/85, p. 7). Such things as humanities and culture are at best fragile, but they must be handled and treated as parts of the world around us; to keep them in the cold storage of the past does them and the world irreparable harm.

Let me draw a parallel to another organization I have worked with for the past thirty-five years, the American Folklore Society, which I look upon as a modified success story not only in survival but in development.

The American Folklore Society in 1989 celebrated its 100th anniversary, more than twice the life span of the American Studies Association. It was not born out of annoyance with conventional academic disciplines but as a realization that there are many aspects of culture that are ignored by academia and should not be. So in 1889 people in anthropology, English, religion and other areas started studying and collecting the beliefs and practices of society and researching and teaching the materials.

The implications are that there is a folk culture that one must become literate in if one wants to understand a large segment of society that is changing but not disappearing and which is so complex and important that it demands its own literacy and fluency in order to be understood.

Through the years the American Folklore Society has suffered some precarious times of existence. The problem was not so much with how they were doing their work, their quality and standards (though people did have some reservations with some of those) but *with what they were not doing.* Many people felt that there were vast areas of great interest and importance that were simply being kept out of the vital information flow.

In 1960 my discontent boiled over. At Purdue University, in 1962, I held a regional meeting of the ASA, at which I invited people from folklore, music, philosophy, history, aesthetics, etc. When I asked the people in folklore to participate, they at first demurred, asking why they should participate in a program with people from the ASA and other areas when these people would only condemn what the folklorists were doing and would condescend to them. And that is precisely what happened. I will never forget one of the leading scholars in American Studies softly cursing under his breath while the leading scholar in folklore was making his talk. I held another conference in 1964, and precisely the same kinds of things happened again.

I worked for years with the ASA and the AFS and told both groups, especially the former, that we were not doing something right. Something was amiss. I felt we should emulate the lessons taught to us by the aristocracy in all countries at all times and let in some new and different blood. In the animal kingdom this is known as bringing in new stock. I felt our incestuous relations had made our bloodlines a little anemic.

Those who were present at the great revolution in Toledo in 1969 will remember when 200 members of the ASA met one afternoon to talk about forming a Popular Culture Association. There were all kinds of interesting tame-eyed and wild-eyed people present. We discussed what we should do, how we should do it, where we should go with our ideas and what we thought was wrong with the activities of the ASA, of which we were members. There were some with conventional views of revolution, mouthing the party-line. But luckily (as far as I see it) they were not put in control. Those who were had other things on their minds. Not revolution for the sake of revolution, not change for the sake of change, but a realization that, to paraphrase Thomas Paine, we could almost think as though we were in on the creation of a new world. We might not *act* as though we were in on the creation of a new world, but we could *dream*. And I think it was the beauty of this dream which activated us; it put in stars in the eyes of many of us there that afternoon. And I suspect it has sustained the stars in the eyes of some of us for these 21 years. Luckily we did not know what we were talking about. We did not know what we meant by popular culture. We had no idea where we were going or even wanted to go. We would bring our biases and prejudices with us, our strengths and limitations, but we could work in exciting areas, developing exciting ideas that we had long entertained. It was, I suspect, as exciting as Daniel Boone looking over the mountains to the west and realizing what a brave new world existed there. The times were young and exciting, and we were strapping youths of all ages. Tomorrow was a bright day.

Where are we twenty-one years later? Were we youngsters who would too soon grow old? Were we visionaries who would soon discover that the world we looked upon as our cookie was in fact half eaten and belonged to somebody else? Did we discover, as Daniel Boone did after he went through Cumberland Gap to Kentucky, that the world of reality is not so easily conquered as we had thought, and that human nature being what it is would modify our dreams?

The answers are yes and no. As Jefferson said about the maintenance of liberty, we must be ever vigilant about seminal ideas in academia because some people won't want them to thrive. We have come, as Lincoln said in the Gettysburg Address, to a great test to see whether the dreams of that October 1969 afternoon will stand the test of time and our own ideas. Conventional people are raising two or more great fire-breathing dragons and are trying to sear the dreams of the Popular Culture Association, or, perhaps less dramatically stated, are trying to direct and channel the thinking and thus the activities of the PCA. The two dragons are, naturally, those that have smoked and fumed in the forest all these years: Quality and Methodology.

With the first no one disagrees, as long as we admit that quality, like beauty, is a personal evaluation. Some people seem handsomer than others, some food tastes better than others, some movies are more enjoyable than others, some books and some works of art are more "artistic" than others, some ideas less evanescent than others to individuals. But these qualities inherent in the eyes of the beholder are learned and culture-driven evaluations, not innate qualities. They are arbitrary and change as rapidly and as unexplainably as opportunity and self-serving interests warrant. They recapitulate a sad litany of people fighting to achieve or maintain advantage over other people. Throughout history literate people have tried to deny literacy to the illiterate because in literacy, as they recognized, lies tremendous real and potential power. "Standards" are really mostly another contemporary word for esthetic literacy. If all people's sense of esthetic quality were the same, there could be no distinction between people's "tastes" and their recognition of "quality;" therefore, there would be a levelling in standards, esthetics and quality that would essentially make all people equal. Indeed, people resist such levelling in every way.

But necessity can show the seams in the strands of quality—and sometimes with the most delicious irony. Such an irony is now unfolding among the landed gentry in England, who, because they are unable to keep their giant country mansions and estates alive, have had to open them to the paying public. Sometimes the blue-bloods and blue-stockinged gentry mix with the red-bloods and no-stockinged hoi-polloi and are not recognized for the superior individuals they actually are. Some of the landlords also feature dinners with the superior individuals for such amounts as $300. Perhaps no finer double irony can be found than in the attitude of many of the people who visit these estates and buy these dinners: the feeling, often expressed, is that it is a shame that these families which sometimes reach back hundreds of years have to resort to mixing with the everyday people. With such an attitude, no wonder the trademark of "standards" (like the Brooklyn Bridge) are so easily sold to the gullible. No better example presents itself than Washington, D.C., the capital of the world's greatest democracy. It is ironic that the power elite in the capital of democracy is perhaps the most snobbish in the country when it comes to taking opportunities to fawn over so-called "quality" and undemocratic people and life. One of the more amusing examples is the visit of the Prince and Princess of Wales to the Capital in November 1985. Most quality Washingtonians were agog with hopes of meeting these "elite" people (such is the world where "quality" and standards obtain). But luckily, in a gesture that was consciously or intuitively correct, President Reagan peopled the stellar dinner honoring the couple not with Washington political stars, but with movie and TV stars from Hollywood, as indeed he should, since both they and the Prince and Princess are strictly engaged in show-biz. But not all Washingtonians were interested in this kind of national display over "quality" and "standards." The man and woman on the street, interviewed by newspaper reporters, quite properly said that they were much more interested in finding a way to make a living than in seeing what these people were wearing or talking about. Even more defiantly, a survey conducted by a Washington radio station revealed that Washingtonians in general by a vote of four to one would rather have a ticket to the Redskins-Cowboys professional football game than to the Presidential party. You can perhaps fool some of the people all of the time...But you can't fool sensible Americans about the relative value of spectacle, especially when running back John Riggins, star of the football field who was invited to the White House, probably uses better grammar than the star of the party.

So quality, I take it, is what we say it is. And I thought one of the shibboleths we abandoned long ago was that we are interested in studying only those things that we are dedicated to, that *we* think beautiful and worthy and elite. I thought we decided that civilization and culture are too important to leave in the hands of the esthetes and "quality" people, those interested in and capable of judging what quality is, which generally means things a particular individual is interested in. I thought we decided that since all aspects of culture are grist to the mill of academic examination, it was our function to examine these elements in all their aspects, dynamics, roles, impact—even their esthetic accomplishments, yes, but only incidentally. In other words, we were trying to put our individual sense of enjoyment aside for the voodoo of the privileged and powerful.

I had understood that since we were setting foot on *terra incognita* we would develop our tools of exploration, what could be termed our methodologies, as we went along, shaping them from the land we were exploring. We would not bring old, possibly outmoded methodologies, even old and possibly outmoded notions of the value of methodologies, into this new land. We would create new machines for our new gardens.

Alas and lack a day. How soon go astray the best laid plans of mice and academics. Somebody is trying to inoculate the PCA with the serum of middle-age timidity or senility while we are in the prime of life. Somebody is trying to tell us that we have swashed through Kentucky in our buckskins long enough, and we should graduate to better quality clothes—decency, society and peer pressure demand it! All along I had thought that *we* would set the standards, not have them imposed upon us. The standards I thought *we* were setting are sometimes derogated by some people as "mere description" or "mere entertainment." I could use dozens of examples, both voiced to me in private and public and printed in various places. I shall use, however, only one, by a friend who when he wrote the words was Assistant Secretary of Education, a sometimes participant in PCA, which he articulated in a talk given to the Popular Culture Association of Japan.

This scholar's concern was with what he called "the rudderless drift that much of the work that American popular culture scholarship has evidenced" lately, scholarship which he says is essentially "descriptive cataloging." "We clearly have documented rather completely the minutiae of our era—from carnivals to gangster films. Al Jolson records to baseball trading cards. A social anthropologist from the future would surely find a treasure trove of trivia about our daily lives." Although the critic may think there is, there is nothing really negative about these observations. Many of us have felt through the years that before we could really manage the world around us we had to recognize and describe it. The question would not be how beautiful it was or how pleasingly we could describe it, in terms of elite and vernacular culture, but how accurately, how realistically. Viewing the terrain, many of us felt, was necessary before accurate maps could be drawn. Everything in due order.

But there may be a disservice in the mis-information and mis-conclusions included in the above quote. It simply mis-states the activities of the PCA. Ninety-seven percent of our activities are devoted to more than "the minutiae" of our world. We should not allow poetic language, cliche, prejudice or embarrassment to induce us to misrepresent the case.

The second fire-breathing dragon in the forest has always been Methodology. Now that dragon has got at least its shoulders in the PCA tent and is pushing hard to muscle in and take over.

The signs of the dragon run the gamut of all known approaches and idiosyncrasies and hobby-horses. People are always looking for the panacea methodology that will open the lock to all secrets and provide the frame on which to hand and air all answers—*not a useful method* but *the methodology.* Structuralists told us a few years ago that structuralism was the true way to study everything, including popular culture. Semioticists tell us that semiotics is the golden key. Linguists assure us that the linguistic approach is sure-fire. Marxists insist that methodologies using any other approach than theirs are headed for the ditches. Sociologists, and others, treasure content analysis. The ASA scholars have counted on the Myth and Symbol school for thirty years. Literature people still use the New Criticism, which was invalidated years ago, and Freudian and Jungian methods, among others. Where are the snows of yesteryear? We continue to use John Cawelti's valid formulas and conventions approach as methodology. We continue to ride on the back of the turtle of methodologies and outstanding scholars long after they have been proved wrong-headed or inadequate, or we teeter on the shoulders of our hero-scholars long after society and academia have bypassed them. Sometimes we rediscover the well-known or reinvent the wheel. Historians are now leaping on their newly invented area, called Public History—which for decades existed as Material Culture. What's in a name? Millions of dollars, that's what. Plus respectability!

What should have been stepping-stones or building blocks become instead mill-stones around our necks which, instead of giving us a clearer vision into the future, bend us backwards toward the past. Sometimes we should never have used the guides. For example, people continue to swear by Herbert Gans' notion of popular culture and high culture without realizing that his book was ten years behind the times the day it was published. Other publications suffer from tunnel vision, especially those by foreign scholars. For example, *Understanding Popular Culture: Europe from the Middle Ages to the 19th Century* (ed. Steven L. Kaplan, Mouton, 1984) is virtually built on one book, Peter Burke's excellent *Popular Culture in Early Modern Europe* (1978), with the authors apparently oblivious to American scholarship, and with one approach, the study of popular culture through language. So, many of the books used as models and "standard texts" are historical monuments but hardly maps of the present and future. I am disturbed, further, by the study of popular culture though the "father" or "master" approach, that is using such people as Aristotle, for example, as the "father" of modern communication studies. Forerunner, perhaps, but father no. We easily take this ancestor worship too far. I have always felt that if communication studies have gotten no further than the theories of Aristotle on rhetoric, then perhaps the whole thing is a corpse that should long since have been interred.

I am inclined to agree with part of what my friend Ronald Kimberling says in the article from which I quoted earlier. His conclusion is that of all methodologies, the rhetorical approach is superior to the others, "that it is a good beginning place, not only because it is the most comprehensive alternative yet put forward, but more importantly because it is *inclusive of*, not *exclusive of*, other approaches. The rhetorical methodology is not really a traditional methodology per se but a *heuristic*, a generative model which enables us to raise relevant questions on the topic of popular culture."

If the methodologists are fighting, as they always have, over which is the proper methodology for the study of a particular area, should we not recognize that there is *no* proper methodology and so use them or not use them all as we see fit? If the rhetorical methodology is the best precisely because it includes all the others, then is not a better one yet that which says the best methodology is no one methodology but all of them? Interdisciplinary studies demand inter-methodological or supra-methodological approaches. Isn't the question of methodology essentially similar to the question of transportation? Which car or airplane shall we take as transportation? But we must keep our perspective. If the mode of transportation becomes more important than the object of our travel, then are we not in serious trouble?

Students of popular culture ought to continue to realize, as I think we have through the years, that our study of popular culture is general not private, cultural not academic, far above the rather earth-bound and mean question of quality and standards and methodology. We have other and larger fish to fry than the questions of whether something is, in the Puritanical words of most critics, "good" or "bad." Good or bad, we should realize that it *is*. It is—*therefore it is important*. Not *cogito-ergo sum*, which is too egotistical an attitude for us, but *it is*, therefore it is worthy of study.

The PCA is not the center of the universe—but scholars in the PCA are trying to understand the universe. Therefore it is imperative, I think, that we continue to defy those people who, for right reasons or wrong, insist that we must search for the golden needle of the right methodology. We need to stand on the shoulders of all the hero-scholars who have thought on the subject of approaches and ways and means to shed light on the vernacular culture. We need to keep an active and open mind, and nimble feet. We need to keep our minds and our feet moving. If we stand too long in the wet cement of debatable and outworn methodologies, we will find our feet (as well as our minds) are stuck fast because the cement has hardened, and we are transfixed in one mind-set and method of approaching truth. Such immovability as that will be detrimental to our minds as well as to the subject itself.

The solution is fluency and mobility—fluency in all the various aspects of the humanities and mobility in moving about among them.

Chapter Twelve

The Expanding World of Literacy

In our exceedingly complex world, we strive to facilitate communication by holding on to our storehouse of knowledge derived from the past. This link to the past provides our stability and thus our ability to cope with the new aspects of life with which we are confronted. As the editors of the *Literary History of the United States* assert: "Each generation must define the past in its own terms," as well as the present. Thus the language of past definitions changes as the need arises.

Language is in a constant state of flux, as is life. As the state of flux changes media, so too change the areas of needed literacy. True, the written word as it is used in various media of communication, in the past and the present, is the basis of communication. For most of us the printed word comprises the set of signs and symbols that constitute the stable form and the known and accepted language of a certain set of people. If that certain set of people communicate through the written word, the literacy of that group equals the ability to read and write that language.

But most societies throughout history have relied primarily on the spoken, rather than the written, word for communication. In preliterate societies non-verbal forms of communication consisted of signs and symbols. Among the subgroups made up of the blind and the deaf in contemporary society, literacy means the ability to communicate in more than braille and heard language. Thus, imposing conventional *literacy* as the ability to read and write fails to recognize the principles of cultural relativism and the conditions under which communication takes a variety of forms.

At the present time all specialized groups and professions have their literature and their forms of literacy. For example, sociology has its literature consisting of materials written for and read by sociologists. Historians have their literature, as do anthropologists, medical doctors, astronomers, geologists, fishermen, carpenters, carny, circus and museum people, primitive sailors, etc. These literatures have vocabularies that are known and understood only by specialized and selective groups.

155

The term "literate" reaches out in a thousand ways. Nobel-Prize winner physicist Leon Lederman, at Chicago's Kersten Physics Teaching Center, is trying to have non-scientists become "literate in protons and quarks." "There's the issue of science literacy, which involves the challenge of educating a work force in an industrial society. It requires a higher level of mathematics and science understanding than ever before. We live in a democracy, and we want citizens informed so they can vote on issues that have scientific and technological aspects—global warming and the environment, defense spending, the space station—and increasingly people aren't prepared to discuss these issues. There's a societal dichotomy in which we want to preserve democracy but the language is Sanskrit to some people." On a more immediate level, Anthony D. Cortese, dean of a newly established Environmental Literacy Institute at Tufts University, which he wants to teach environmental literacy. "The notion of environmental literacy is to give all students a broad, continuing and repetitive exposure to environmental issues throughout the curriculum," he said. He adds: "In a way, what I'm about is changing the three R's of reading, 'riting and 'rithmetic to also mean reduce, reuse, recycle." They might just as well mean reexamine, relax and rehabilitate, making cognitive the R & R so ritualized in Army life. Specialized vocabularies facilitate communication and understanding within subgroups but do not comprise a form of knowledge shared by the general population, as Emile Durkheim noted years ago, the primary source of unity in modern society is not shared knowledge but specialized knowledge growing out of the division of labor. We become dependent upon each other because of this specialization. Communication becomes essential not because of common or shared knowledge but because of the need for aligning our own behavior.

Anthropologists recognize more and more the near-universality of language as manifested in the various activities of humankind. "Objects certainly 'speak', that is they directly communicate a message through visible and tangible qualities such as form, color, texture, size, and so forth," says Victor Turner, a leading anthropologist. In Pueblo Indian lore, says Barbara A. Babcock, every piece of clay "sings." And folklorist-anthropologist Roger Abrahams insists that there is a "language of festivals" just as there is a "language of arts." "The vocabulary of festival," he says, "is the language of extreme experiences through contrasts— contrasts between everyday life and those high times, between the different parts of the occasion" (Turner 162).

The language of all aspects of human experience and environment are all around us. Cultural historian Gunther Barth develops the thesis that there has always been a tension between the American people and the nature on which they thrived and depended. In a new environment, he suggests, people can exploit the passive environment, just as a dominant strong people can exploit the weak (minorities, slaves, children and women). During that time of exploitation there is no need for communication. The strong speak *to* but do not listen to the passive. They speak *at* their weaker members, not to communicate but to deliver orders.

Such behavior in America has been the economic capitalistic voice of the Bible, which taught its people to go forth and multiply and conquer the earth. This was the voice of Genesis 1:28-29: "Be fruitful, multiply, fill the earth and conquer it. Be masters of the fish of the sea, the birds of heaven and all living animals on earth," and of Genesis 2:15-16: God settled man in Eden "to cultivate and take care of it."

But the Bible also speaks out of the other side of its power in a gentler voice. Matthew 10:31 associates people with the other animals God has created. "Fear ye not therefore, ye are of more value than many sparrows." One fine Protestant hymn takes up this non-animal association and sings of God's care of mankind. "I sing because I'm happy/I sing because I'm free/For his eye is on the sparrow, and I know He watches me," (Civilla D. Martin and Charles H. Gabriel), which teaches respect for the earth.

When the opposition to the powerful becomes strong enough to insist on being heard or nearly exhausted and, therefore, must be cared for as the earth is today, then there must be communication with the opposition. In this situation the earth must be allowed to speak. Not to develop this communication with the earth—not to be literate in the language spoken by the physical surroundings—is to invite and encourage disaster. As Barth suggests: "With the ongoing destruction of irreplaceable natural resources, an assessment of the relationship between nature and culture ultimately involves the issue of life itself" (XVIII)—i.e. literacy in the communication skills between man and earth.

Naturalist Gerald Durrell, head of the survival zoo on Jersey Island in the English Channel, speaks to another kind of survival and language: "A zoo is as important as a library," in offering sources of information vital to mankind's survival, he says. He might have been more inclusive, for a zoo is the life from which libraries are made. A zoo therefore contains more languages than a library—and demands fluency in all of them if mankind is going to be successful in communicating with the forces that constitute life on this planet.

These languages that we must read swirl all around us, throughout culture. We read cards, signs, charts, actions, the heavens, attitudes, "body language" and movies. Sports figures "read" the formations of their opponents and adjust to them. Eskimos read snow, detectives read clues, ecologists read trends in nature, political figures and pollsters "read" their "grass-root" sentiments, environmentalists read long-range trends and meteorologists read air currents. Belatedly we are trying to learn the languages of other animals, which we finally recognize constitute an important medium of communication. When sounds or silences of animals are recorded and raised from low frequency or reduced from high frequency to our middle-range frequency, the world of animals becomes babbling cacophonies of communication. Elephants apparently talk to one another all the time on a low frequency not audible to human beings. The sea is filled with talkative dolphins and whales; even the most lowly crabs talk to themselves and others of their kind. And in the world of artifacts, each is assumed to have its own language. For example, a very fine documentary recently broadcast in 1991 on television's The Discovery Channel was named "The Language of Antlers."

The outreach is becoming more and more natural. The 1990 presentation of the *High & Low: Modern Art and Popular Culture* exhibition at the Museum of Modern Art demonstrates well this blurring of the lines between "Languages." In the news release—to which apparently none of the thousands of elite critics would protest despite their objections to the art presentations—there are several unconventional uses of the term language. Graffiti, for example, is called "untutored public 'writing'," and "crude language of anonymous street vandals." "Caricature, like graffiti, is a language," says the author. "Language of comedy can become language of tragedy," says another reference to the many tongues of language.

Ronald Barthes properly observed that "myth is depoliticized speech" (*Mythologies*, 1972). Historian Daniel Boorstin wrote in the Introduction to the autobiography of Western historian-novelist Louis L'Amour: "Louis was a good listener, as eager to learn from the speaker as from the printed word." Nineteenth-century essayist-philosopher Thomas Carlyle felt that "Music is well said to be the speech of angels."

On a larger scale, Don Handelman observed the language of the ways of life of a people and their ability to communicate, and he summarized: "The further one penetrates the ways of life of a people, the more the likelihood of achieving a worthy, if approximate, translation of these into the language of anthropology." On a particular type of human behavior he said: "Public events are locations of communication that convey participants into versions of social order in relatively coherent ways. As the flow of living often is not, public events are put together to communicate comparatively well-honed messages" (14-15). These meanings, he might have added, when strung together constitute a language. Paleontologists insist that fossils tell narratives which must be read from beginning to end.

Belatedly we are trying to learn the languages of other animals, which we finally recognize constitute larger vocabularies and languages. We all read nature in more or fewer of its manifestations. Phenomena and artifacts both great and small speak volumes. For example, a marine sand dollar is a small language, and the ocean is a whole library of languages. One layer of mud to an archeologist is one small language; the Grand Canyon is a Babel of languages a mile high turned upside down which speaks a thousand languages of millions of years duration. These languages constitute substitutes to the printed word. In fact they are printed languages, just not in the conventional form. If each artifact is a microcosm, as Gowans maintains, then each series of artifacts constitutes a language in which one could become literate and thus draw on as a form of communication. Unfortunately, we often terminate education almost before it has begun.

Too often, looking upon education as something we "get," not unlike a physical entity, instead of a life-long process, we are hidebound by that education and training and refuse to learn anything new that is outside the confines and directions of our training.

Regrettably this is discouragingly true of people in the humanities and social sciences. For example, Richard Rudisill, Curator of Photographic History of the Museum of New Mexico, correctly points out that "far too many historians regard pictures, especially photographs, only as a means to decorate an otherwise totally verbal" statement (1). Alan Trachtenberg, a leading interpreter of photographs as documents, along the same line observed that photos are in fact "words" resembling entries in a dictionary or facts in an encyclopedia, and when used together become literature and books. Individual photos strung together become sentences just as words grow into paragraphs. As Trachtenberg noted, "To recognize that an image is a kind of writing prepares us for the larger challenge of reading or making sense of a group of photos." "A film is a kind of book, a kind of language, a kind of speech act...an expressive cultural act," says Lawrence W. Levine, folklorist and noted historian (52).

The implications of these recognitions of the language of photos and films are immense and far-reaching and need amplification. The truism that a picture is worth a thousand words is valid only if the viewer understands the language of the picture. People who are not literate in the language see the picture as a sign or symbol. To see beyond the symbol, the viewer must be literate in the language of the picture. The viewer must realize that, as what Rudisill calls "a sample," the picture is three-dimensional, the third dimension being the dynamic of what is pictured. In order to comprehend the full language, the viewer must understand the mechanics of photography: use of light, shadow, angle, type of camera, period of exposure, cropping, double exposure, etc. In addition the viewer must comprehend the "social mechanics:" the artifacts present, the social attitudes, the moods, the feelings, the atmosphere, the history, the geography, the emotions, the human actions and the reactions. The demands of the language of photography are almost mind-boggling. In fact the major reason most of us are photographically illiterate is the demands of the medium. To have fluency in photography, one must be expert in everything that can be included in a photograph. The same demands for photography are present in the various other languages we can be fluent in. Movies demand this fluency plus the infinitely more complex fluency in pictured narrative.

James Deetz has observed many other kinds of books, often ignored or despised, in which we need to be literate. He notes: "In ways great and small, gravestones, grape pits, houses, refuse, cuts of meat, recipes, ceramics, furniture, and cutlery inform us that a great change was worked between 1760 and 1800 on the world view of most Anglo-Americans." In a similar vein, Robert Blair St. George observed that "houses, furniture, teacups, probate inventories, diaries, account books, newspapers, and tax lists may all warrant investigation in the course of a single topic." In other words, these media demand and reward literacy.

Both might have been more inclusive. All artifacts and static evidences of culture are words in various languages. The life that these artifacts have or once had are the language that articulates them. The artifacts are the words, the arrangements in society are the grammar and the impact is the language. So all evidences of the existence of mankind—archeology, history, contemporary artifacts—are vast congeries of world languages. All such evidences world-wide have much in common in words and actions but many differences in the grammar and interpretations. "Ground floors, upper chambers and garrets are fragments of a playful language that gives shape to complex ideas," observed St. George. French historian Braudel felt that "Costume is a language." Indeed everything is a language, or part of a language. "Everything," says Braudel, "is connected." To understand the connections, one must learn all the languages.

From the preceding concept it is only a short step from seeing the conventional book on a subject to regarding the subject itself as a book. For example, it is only a short step from a book on architecture to regarding the architecture itself as a book; from a book about a building to seeing the building as a book. Jules David Prown acutely observed that from his analysis of material culture, "Objects are signs that convey meaning, a mode of communication, a form of language." From a study of buildings as records of evidence, Phyllis Lambert notes that, "The buildings which a society constructs convey information at a symbolic level." Individually and collectively, Lambert goes on to say, "they are formal expressions of its needs, values, and aspirations." Such analyses suggest the logic of moving from a book about a shopping mall to taking the mall itself as a form of communication; from books about automobiles to automobiles themselves as means of communication. Thousands of

The Expanding World of Literacy   161

other material objects convey messages that must be understood if one is to be literate in modern culture.

On its simplest level, literacy necessarily must begin shortly after birth. Infants early on become literate in the language of their cries, and adults must be literate in being able to read and interpret those cries. When 19th-century poet Alfred Lord Tennyson lamented about being "an infant crying in the night" and with "no language but a cry," he was echoing the observation of such ancients as Pliny the Elder and the author of the Wisdom of Solomon and many more modern observers who have recognized the need for literacy in the primordial forms of languages.

Fluency in the many media of visual and oral communication was the functional equivalent of literacy in the days before the written and printed word. The context within which men and women live has always been filled with many languages, and individuals must become "literate" in those languages or perish. If citizens of our generation know less about what they need to understand in order to function effectively in society, it is not primarily because of a failure of the educational system, but because of the dramatic increase in the complexity of the world in which they live and society's unwillingness to let go of the old and grasp the present and reach for the future. With historical increases in the scope and intensity of information in the 20th century, the knowledge of any given individual represents a declining proportion of the totality of that which is available to be known. "Be not the first by whom the new are tried/Nor yet the last to lay the old aside," cautioned conservative 18th-century poet Alexander Pope. The middle ground promises at least some movement forward.

In February 1990 the Presidential Commission on Education stated as the goal of the United States that by the year 2000 everybody in the U.S. will be literate. Apparently, the commission was meaning literacy in the conventional sense of the word and in the conventional print medium. Many questions arise over the stated goal. In the first place, it surely is a politically motivated and completely unrealistic goal—in many ways one of the abuses of conventional literacy, when the words are there but the meaning entirely absent. It surely is a politically motivated effort to placate people who are genuinely concerned about the state of literacy in American society today. As a national priority, however, it is sufficiently weak and vague to allow it to die out in the corridors of time and be completely forgotten. The goal will be recognized as unattainable, and by the year 2000 this goal will have been forgotten or replaced by dozens of others, all of which are equally unattainable in the conventional medium.

Whether the goal is desirable is another question of perhaps even greater importance. The question is, literate in what medium? Is society determined to be literate only in the printed word, and is that goal proper? If so, is that goal an effort to make people proficient in a medium that by the year 2000, or soon thereafter, will have lost much of the power it currently commands? That is, is the goal of the President's Commission to make people proficient in a medium that is no longer the leading medium in society? For example, do the recommendations resemble suggesting that people be made proficient in the typewriter when it has been replaced by the computer; in the conventional book, when it has been replaced by electronic media of infinitely more power? Is society going to be taught to use the conventional library when the conventional library has already become an historical anachronism? In other words, is conventional literacy being held in the steel vice of vested interests and unimaginative bureaucrats and being foisted off as fundamental and imperative when in fact a new currency has been introduced into the commerce of life and new coins of literacy are daily being used throughout the literate world? Reality poses a new question. Why concentrate all energy and emphasis on print literacy when other media of communication are working effectively?

It seems clear that as American society becomes more democratic, and every person therefore a more powerful entity unto himself or herself, there must be some way to make literacy more appealing, more indispensable, than it apparently is at the present. We are bolstered in our present-day drive to make everybody print literate by the memory of an earlier time in which a large percentage of Americans were print literate. In reality, America is now and has always been a literate nation. In colonial America foreign travelers were amazed to discover how many books were made available through a multitude of bookstores. In Ben Franklin's Boston, for example, there were fifty bookstores providing reading material for a people thirsting for information and knowledge. Every ship was met wharfside by booksellers to discover what books were available for them to supply to an avidly reading public. It is assumed that nearly every Puritan in the early Bay settlements could read and write. In those days, as Russel B. Nye pointed out, it was imperative for anyone interested in saving his soul, getting ahead in the world, or just getting along to be literate in the printed word.

People were taught literacy generally through methods that emphasized specific facts and rote memorization. Everybody wanted to become literate and was willing to undergo any method in order to achieve that goal. Today reliance on the old methods has not prevailed simply because the alternatives to print literacy have proved more appealing.

Print literacy today, however, is not nearly the fading art it is feared to be. In the United States yearly some 50,000 books are published, with the total number of copies printed rising to 2 billion. With multiple readings of these 2 billion books, we must conclude that some 4 billion are read annually. True, these books are read by a minority of the total population, but at least potentially not as small a minority as many critics of our educational system try to maintain. The real and potential size of the reading public should be recognized and enlarged, and this can be done by our redefining what the reading public is literate and illiterate in and by being realistic and non-elitist about what constitutes literacy.

As long as custodians and definers of literacy are people like E.D. Hirsch, Allan Bloom and to a certain extent Lynne Cheney, Chairman of the National Endowment of the Humanities, and their many followers, literacy is going to be mis-defined, is going to be described as a distant mountain reachable by only a select few, and as a result will not be desired by many who would be eager to climb the mountain from illiteracy to literacy if they realized the gradual ascent and the level from which they start the climb. Hirsch, Bloom, Cheney, et al, no matter how much they mouth the lures of learning, misunderstood the primary rule of motivation. "Learning is not a game," Cheney writes in her *50 Hours: A Core Curriculum for College Students* (1989), "but an undertaking that compels mind and heart." She seeks to accomplish her goals at the end of a whip, a cat-of-one-tail, rather than through an exciting adventure. In fact learning should be a game. It is with children and could more profitably be with adults. We know that learning on all age levels does not "compel" anything and that learning is most easily accomplished when it is a game; in fact, the greatest learners and thinkers are those who see learning as "fun." Cheney does no good service to the desired goal of learning when she insists that there is simply not enough room for all people in her little yacht of learning. As a result, as many readers have seen, her suggestions, in the words of one observer, "do not represent an improvement in the environment for essential learning in university-based liberal arts colleges" (James W. Reed, Dean of Rutgers College). Or, he might have added, anywhere else. Cheney tries to foist off as desirable learning fluency in materials she considers canonical and therefore sacred.

The blindest offender in such misguided efforts is everybody's whipping boy, Allan Bloom. He must live on honey-dew and lotus, he is so little a citizen of this world. He is a two-book man. His attitude towards the role of books in our world is so silly that is deserves quoting at length just for grim laughs:

Men may live more truly and fully in reading Plato and Shakespeare than at any other time, because then they are participating in essential being and are forgetting their accidental lives. The fact that this kind of humanity exists or existed, and that we can somehow still touch it with the tips of our outstretched fingers, makes our imperfect humanity, which we can no longer bear, tolerable. The books in their objective beauty are still there, and we must help protect and cultivate the delicate tendrils reaching out toward them through the unfriendly soil of student's souls. Human nature, it seems, remains the same in our very altered circumstances because we still face the same problems, if in different guises, and have the distinctively human need to solve them, even though our awareness and forces have become enfeebled. (*Closing*, 38)

It is frightening indeed to realize that such thinking directs the teaching—though on a restricted scale, thank goodness—of our future citizens. It is a sad commentary when those people who declare themselves our teachers have not been able to free themselves of the myths they accepted in graduate school as truths, and therefore remain myth-bound, looking backwards instead of around themselves or into the future. Too many in the American educational system unfortunately still revere particular authors and books—such as Matthew Arnold and *The Republic*—as icons instead of the system of thinking that those books and authors should have developed in them. Education should be *thinking*, not remembering, stretching above our training, not squatting on it. Education should be a launching pad, not quicksand to hold us earthbound. Literacy is not the mere fingering of books like beads on a prayer chain. Literacy demands and promotes action. Of the two kinds of literacy—passive and active—the latter is infinitely superior. Still, we tend to be afraid of active literacy and to cling to the passive variety. Memory clings eternal to the human breast.

One is reminded of the months after publication of Bloom's book when presidents of universities and colleges had themselves photographed in their offices with a copy of the book conspicuous behind them. Such use of the icon was an obvious substitute for competence. Had they read and understood the book they would not have had it signalling their set of values and plans for the future unless they were presiding over Old Times University and dedicated to closing the American mind. Possible donors and benefactors must have given—or should have given—second thoughts before committing their good money to such educators so blindly clinging to the past. With such intellectual sterility guiding American education, how can the country possibly succeed in trying to make every citizen literate by the year 2000? Or even survive? In such attitudes American educators demonstrate their shortcomings.

For example, for years in the speech department of a university I was at, a professor taught Aristotle's *Rhetoric* as his only text in a course on rhetoric—not classical rhetoric, but rhetoric. When I suggested that either somebody had in the past two thousand years said something useful about rhetoric or it was a dead subject, he protested, saying that after Aristotle nobody had ever had anything to say to equal the early study. Could there possibly be a sillier denial of reality than this attitude?

Bloom's account in *The Closing of the American Mind* of the awe inspired in his soul the first time he walked onto the campus of the University of Chicago and experienced the impressive old buildings there parallels the experience of many naive idealistic young minds when they first step into the presence of facilities that bespeak the locale of intellectual activity. Of course, the buildings are impressive and represent tradition, just as they are intended to be by the designers and the faculty. Academics, like everybody else, realize that impressive packaging helps sell products.

Physical surroundings are meant to be "read" as messages, and they apparently are. The Parthenon, the entire Acropolis, the buildings of classical Rome were intended to be "read" by the populace, and they undoubtedly were, but probably not nearly with as much awe as the people who were in the business of peddling them hoped. In our time, the massive structures of the federal buildings in Washington, the monuments in our Nation's Capital and throughout the world, the giant buildings in our cities—all create physical worlds which impact on the culture and psychology of the people who experience them. All call forth reactions and behavior. But not so impressively as they once did or as they were intended to do. It is the suggestible and naive mind, like Allan Bloom's, that does not recognize the physical surroundings for precisely what they are, that is, physical and psychological packaging. Bloom is one of those people so unaware of the world that he never accepts its impact upon him. He remains virginal in mind though a thousand times ravished.

Impressing the naive is good business. The air is filled with examples. Of course Harvard University likes to perpetuate the myth that it is the country's greatest university. It may or may not be. But it is in the interest of the alumni, the university, the faculty, the current students and the power elite in the government in Washington to keep the myth alive. In myth—and the ignorance in which myth thrives—there is power and control.

In education—in the understanding of the ploys of power—on the contrary, there is supposed to be freedom, the power to think, the ability to progress and the development of education. Education is requisite to freedom. Jefferson stated the need 150 years ago: "If a nation expects to be ignorant and free, in a state of civilization, it expects what never was and never will be." Countless perceptive people have echoed this need. But freedom, progress and education do not flow from the worship of buildings or libraries, or, for that matter, professors as icons. People in charge of directing and paying for education simply must—sooner or later—realize that *The Republic,* Matthew Arnold and other icons may be useful stepping stones and milestones but in our world cannot be destinations. To say that does not denigrate in any way the value and pleasure of reading such authors and books and the value they may have had in the past. But the past is the past. We cannot return to it, nor would we want to. Those people who cannot leave it are living in a fantasy world that seems doomed to be filled with frustration and disappointment. They are moving down the fast lane of contemporary society backwards. Little wonder that they are constantly jolted and surprised.

The fact that Harvard's library contains eleven million books, and manuscripts actually touched by the hands of Cotton Mather and his illustrious contemporaries does not make it a temple where reverent scholars must be intimidated by the weight of the past. On the contrary, the library presents an opportunity for people to develop so that they can, as a result of their thinking, add to the treasures held therein. Other treasures inculcate the proper attitude. The Library of Congress is the greatest collection of books in the world. Though, like all bureaucrats and people in power, the librarians there occasionally try to intimidate the users, generally, at least while Daniel Boorstin was Librarian of Congress, the clerks recognized their role and tried to assist the users. Their function is to make the materials available, not to protect them from the public.

Years ago when I was a constant user of the Library of Congress Rare Book Room, I was impressed with the way rare books were made available. But not without protests. One day a user from a large college library asked the Rare Book Director how he managed to keep his books from being used by the public. The Director responded that he did not mean to keep the books from being used. He wanted to make them available. He was absolutely correct. Books by definition are things to be read, not touched and revered, like the Ark of the Covenant. They must be read to be effective.

These two opposing attitudes reflect essentially the two ways of looking at literacy. Members of the literacy club really think the advantages they enjoy should not be made available to everyone. The people on the other side insist that freedom to achieve membership in the club comes with the U.S. Constitution, and that people should be assisted in achieving the necessary skills. They should not be openly or covertly, deliberately or unwittingly, deterred. The prejudices against universal literacy are sometimes subtle, though real. They are not, however, tolerable in a world which demands literacy and fluency in communication of one form or another, and therefore must be recognized for what they are and broken down.

Democracy demands and thrives on literacy in democratic materials. To try to force democratic people into literacy through the needle-eye of elitism is to deaden incentive and therefore to exclude many potentially literate people from their desired goal. A major part of the reading material in a democracy is non-elite and conventional. It is such things as comic books, best-selling books, baseball cards, the simplest forms of printed materials, television, movies, sports, all the forms of society which carry messages. All forms demand literacy as the key to participation. And we, if we would build on the obvious, could use these primary forms of print literacy as beginnings for development into more conventional forms of print literacy. The mere accumulation of facts, again, might be useful and even desirable. But facts alone are a sad evidence of the real dynamics of literacy. Hirsch's 5000 facts are merely the lumber with which thinking builds. The thinking, enquiring mind can construct with its great techniques though it has only a few references, whereas the full complement of canonical references has little room for new ones and often has no realization or the need for more. When your cupboard is full, who needs new stocks? Nobody but the person who thinks!

In our search for effective means of developing literacy, we may be instructed by the selective aspects of American culture that are used by other, "non-elite," cultures such as China, eastern Germany, Mexico and Central and South America. These nations have long recognized intrinsic interest as the simplest doorway to literacy and have exploited the vernacular to the fullest. In these countries basic and simple forms of literacy are being utilized to develop both linguistic literacy and knowledge about the United States as a nation. For example, the People's Republic of China has for years translated American best-sellers, such as Horatio Alger, Alex Haley, Irving Wallace and Louis L'Amour, into best-sellers in China.

The purpose has been twofold: to increase the reader's fluency in English and to develop the reader's knowledge of American culture. The same methods and materials are used extensively in the other countries mentioned, as well as many others. No medium is too popular to be utilized. The American culture sought is not that of Thomas Jefferson or the Constitution, but that of Lincoln's democratic Americans in their everyday lives. The force that brought down the Berlin Wall and led to the dissolution of the U.S.S.R. was not the call for the concept of "Liberty," but that for everyday "freedom," the power of McDonald's hamburgers, television's *Dallas* and Rock 'n' roll. The citizens voted with their growling bellies and the realization that they cold demand and get better. For Americans who are seeking to increase literacy inside this country not to observe profit from the power of popular media utilized for similar drives in countries outside America is to act blindly and to waste golden opportunities. In not utilizing popular media as stepping stones to literacy, educators exclude and exile many potentially literate persons to the slums of non-acceptability and thereby do literacy and democracy a great disservice.

The power of McDonald's restaurant might be difficult to demonstrate immediately, but its long-range effect is beyond doubt. People have always relied on catching a bite to eat on the run—out of convenience or necessity. Packets of jerky in the pouches of pioneers or chocolate bars and soft drinks for the instant revitalization of athletes come to mind immediately. But McDonald's ultra fast food has made a major contribution to democratizing American culture and is having its impact on that of the world. Cadillacs and jalopies pass by the same drive-thru window, the occupants eating the same kind of food and drinking the same drinks. The effect of this common food overseas, though often resisted by the elite, is the same: the universalizing of eating habits and bringing together the elite and the commoner over the need or desire to get good, sanitary food in a hurry at an economical price.

Introduction of the world's largest McDonald's into Moscow where it serves thousands of sandwiches hourly initiated a trend with many implications that cannot be denied or reversed. The world behind the Iron Curtain was changed irreversibly by the lowly hamburger. So too is that behind the Bamboo Curtain going to be changed by introduction of Pizza Hut into Beijing in the summer of 1990. As an army travels on its stomach, often the way to literacy can be through the stomach culture.

The power of rock music has been evident from the first when Elvis Presley first appeared on the Ed Sullivan Show and was filmed only from the waist up. It was clear that the forces he had discovered and was releasing would have traumatic effects. These forces have been and continue to be resisted—but all to no avail. In the relatively free society of the U.S. the results of rock music were strong. In the tighter and more authoritarian societies around the world, the results have been no less than shattering and revolutionary, releasing individual and mass forces that completely change mindsets and ways of life. Sometimes the results have been delayed, but underground they smoldered. Behind the Iron Curtain, for example, rock music came over airwaves that though jammed could not be silenced. All kinds of musical and cultural responses grew up. In Leningrad, for example, in 1983 there were an estimated 4000 rock groups playing furtively and underground, yet blowing on a long banked fire that would eventually blaze into an international conflagration. In 1990 there were an estimated 250,000 rock bands playing in the Soviet Union. As the music of people marching around the walls of Jericho finally brought it down, undoubtedly rock 'n' roll had a great influence on the disintegration of the Soviet Empire.

Television has had an equally profound if not profounder effect on the equalization of society, and eventually of nations. TV is the right medium at the right time. It has the correct mixture of animated pictures and sound. It is, in other words, very much like audio comics. It can be instantly available and responsive. As nearly all people have predicted since the earliest days, TV was born to change the nature of communication and society. It is instant movies home-delivered and seemingly free.

All television, especially American news, entertainment, commercials, sports and documentaries, has had and continues to have a profound effect on the world's societies. But perhaps none has had so dramatic effect as the TV weekly serial *Dallas*, the saga of the life and disasters of the Ewing family living in their baronial splendor outside Dallas, Texas, and doomed in acting out the apparent American success story to be beset by unhappiness, frustration and failure.

The success of *Dallas* was worldwide. Over ninety countries aired it weekly and continue to run it. The lure of the story was so great that streets around the world emptied, businesses adjusted to it, farm workers halted, classes were scheduled around it so that nearly everybody around the world would journey to Dallas for an hour a week to suffer with the Ewings. *Dallas* was the *lingua franca* and the secular mecca. Following the season's final cliffhanger when J.R. Ewing was shot and viewers had to wait throughout the summer until the series began again in the fall to see who shot J.R., Americans throughout the world were asked constantly by a worried international public, "Who shot J.R.?" It was perhaps the most worrisome mystery of the summer. The final episode in 1991, when the empire collapsed, drew TV's largest audience ever.

But the accomplishment of *Dallas* and the magic of television was that viewers did not have to move to Dallas nor did Dallas have to come to them. The television show was far more than mere entertainment. It was a metaphor for man's self-fulfillment, the land of heart's desire. It delved into and worked in mankind's deepest mythologies, themes and formulas of life's potentials. And it tapped those potentials on the most stimulating of all points—the frontiers of geography, mind and opportunity. *Dallas*, as Liebes and Katz point out is a "primordial tale" (141), paralleling the Biblical Genesis. But in fact *Dallas* may touch on an instinct older than Genesis, one that was responsible for the creation of Genesis—mankind's ambition to stretch in understanding and capabilities, to break through the apparent static limitations and thus to see beyond the Western horizon of mankind's possibilities. *Dallas* is a frontier story inviting all to journey through the past into the future. As such, no wonder that it exerted such a profound effect on the world population. It spun on the axis of mankind's common core. *Dallas* in several ways was the center of the universe. Understanding it required literacy.

At least one group, the Association for Media Literacy, recognizes the importance of fluency in this medium. Dedicated to increasing awareness of the need for people to learn the language of television, the AML now holds yearly professional meetings, publishes a newsletter and a journal, and insists that literacy must grow to the size of and keep up with the development of technology. Media literacy embraces media ecology and rushes toward complete understanding of the technology and humanities involved.

Educators need to be alert to those kinds of *lingua franca*—the powerful popular forces and movements—and to utilize them in developing universal literacy as the occasions present themselves. To fail to do so is to miss a spaceship that is sailing into the future of literacy.

Many forces in the U.S. are coalescing to create powerful forces for developing literacy. For example, in 1990 there was a sudden and much needed resurgence in the publication of Classic Comics, a business that thrived during the 1940s and 50s but was always discouraged by elitists who condemned the enterprise as vulgar and demeaning to literature and people.

But the opposite was and is true. Classic Comics bring to a wide audience the proved appealing and entertaining stories of old. These are necessarily not all elite—thank goodness—but do include some valuable classics that have proved their lasting values, such as *Moby-Dick*, Shakespeare's works, *Paradise Lost* and numerous others that proved entertaining in the past. The value of this resurgence in the publication of Classic Comics can be immeasurable if properly handled. The point these new publications make vividly clear is that such a medium as the comics should no longer be despised, but instead should be socially and educationally approved and brought up to the status of a major tool in the development of literacy. It makes little sense to profess an interest in promoting literacy and then, because of background or personal bias, to downgrade and insult a medium that has been demonstrated effective.

The effectiveness of the simple picture-text has been proved since the cave art of prehistory. Nations have been helped in their attempted rise from illiteracy through the "cheap" forms of simple publications. Russia was brought to literacy in the 19th century through inexpensive popular literature, and contemporary China, Mexico, South and Central America are utilizing the simplicity of comic books to open the door to literacy.

Japan, which is supposed to be more literate than the United States, makes extensive use of comics. The tradition in Japan dates back at least to the 12th century, when a Buddhist priest named Toba (1053-1140) drew Chojugiga scrolls, "humorous pictures of birds and animals," which were a kind of pre-Walt Disney figures of monkeys, rabbits, frogs and other animals bathing in rivers, wrestling, worshipping and practicing archery. Japanese cartoonist Tezuka Osamu does not think of his figures as comics. "I don't consider them pictures—I think of them as a type of hieroglyphics...In reality I'm not writing a story with a unique type of symbol," the individual Japanese ideogram, he says. The Japanese comics have flourished ever since, among both children, who read them for the same reasons American children read them, and adults, who take the comics with them from childhood to adulthood. Japanese respect for the comics could profitably be copied by Americans if we could ever flush out of our cultural system the Puritanical concept of some things being "better," some "worse" than others.

Americans are disinclined to recognize that most values are relative, not absolute. To American educators, as to Americans in general, there are "proper" ways to develop literacy; and all other ways, no matter how obviously fruitful their results, are considered irrelevant or beside the point. So we continue to despise the comics, despite the fact that comic books and strips are the most widely-read of all literature in the United States and around the world. (Lawlor 22). The comics, in the broadest sense of the word, were the early equivalent of television. "The picture story, which the critics disregard and scholars scarcely notice, had great influence at all times, perhaps even more than written literature," observed Rodolphe Topffer (*Essay on Physiognomy*, 1845).

Four U.S. Government agencies are now experimenting with the effectiveness of the comic book to promote a point of view and behavior. It is ironic that these agencies, rather than the Department of Education or the National Endowment for the Humanities, should turn to the comic book to promote literacy and through it change behavior. In 1990 these agencies teamed with Marvel Comics to produce a 16 page comic book called "High Heat," which tells the story of a high school baseball player who takes drugs offered to him by an alien creature out to prove the weakness of human beings. Captain America counsels the player that "Drugs just destroy the gifts you have." Says William Sessions, FBI Director, about the experiment: "There is no easy answer to the plague of illegal drugs in this country, but there is the opportunity to improve the situation through education." Sessions and the several organizations are obviously using a medium of communication in which most kids are literate to communicate with them and to attempt to make suggestions for their behavior. The whole effort seems to make sense (UPI, July 28, 1990).

One of the more amusing—not to say far-out—comic books is called *The Wasteland* by Martin Rowson. It is a mixture of Raymond Chandler's works and characters (for example, "Chris Marlowe" is there), and the characters who played the movie version of Hammett's *Maltese Falcon*. T.S. Eliot is on the cover and wanders through the pages. The names of the chapters parallel sections of Eliot's poem *The Waste Land*. The text is in English, pidgin German and Latin. There are notes, as in Eliot's work, explaining the text. One note by "the minimalist poet D.H. Eva" is a two line poem:

I knew a man called T.S. Eliot
Who wanted to write "Waist Land" but couldn't spelliot.

This elite spoof demonstrates to what uses the comic book can be put.

It should be kept in mind that non-print media can serve as stimulants and stepping stones to print literacy. English author of crime fiction Ruth Rendell tells how she has always been struck by the excitement created by the dramatization on television or in the movies of one of her novels. The sale of a particular book has jumped considerably as viewers have enjoyed the dramatized version and have wanted to further enjoy the printed version. So the cliché that one doesn't want to read a book because he or she has seen the movie does not hold. The excitement is just as great in reverse: One wants to read a book *because* of having seen the movie. Likewise with other media. Seeing pictures, photographs, furniture, fashions, farm implements, parades and automobiles can create excitement about books which feature them and cause people to want to become print literate so they can read books about the materials. Wide sales of the book *Cooking From Quilt Country* (1988) by Marcia Adams, have resulted from the PBS series "Plain Cooking," aired throughout the country. Other excellent examples are the scores of books written to accompany successful television series on PBS and The Discovery Channel, among others. The close tie among the media is obvious.

Finally realizing the close links among the media, a group of TV companies have established KIDSNET, a clearinghouse for children's television and radio programming which is based in Washington and dedicated to launching a new public service campaign promoting realization of the symbiotic relationship between television (and presumably by extension other media) and books. At first the group will air two 30-second announcements pointing out the ways TV and video are closely allied to reading. At the launching ceremony, First Lady Barbara Bush said: "When a good TV show makes you want to find out more, find it in a book. TV and books together really take you places." This TV and Books Campaign, part of a united, nation-wide effort to provide resources and products to parents and educators and to encourage them to work more closely together, is backed by several TV companies: Arts & Entertainment Network, Capital Cities-ABC Inc., CBS, The Discovery Channel, The Disney Channel, Fox Broadcasters, the Family Channel, NBC, Rainbow Program Enterprises-Bravo, Showtime and USA Network. It is unfortunate that in her introductory remarks Mrs. Bush stressed "a good TV show." One should think that any kind of stimulus from TV to encourage a person to read would be welcome. One would surely hope that the backers of KIDSNET are not going to insist on "good" TV shows and "good" books, whatever those have to do with literacy. Elitism, deliberate or unconscious, stifles instead of promotes literacy today.

Educators are coming more and more to realize the educational potential in television. Various TV networks, ABC, CBS, NBC and Fox announced in August 1990 their plan to begin in April 1991 to devote at least eight hours per week of prime-time programming to educational themes, a plan sponsored by Brandon Tartikoff, chairman of NBC's Entertainment Group. In commenting on the plan, Ann Lynch, president of the National PTA, said to the Network executives: "...I'm here to tell you you're the motors and developers of this nation..." She concluded, "you are more powerful than you will ever know."

In commenting on the power of television, Carol Isenberg, a co-founder of Education First, unconsciously touched on perhaps the greatest and most powerful lobby—that of the tradition of the power of print literacy and resistance to recognizing the value of others—in her observation on the interconnectedness of television and other forms of education and literacy: "Unfortunately, the American public doesn't recognize this illiteracy as a problem that touches them personally. But it does. It doesn't matter if you have children or not. It doesn't matter if you're rich or poor. Our lives are interconnected. The child of the ghetto who is uneducated touches our lives tomorrow. And time is not on our side."

Indeed, she might have broadened her observation to note that uneducated adults have a more immediate and profound effect on our lives and civilization. Their problems and power impact on us now. Armageddon seems just around the corner, not in the next generation.

Another telling verification of the symbiotic relationship among the media is provided by Black Elk, a Lakota Shaman of the Indians who defeated Custer, who in his autobiography commented on how literacy in one language does not prevent understanding in other media languages: "Everything that I see, hear, smell, or taste—I have a little color TV back there that records it [pointing to his head]. That's how I came to know what I know. Everything I saw and everything I heard was recorded [in my head], and I could rewind it and replay that little picture."

Literacy should mean fluency in a medium, the ability to "read" and "write" in a medium, regardless of what the medium is. Consequently we should recognize that there are many media in which we can and should promote literacy. We should recognize literacy in media other than print that are valid alternatives for literacy in print: music, art, photography, television, movies, archeology, mechanics, plumbing, medicine, "rapping," pottery, weaving, cooking and scores of others. So we are looking to achieve fluency in these media—that is, "mediacy" in general for the electronic media. Many of these forms are already recognized as reasonable adjuncts or alternatives to print media. More should be and will be.

Undoubtedly the switchover from print literacy to fluency in other media is going to be resisted by many traditionalists who will hold that print literacy has been sufficient for over two hundred years and seems to be a basic and core medium for the future. Indeed print does seem to promise a stable foundation of basic media for the 21st century. However, in many ways that concept is like a fade-out image on the TV screen. The print medium may be likened to the wheel in transportation. The wheel is basic, is useful in nearly all forms of transportation and may even be integral to all forms of transportation. But there are developments in transportation that do not rely on the fundamental historical concept of the wheel touching the road; the wheel can be fundamental without being integral to present needs to trasnporation. Likewise with print literacy. There are forms of literacy that transcend and supersede traditional ones, and we must be aware of these new forms and take advantage of them or we will be left holding the traditional book when it had been relegated to a niche in the communication archives.

The issues we have so far addressed in our analysis do not relate to the basic definition of literacy as the capacity to read and write. The value of this form of literacy is self-evident and easily documented. On a personal scale, the British crime novelist Ruth Rendell tells a sobering story in *Judgement in Stone* (1978) of an English Country housekeeper who is left notes of instruction every morning as her employers go to work. Unable to read, she follows none of the instructions; and since she does not want to admit her illiteracy, she repeatedly lies about not seeing the notes. Finally, as her employers press her for a more reasonable explanation, unable to stand the ignominy of being illiterate, the housekeeper kills both her employers. Conventional illiteracy and the social shame and exclusiveness it brings are costly, unnecessary and only partially as real as it seems.

It used to be an article of social privilege and tyranny that aristocracies were proficient and joined international communities in several "languages," which included art, music, dance, fine cuisines, privilege, taste and esthetics. Common people, because they had not been trained in the esoterica of these media of communication, could not speak and appreciate these languages. These concepts of literacy were obvious and blatant conspiracies to exclude people from certain areas of life, as obvious as the British aristocracies in India during the nineteenth century. Members of the ruling class were joining themselves into powerful and exclusive cliques on the basis of their communication; they were literate in their excluding languages.

Their circle of exclusivity was broken eventually by the democratic thrusts of too many people becoming literate in too many media of communication. Like the shock of recognition when the emperor in Hans Christian Anderson's fairy tale was reminded that he wore no clothes, the secret was secret no longer. In effect, the myth of magic clothes and magic literacy had been made real and universal. The charade had been shattered by the literacy of everyday experience.

Conventional forms of literacy have always been used as a means of drawing boundaries of separation and exclusion in the social realm. The contemporary emphasis upon certification and credentialism in formal education is a modern counterpart to the masks that once shielded the aristocracy from the rest of the population. The essential component of professionalism was a demonstrated mastery of vocabularies and reading skills that give special privileges to members and set them apart from non-members. The near universality of reading and writing skills as a conventional criterion that accompanied the elaboration of public education in an effort to remain distinct and different has led to the emergence of a new set of criteria more realistic in the age of multiple media for determining who is literate and who is non-literate.

As many people have come to recognize the potential breadth and depth of the term *literacy* today, the conventional narrow meaning has been relaxed and broadened to include various concepts associated with fluency in the various media of communication—verbal, visual, imitational and exampled.

Examples are as numerous as life's experiences. Baseball, for instance, assumes certain artifacts and literacy needed for the game. If one does not have these artifacts and does not utilize them in the means of communication as defined by the rules of the game, one cannot play. A medical doctor assumes certain pieces of equipment necessary for his practice. If one does not have those pieces of equipment and the literacy for their proper use, he or she cannot engage in the practice of medicine. Astronomers assume certain pieces of equipment and rules with which and by which they operate. Without them people stand mute in awe and amazement in the presence of the stars.

In our world of specialization, the multiplicity of languages and forms of expertise have carried us almost to the point of mutual unintelligibility. We cannot assume facility in the use of a common language in view of the difficulties we have in communicating across the various special groups and their specialized languages. The written word, long held to be the one common denominator among the various languages, is clearly failing in trying to remain the one and stable constant. The stable core is constant no longer. The written word is being put under greater stress than it can bear even as we create neologisms to fit expanding technologies and new grammars to accommodate liberties taken in the construction of language. Under this stress, the words, grammatical rules and meanings are being stretched and twisted into unintelligibility and a failure to communicate.

Likewise, the other media are tearing at its flanks and demonstrating that in the present world of instant and varied communication, the printed word is not sufficient in scope, speed or utility to carry on the functions suitable for a complex world. In a culture where the language of mathematics, the language of computer, the signs of mathematics and the bleeps of the electronic world are working around and without conventional language and demanding their own forms of literacy, it becomes increasingly apparent that the conventional fields of literacy are no longer sufficient. Imperatives cry out for solutions.

There are serious questions that need to be raised about the desirability of trying to maintain the print medium as the exclusive or main language of communication. To do so may well involve relying on a past or passing medium, one that because of its very nature is unable to cope with the world's variety of needs for action and understanding. New and future means of communication are questioning the dominance—or demonstrating the lack of dominance—of the printed word. Movies, television, photographs, billboards, pictures, music, fossils, graffiti, body language, sign language, sports and outdoor entertainment, each challenging the exclusive superiority of the print medium, represents a culture that to one degree or another requires its own expertise and literacy. Each opens up its own world.

We in turn must be aware of all these worlds, and if we are to take advantage of all we must not think in too narrow confines; we must not think conventionally after merely broadening the range of the media to fit our own needs. To a certain extent the otherwise commendable group called Media Literacy tends to make that mistake. They are dedicated to promoting literacy in the mass media, which is proper and urgent. But there are media that are just as important to culture, as the electronic media, though not as showy. Rock 'n' roll, for example, is important in society, but so is the cooing of lullabies to babes in arms. Johnny Carson has had an influential TV show for years, but then so have many folk-humorists who have developed and perpetuated the essence of humor in another stratum of culture. If all the world is a stage, then indeed all of it is, from top to bottom, from side to side. And the stage actors speak many languages.

The American literary world has always derived its strength from the vitality of American semi-literate people and traditions—the folk and popular, frontier, so-called Southwest humor, from life and people too large to be contained by their degree of conventional literacy. As Leslie Fiedler and David S. Reynolds, among others, have pointed out, American culture has always been subversive, expansive, challenging the order of things, burly, big at shoulder, not containable in conventional forms and dress and always developing new expressions. Many examples come readily to mind. Perhaps one of the more instructive was Captain Edgar ("Ned") Wakeman, whom Mark Twain met in 1866 and never forgot.

I'd rather travel with that old portly, hearty, jolly, boisterous, good-natured sailor, Capt. Ned Wakeman, than with any other man I ever came across, Twain wrote in his notebook. Twain's enthusiasm for this volcano of a talker, whose flow of glorious irreverence and blasphemy never slackened persisted throughout his later years. Voluminously fluent verbally, Wakeman lacked most of the subtleties of the written medium, as a short example from a letter he wrote to Twain's friend Joseph Twichell reveals: 'last Eve right in the Midst of Enjoying all the pleasure there is or can be, round the Christmas tree that unlike any other Tree I Ever see, Bears Fruit in Every Clime which is the finest and the greatest variety and of Most Excellent Flavour that I ever knew, it is a Golden fruit of a Devoted Mother's Love and Effection towards five of the Most Beautiful children you ever see, and in effect far excels any other tree. There is in the world, as I was enjoying, hugely the happy emotion of the Bigger children as they with difficulty restrained their Joyish feelings, as they Plucked the fruit that God had sent them and turning towards their mother with all the tenderest words of Love and Effection, and with Eyes that was beaming of what my Poor Pensel cannot Portray...(Browne)

The individual in contemporary culture can live a happy, useful life without being expertly literate in the printed word. Yogi Berra and Sam Goldwyn, of baseball and the movies respectively, are two excellent examples of effective communicators who drew upon non-standard forms of literacy. Berra could communicate only with some difficulty in conventional English, but he was a distinguished baseball player and coach. His "It ain't over until it's over" would hardly be classified as clear communication in conventional English. Movie producer Sam Goldwyn gushed a lexicon of malapropisms, among them: "There's a statue of limitations," and "You can include me out." But Berra and Goldwyn towered above their malapropisms and fractured conventional literacy in the printed word and were adroitly superior each in his own medium, as millions of others throughout society are.

If in a democracy one can survive and succeed without print literacy, then many people are going to wonder why they should go to the trouble of becoming print literate. Obviously also many instructors are faced with the question of why expend their energies in trying to excite people to become literate when the rewards seem incommensurate with the effort. In our society when a youngster illiterate in print can make millions of dollars a year playing a sport, why should he bother to become print literate, perhaps only to see his valuable income decrease by the degree to which he is literate!

Educators have so far been unable to convince athletes to remain in school until they are print literate when the rewards within the bounds of illiteracy are so great. The superiority of the combination of poverty and literacy over the cartel of wealth and illiteracy is difficult to prove. Sometimes literacy, like beauty in Emerson's poem "The Rhedora," must be its own excuse for being.

What then are the troubles and the possible means of demonstrating the flaws of illiteracy and their alleviation? The answer might lie simply in the fact that in a free society, driven by free-enterprise and rewards as rich as the market will bear, conventional learning will always suffer from lack of respect. Virtue as its own reward does not buy many mansions or sports cars in America today. And so far the cry of virtue with financial reward has not curtailed the acquisitive drive of many people. So it should be clear that there are two possible routes, one perhaps depressing, the other probably promising.

The most obvious route is to make learning intrinsically rewarding. That drive has not succeeded well. The rewards are too few and immaterial. The other is to make literacy have a demonstrated relevance to the world around us and provide insights into the changes that are occurring, ways to cope with a world that is almost never the same at the end of the week as it was at the beginning.

In this new realization, instead of trying to go back to "basics" in order to teach literacy in a far from basic world, we should turn to the basic technology available to us and capitalize on it. *Sesame Street* has demonstrated for twenty years that conventional and electronic literacy can be taught on television. Channel One on TV is now being offered in schools throughout the United States in an effort to use the medium as a means of encouraging and developing literacy in the written work. Ted Turner is offering an alternative to Channel One in his effort to utilize television to its fullest in the educative procedure. With them television draws people together.

Commercial companies are utilizing television and audio tapes for what they claim are startlingly successful results. One company, for example, calling its programs "Where There's a Will there's an 'A'," has issued video and audio tapes for three age groups, grade-school, high-school and college; and according to their testimonials on TV, have achieved phenomenal results. The company now claims that the tapes have taught literacy to a million people.

Those who are at a disadvantage in modern forms of communication are not those lacking in a knowledge of canonical literature and history. Instead, estrangement from modern society and the culture it manifests is disproportionately found among those who have cut themselves off from modern forms of communication, from watching television news, from reading a daily newspaper, from going to the movies, from watching television and from being knowledgeable about and participating in spectator sports and other forms of outdoor recreation. These are not the elite forms of culture, not the type that the conventional print-literacy advocate feels are indispensable. But they reflect the kinds of cultural involvements that characterize most people in our time and place. If literacy is to be defined realistically, then it must include developing an awareness and appreciation of the activities and daily interests of most people most of the time in contemporary society.

The problem of most people is not the lack of knowledge, but the question of how to manage the scope and intensity of information encountered on a daily basis. Average Americans are exposed to environments in which they are bombarded with 5200 commercials each day, and there is a need to be literate in evaluating and resisting the multiple demands placed upon personal time, resources and energies.

The typical weekly edition of the *New York Times* contains more information than the average individual encountered in a lifetime in 17th-century England. The diversity of information presumed to be newsworthy reflects the increased size and complexity of modern society. Sophisticated means of communication and transportation now provide social linkages over large geographical areas and embrace millions of people, thus generating forms of social awareness that were not possible prior to the 20th century.

With the increasing complexity of the world come many opportunities. One is the possibility of having the community of the world bound together through world-wide instantaneous communication. Just possibly in a world that is bound together through communication and understanding, the people will discover it is to their advantage to communicate instead of to destroy one another, and they might not destroy the earth. U.S. presidents and Soviet leaders have for years maintained telephone "hot lines" for instantaneous communication on important issues. So far they seem to have been useful.

But since there are thousands of media of communication operating throughout the world, and we must all be literate in one or more, it behooves us all, and especially the power-brokers, to recognize that literacy comes in more colors than a laser show, each with its own value and importance.

To prepare the U.S. citizen for the world of the future, we must quit trying to revivify the conventional print literacy to the exclusion of others, and instead embrace all forms of literacy, dignify them and try to use each and every one in getting society to work. Donald Kennedy, ex-Commissioner of the Food and Drug Administration and currently 8th president of Stanford University, recognizes the value of non-print literacy. "I do rudimentary word processing," he remarked to an interviewer. "Otherwise I'm semi-illiterate." His point should be recognized and emphasized.

Literacy comes to the mind through many media. All influence the future. All should be recognized and accorded their places as media of communication in which people should be literate. The fate of humankind is too important to leave in the hands of anachronists. They react to a world that may never have existed and which surely no longer is reality. The world needs people who at least are empirical enough to recognize reality when they see it.

Chapter Thirteen

Reading Below the Surface

The trouble with our method of developing the human mind is that in general we work from the wrong starting point, proceed in the wrong direction and come to the wrong destination. Instead of realizing that education is a ground-up, hands-on process that develops from the small to the large, from a beginning point through phenomena toward some complete understanding, as our experience with children should demonstrate, we assume that to know the theory and methodology for dealing with life is to know the nuts and bolts of experience. We think that with theory and methodology there is no need for knowing nuts and bolts. As a consequence, we build from the top down rather than from the bottom up. We cook pie in the sky before we have learned how to work in the kitchen. We try to reap the harvest before we have planted the seed. It is like looking at the frozen-over lake and assuming that the ice on top is all of the lake, without ever plumbing its depths to see what kinds of life exist below the surface. This approach leads to a superficial reading, as we are learning now as sophisticated equipment allows us to drop to great depths in the waters of the world to discover forms of life no living person has recognized before.

Looking at the macro—the large—forms of phenomena, we are trained to generalize before we understand the specific. We will be interested, for example, in a specific symbol, an action, a particular phenomenon. We will examine that isolated component until we have extracted all that is valuable and meaningful in it. Then we will go on to another macro example and study that in vacuo.

In this specialization we always see more trees than forest. We have been cautioned not to miss the forest by concentrating on the trees, but that is precisely what we do. Our drive is to become overspecialized too soon.

Realizing the danger in this mode of investigation, many educators, especially those in the humanities, are urging people to learn in the reverse direction, to build from the ground up, to move from the large to the small. Then, we should be taught, we ought to move back from the specialization to the general. With this movement, the cycle of learning will have been completed—general-particular-general. Such a direction of learning moves in a three-level penetration. First one understands the general, then penetrates into the specific, then converts the specific back into a broader and better informed general. In scientific terminology, this is moving from a macro (general), into a micro (specific) and back into a blending of the specific into a better informed general.

Excellent examples can be found in the world of music. Music has long been recognized as one of the few expressions of communication common to nearly all people—and nearly all animals. Music is a lyrical expression in some kind of melody. It is also a means of expression, a language which regardless of word content speaks of joy, sadness, love, hate, adventure, patriotism, humor or just communication. The media are the human or animal voice—or some other kind of instrument: a blade of grass held between the thumbs and blown over, a hair comb with waxed paper over it, the pan-flute up to the mighty pipe organ. Why do we use music? To better enhance our message we wish to communicate.

To a certain extent all music is the same. That is, on the type level all music is the same. That of the Tibetan lama, the Papua New Guinea single string fiddle and the American Indian drums all have basically a common language. There are, to be sure, dialects in the various musics. Tibetan lama music may not be understood and appreciated by people outside the tradition, and this type of music is generally held to its tradition through acceptability and the desire of its users not to stray from that tradition. Music, like most of the media of communication, is forced by the people to be repetitive and conservative. In the U.S., for example, composer Irving Berlin wrote a thousand popular songs which although they varied widely in subject matter pretty much were held to the "popular" formula in subject and development.

Although music is thus kept to sounding the same in the large, there are fundamental differences on the micro level. No two of Berlin's songs were exactly alike, nor could be. No doubt there is a Russian ingredient shared by the intensely Russian composers Tchaikovsky, Rachmaninoff and Alexander Glazinov. We recognize this "Russianness" resonating through the works. There is a Nordic quality shed by the Norwegian Eduard Grieg and the Finnish Jan Sibelius; an American quality shared by Ferde Grofe, Victor Herbert, the Czech Antonin Dvorak in his "From the New World Symphony" and his "American" quartet, Aaron Copeland, George Gershwin and the many composers of American jazz: it is a jazzy, brassy, open-land ingredient containing what we think is the essence of "Americanness." There is a common element in the Gospel sound heard round the world, whether sung by Finns, Japanese, Australians or Americans; a Black sound with qualities native to American, African and Caribbean blacks. All native American ballads and folksongs have common elements, yet are distinguishable one from another. Most immediately obvious is the sound common to rock 'n' roll, wherever it is found on earth; but to the discerning ear all pieces are different from one another.

Though these various composers share types and motifs (themes), all develop their music with striking differences which individualize one's works and distinguish it from the others. Rachmaninoff did not say that he intended to duplicate Tchaikovsky's work. Copeland did not search for the essence of Dvorak so that he could duplicate it. Black composers do not search for the essence of their music so that they can merely copy it. Presley did not mix Black, Southern and folk music so that all three voices could still be heard. Composers could not merely imitate if they wanted to. Copeland's genes and genius spoke in unique, personal voices unlike any that have gone before. Sergei Prokofief tried to emulate the 18th century with his "Classical Symphony," which though it is a reasonable facsimile to the untrained ear, to the person who knows both the 18th-century symphony and 20th-century effort to emulate it, the ring is not authentic. In order to make the reasonable facsimile, the composer must understand fully the work, the type and the milieu he is trying to emulate, and he may come reasonably close. But in truth just as one individual cannot go home again to become the child he formerly was, one cannot write the music of a former period.

What is true of music in general is especially true of rock 'n' roll. The impact of the early giants, Presley and the Beatles for example, in rock 'n' roll was so great and lasting that their influence is still overriding. Their rock 'n' roll still predominates. Their rhythms, thoughts, sounds and combinations are still present. But that is true mainly because rock 'n' roll is still only a fledgling style of music only thirty years old. We still see Elvis' ghost in shopping malls and elsewhere, John Lennon is only 10 years dead and Paul McCartney is still performing. The generation of the creators is just closing. Their hands and voices are still heard in the land. Ordinarily a type should grow further from the fountainhead in order to be free and independent.

Though these generalizations are valid, not all rock 'n' roll artists are the same and not all such music is a mere duplicate of the rest. In fact, it could not be. The Beatles were different from Elvis Presley, just as Presley had been different from Buddy Holly. The Supremes' sound was different from all their predecessors. And the thousands of groups that have grown out of and broken off from the early rock 'n' roll groups create their own variations, their own sounds and their own individualized versions. Their types are the same, even sometimes their formulas and motifs. But their micromotifs are as different as the individuals who created them.

At times creators must work with thousands of variations. The French crime writer George Simenon with his more than 90 novels was "disdainful of pretentious philosophizing or didacticism," according to an authority on the author, George Grella, and used his "canvas" of novelizing to communicate "the power and inevitability of life itself" (83).

Picasso with his 10,000 works was the Simenon of painting. Novelist Kathryn Marshall quotes Picasso as wanting to "draw the [viewer's] mind in a direction it's not used to and wake it up," desiring to "set things in movement, to provoke. . .contradictory tensions, opposing forces" (83). These forces he brought to bear in his works, most of which look to the average viewer strikingly like all the others, just as do most of the pictures of most unrecognized and unacclaimed artists. But the tens of thousands of paintings of rural America, awe-inspiring mountains, rural scenes and haystacks may seem the same to the undiscriminating eyes. But to the perceptive, inquiring and unbiased close observer, striking differences immediately become apparent.

So too in the other media. Television talk-shows, for example, although similar in formula, are individualized by the different participants and the hosts. They are known by their hosts—Phil Donahue, Oprah Winfrey, Geraldo, Joan Rivers, etc.—who call upon their individual guests to be as strikingly individualistic as possible. The hosts live on the differences. Comedies, soap operas, game shows and news shows, though identified by name as a matter of convenience, are really known by the characters they keep. Hosts and characters distinguished all shows from all others.

Thus popular entertainment—and all communication—and popular culture in general, perhaps of necessity in a democratic society, is highly individualized. Anonymity is not a cloak eagerly sought by today's participants in life, nor is losing oneself in the common stream of formula participation. For confirmation one only has to look at the individualizing statements published throughout the land in every medium. The chic crowd wear designer clothes to distinguish themselves and then wear individualizig items within the crowd. Sports players wear their names and numbers on their jerseys and perform ritual dances at the end of every identifiable play they make in order to give themselves more "stage" time in the public eyes. Performers everywhere have to be listed on announcements of their performances through "credits." On television everybody who even breathed in the production—even the first grip— has to be named. On a National Geographic Special aired December 13, 1990, credit was even given to "Tigger the Fall Cat," for his performance. *People Magazine* is dedicated to people. People sell well to people. Capitalism is ego-driven. Anonymity does not prosper.

There is a valid question of whether with 5-10 billion people and with all the animals and plants asserting their individual rights the planet can survive. Regardless, it surely is a stage that must be worked with and worked through. The number of players crowds the stage. All the lists of players obliterate the landscape.

Nationalities may be similar and have similar characteristics. But the people have more individual differences than similarities. Majorities are not alike in their majority. Minorities are not alike in their minority. Ethnic groups generally are aching to lose their covering mantle of similarity. We are discovering that even animals that we used to think of as one ball of distinguishing marks—zebras, leopards and cheetahs—and animals that run in packs—wolves and lions—that seemed indistinguishable are in fact very much individualized in characteristics and behavior. Animals recognize individualization. They smell out their own offspring, recognize dominant individuals and learn how to act in the group.

Even the most casual observation should have told us these facts. But people generally observe to confirm a prior conviction, not to learn. Mark Twain once said that it is astonishing the things we can look at without seeing. As a result we make long-lasting mistakes based on ignorance. For a thousand years imperfect observation confirmed the assumption that ostriches bury their heads in the sand, when in fact they merely feed off the ground. For years it was the practice for zoo keepers to put together a male and a female of a species and expect them sexually to make "like animals" and produce offspring. But we are finally discovering that animals have their likes and dislikes in the mating game just as *homo sapiens* do. Sometimes they do not like the partners that have been assigned them. We are finally realizing that arranged marriages even in the animal kingdom at times seem to result in unhappiness, incompatibility and sterility.

In order to understand these differences we must see beneath the stereotype into the particular. We must be able to read beneath the surface. We must learn to see below the type to the motif and beneath the motif into the micro-motif. There we will see a new world opening up, a world of reality that charges one up to the new sensitivities and awarenesses. Mind-expanding drugs may create areas of sensitivity and awareness. So too can the realization that the everyday world is by no means what it seems to be to the untrained and prejudiced eye. A drop of water from a brook placed beneath a microscope teems with life. A group of American teenagers—all of whom seem to be running the same formula of behavior—mill in a thousand directions of behavior.

To say, as we do, that having seen one Western, having watched one television show or having read one detective or romance story that we know the lot is a gross blunting of human intelligence and a perversion of experience. When poet Gertrude Stein made her oft-quoted statement that "a rose is a rose is a rose is a rose," she elevated poetic license to the plane of ignorance and nonsense. When anybody, believing that poets by nature possess an unusual wisdom necessarily valuable to us all, thought that there was any sense in Stein's observation, he/she compounded ignorance with blind, formulaic unthinking. Perhaps we should remember that Plato banished poets from his Republic because he thought they were mad. We do not necessarily have to find them all mad, but we should understand Plato enough to realize that we must examine carefully everything they poeticize. To paraphrase Socrates, an unexamined poet is not worth reading.

Perhaps in more ways than one we might aspire to learn from the birds and bees and to become bee-brains. We can learn a lot from nature and might refine our sense of fluency. At least we would learn which sources of wisdom are worth our probing.

An excellent informative parallel to the above generalizations can be found in the study of narrative, both folk and non-folk.

In 1910 Finnish folklorist Antti Arne observed that there are similarities in folk narratives around the world. In order to study these narratives comparatively he called the similarities *types*. For example, the type known as the stick-fast type he found current in 17 countries around the world. In the U.S. this story is best illustrated in the Uncle Remus Tar-Baby Story, where Br'er Rabbit slaps Tar Baby with one foot after the other for insolence and in so doing gets his paws stuck to the tar baby's body. In the 17 countries around the world where this type is found, in several instances there is no tar or resin available, thus leaving open the question of how the story could be credible.

Though this typing is useful for comparative study of folktales around the world, Stith Thompson, renowned folklorist at Indiana University who worked with Arne on his typing, realized that it is too broad and general to be most effective. He needed greater detail for analysis. He found this greater detail by dividing the types into motifs. As he explained his reasoning:

(If) an attempt is made to reduce the traditional narrative material of the whole earth to order (as, for example, the scientists have done with the worldwide phenomenon of biology) it must be by means of a classification of single motifs—those details out of which full-fledged narratives are composed.

Thus a *type* is divisible into motifs. In Thompson's words, a motif is the smallest unit of a narrative. Jan Brunvand, another folklorist, in trying to be a bit more precise, identified motifs as having any of seven capabilities:

1. Motifs may describe objects.
2. Motifs may describe a marvelous animal.
3. Motifs may describe a concept.
4. Motifs may describe an action.
5. Motifs may describe a character (e.g. a giant).
6. Motifs may describe a character type (e.g. a thief).
7. Motifs may describe a structural quality.

These categorizations of Thompson and Brunvand are helpful. The fact is, however, that a motif cannot be identified as the smallest unit that *describes* something. A description is an adjective, a synonym, a parallel or a symbol. A giant, for example, is not a motif, but giantism is; a thief is not a motif, though theft is. Thus a motif must be understood not as a description but as a unit in a work that *generates some kind of action*—physical or mental response. A haunted house, for example, or "hauntedness," or a loaded gun, or "loadedness," is a motif because each generates some kind of response, is responsible for some kind of action, in the person who experiences the phenomenon.

Though types and motifs are both useful in helping one understand the phenomena of life they are too general to be most effective. They are like labels on containers of material rather than individual listings of the enclosed items. There are all kinds of loaded guns, for example; in order for the mere listing of a loaded gun to be most useful in narrative analysis the loaded gun must be described in greater detail. For instance, what caliber gun. Women fire smaller caliber guns, macho males use the .45, police officers the .38 special, mass killers use the machine gun and cocaine dealers currently use rapid-fire guns. Equally important is the location in which a gun is used. The revolver used at the O.K. Corral or carried by Gregory Peck in the movie *Gunfighter* is quite a different gun from that strapped to Billy the Kid or the cocaine-dealing punk on the streets of Detroit. The .22 caliber pistol carried by a woman on the streets of New York City for her own protection is quite a different motif from that of a hired assassin stalking the streets of London waiting for a chance to kill some government employee.

All these differences are significant. Though they all constitute the motif of the loaded gun, they should be broken down into micromotifs so that their true nature and purpose can be expressed. Each micromotif has its own distinct characteristics and develops along its own lines with a consequent beginning, middle and end. Each micromotif directs the development of its own individualized constituents.

An excellent example of the needed breakdown of the motifs into micromotifs can be found in the ever-popular Dashiell Hammett novel *The Maltese Falcon*. The story's formula is of course the Private

Investigator detective fiction. Within that formula there are several motifs: the magic symbol as a lure to crime (the bird); one man's revenge for the murder of a friend/colleague; a beautiful woman as a sex symbol; etc. The several motifs are developed in some 150 micromotifs, which set this book off from all others in the genre and from all others Hammett wrote.

These micromotifs range throughout the activities of life. For example: a quiet, shy voice reveals innocence; smoking a cigarette reveals nervousness; curious onlookers gawk at the scene of a crime; a cheap clock shows time in a slum; Sam Spade keeps the police in the dark; the police (power) try to coerce Spade; glancing at a watch reveals impatience; Effie envies Iva's body; Sam spreads newspapers around the bed before sleeping to protect himself; a foreigner depicts evil; the several italicized in the quoted passage below. One example can suffice for illustration of the development of a micromotif in a narrative.

The novel opens in Sam Spade's office, with Sam sitting in his swivel chair behind his *oaken desk*; it must be oaken because the chair the customer sits in is "the *oaken armchair* beside his desk," which is immediately referred to next as merely the "chair's wooden seat." Historically the oak tree has denoted fertility and sexuality. This scene, set against a background of potential fertility, becomes charged with sexuality as Miss Wonderly (one of the many names used by Brigid O'Shaunnessy) walks in for her interview with Spade:

> She advanced slowly, with tentative steps, looking at Spade with cobalt-blue eyes that were both shy and probing. She was *tall and pliantly slender*, without angularity anywhere. Her *body* was erect and *high-breasted*, her *legs long*, her *hands and feet narrow*. She wore two shades of blue that had been selected because of her eyes. The hair curling from under her blue hat was darkly red, her *full lips* more *brightly red. White teeth glistened* in the *crescent her timid smile made*.

Spade obviously responds to her sensuality, but he is primarily the professional, putting professional ethics above sensual pleasure. His office is the place for business, not pleasure. He is currently sleeping with Miles Archer's wife, Iva, but even in that relationship he puts business before pleasure. Miles Archer, however, is the opposite and is used for contrast. Archer puts pleasure before professional ethics. When Wonderly suggests somebody follow her and her companion later in the night, it is Archer who wants the tailing job because he sees potential sexual pleasure in the encounter. For his lecherous attitude he is killed.

Throughout the novel Spade remains the professional. At the end, he forces the law to take its course with Brigid O'Shaunnessy. She had killed Miles, had murdered and stolen and was prepared to commit any crime in order to get and keep the jewel-laden falcon. At the end, she parades sex before Spade and promises him a life of sensual pleasure, but Spade does not hesitate a moment. He remains professional and calls the police: "I won't play the sap for you," he tells Brigid.

At the last scene of the novel Spade has returned, on Monday morning to his office, to the micromotif of the oaken desk and setting. He finds Effie, his secretary, sitting in his swivel-chair behind his oaken desk. She immediately jumps up as he enters. The scene is again—still—charged with sexuality. Sam puts his arm around Effie and begins to fondle her. But she resists, saying, "But don't touch me now—not now." The scene is interrupted with the reappearance of Iva, who has always been Effie's rival. Earlier in the book Sam had told Iva that she should not come to the office—it was not good form. Now she has returned to reintroduce illicit sex into the scene.

But Sam again turns professional, and it is the oaken desk that is the micromotif that develops this single most important element of the book. Sam puts professionalism above personal pleasure and the revealing micromotif is the oaken desk, his generating power that holds his duty, his office and his moral code in place. The book ends with the simple but totally revealing short paragraph:

"Spade, looking at his desk, nodded almost imperceptibly, 'Yes,' he said and shivered. 'Well, send her in'." The micromotif of the oaken desk and the office has tied the book together. It made Sam the person he is and the novel the powerful statement it is. Without the micromotif obviously the power would not be there. The oaken desk and chairs is a micromotif, not a symbol, since it drives the action; it is not something which symbolizes the action. It powers the action. Without understanding this micromotif the reader and critic can never fully understand the dynamics of the book.

What is true in *The Maltese Falcon* prevails throughout popular literature (and all literature). Writers in the broad type of "popular" literature and in the more narrow type or genre they work in—such as crime fiction, romance, science fiction, etc.—know the type and the theme. They know the motifs of "best-sellers," detective, horror, romance, etc. They know that there needs to be action, love and sex—explicit and hard-hitting "American life" style, etc. So on the formula or type level the books in a genre are similar.

But each develops the micromotifs of his/her genre and story in his/her own way. Sidney Sheldon, one of our most popular authors, insists that the reader recognize Sheldon in the conventional best-selling story he writes. And the reader does. British authors P.D. James and Ruth Rendell demand that one recognize each in their detective fiction; they are offended, quite properly, if the reader mistakes one for the other, and only the careless untrained reader would. Rendell's stores are not James'. Only in general are they "alike." Specifically they are quite dissimilar. Joan Hess, Les Roberts, Sara Paretsky, three American writers of crime fiction, insist that one recognize their fictions as being uniquely theirs, different and unique. And they are correct.

In languages other than English and in cultural traditions other than English-American, micromotifs are strikingly different from the English-American and from one another. Umberto Eco's story of murder in medieval Italy, *The Name of the Rose*, Paco Ignacio Taibo II's novel of present-day Mexico city, *An Easy Thing*, and stories of murder in present-day Russia written by American Stuart Kaminsky must develop their own micromotifs and are to the careful reader strikingly different one from another and from all the American works of the same type.

Most readers are not careful. They want to find similarities and associations in all works. Therefore they look for these similarities, these echoes of former reading, the resonances of the past which grip the present. Once they see the similarities, they do not look for the differences. Elite readers and critics are especially guilty of this grip of the past. Readers and reviewers of popular books are likely to categorize them with such descriptions as, "As good as Sidney Sheldon," "A budding P.D. James," "As hard-hitting as Hammett and Chandler" or "Hard-boiled fiction at its hardest."

For example, contemporary crime fiction writer Robert Campbell was described in the *New York Times* as "A master of the hard-boiled Chandleresque manner." In the *Washington Post* he was characterized, "Campbell is, above all, a first-rate storyteller...Like Marlow, McGee, Burke, and...others." Occasionally critics see beneath the surface. In commenting on the Robert Campbell novel *Juice*, Elmore Leonard, a distinguished novelist himself and therefore one who could read beneath the lines, said, "Robert Campbell has his own sound; he's an awfully good writer."

All generalizations that lump popular writers in one pile reveal the sloppiness and inadequate attention of the reader more than an analysis of the book being discussed. Only Sheldon can write like Sheldon. To say that "XXX is a budding hard-boiled writer," is no more revealing than to say that he has two legs, or uses Los Angelos as a setting. It is time that readers and critics became more discerning and discriminating and learn to recognize that authors are different one from another and consequently their works are different one from another. A group may all belong to the same family and be written to a formula, but all differ to one degree or another from all the others. To fail to recognize these differences is to under-read the writers.

Publishers and popular readers recognize that there is a difference. That is the reason books are marketed with the author's name more prominent than the title. Readers buy specific authors—a Louis L'Amour western, an Agatha Christie mystery, a James Mitchener epic of place, a Stephen King horror story or a Danielle Steele romance. It is primarily the author readers buy, not the genre. Not since the Middle Ages have books been sold anonymously on the strength of the story alone. Nowadays, Sheldon, Christie, James, Rendell, Hess, L'Amour, John D. MacDonald and Ross Macdonald all have insisted—they could not avoid it—on writing the so-called formula story in their own ways. L'Amour's Westerns are not just westerns; they are L'Amour Westerns, driven by the author's particular point of view and purpose. A Christie detective story is not just a detective story but her own that could be written by no one else. A Ross Macdonald crime fiction novel is a psychological probing of loneliness in America, written by any other author it would be imitated but not copied.

Sometimes, for various reasons, authors have been willing to write under other names. For the first quarter of the 20th century, for example, Edward Stratemeyer's syndicate had at least ten writers authoring books about the Rover Boys—Dick, Tom and Sam—under the Stratemeyer name; the authors needed the money and wanted to write. In our own time detective fiction author Carolyn Heilbrun published under the name Amanda Cross because when she began writing she was afraid her colleagues in the English Department at Columbia University would deny her tenure if they discovered she was writing that kind of fiction. Many other authors use pseudonyms, sometimes because they want to write different kinds of fiction. Oxford don J.I.M. Stewart, literary scholar, wrote mysteries under the name Michael Innes and "straight" fiction under the Stewart name. Academic C. Day-Lewis wrote detective fiction under the name Nicholas Blake, as did Robert Bruce Montgomery writing as Edmund Crispin. Sometimes authors adopt other names because their publishers want more than one name to place before the public. So Ruth Rendell writes as Barbara Vine, and Ralph McInerny as Edward Mackin as well as his own.

In all these kinds of works, the formula is the motif; the individualizations by the authors are the micromotifs. The authors individualize and mark their works clearly and forcefully. They may write genre fiction but they are not generic authors.

There have always been stories in oral and print tradition that developed along similar lines. Traditional epics like the *Odyssey* and *Iliad* spring instantly to mind. But the greatest surge in America came with the development of rapid printing in the 1800s. In the U.S. such stories got their greatest impetus in the 1940s and 1950s in the form of the dime novel and developed from 1896 to 1957 in such magazines as *Doc Savage, The Shadow, The Spider, Astounding, Black Mask* or the dozens of other detective magazines and scores of other kinds—more than a hundred in all.

Pulp magazines were the infatuation of the young and the blue-collar workers because they brought a variety, an intensity and an adventure to life that was otherwise missing. They were immediately recognizable by their size, their cover and their contents. Tom Sawyer loved them and so did most other kids, except Tom's sissy brother, Sid— not to mention Aunt Polly. These magazines spoke of a way of life that was outside one's physical reach but within the bounds of imagination and the vision of one's heart's desire.

To parents and other outsiders—especially the elite—pulp stories were all horrible—filled with thud and thunder, blood and guts, grotesques and defectives. But the readers of these magazines—those who took the time to learn what they were talking about and to become fluent in their language—had the more discriminating tastes. They knew the treasures bound within the soft-covers, and inside the favorite pulp his treasured author and character. To such discriminating tastes it was nonsense to say that all pulps were the same, that if you read one you had read them all. They, on the contrary, obviously were not all the same. Each had its own dynamic, its own reality, its own style and appeal, its own avenue of growth. Their individual and collective accomplishments were portentous, as Robert Sampson, perhaps the country's leading historian of the subject, attests:

They opened new possibilities and sent excited shocks across the fabric of fiction. They directly influenced the conventions of the day—a new character or a new role, a different way of presenting action, a fascinating variant in narrative structuring. And, almost incidentally, they brought to general use certain assumptions and attitudes that lay implicit beneath the stuff of the writer's work. (3)

In bringing out these certain assumptions and attitudes that lay implicit beneath the writers' work, the pulps, despite what conventional wisdom said, encouraged the development of personalized statements by individual authors. The stable of authors contained so many that they could not be controlled. They were in constant individual development and rebellion against constraint. Pulp magazines thus became the medium for the growth of American fiction of the middle 20th century, which is the envy and model of the world.

The authors could be directed in general; they would write the type required and they would use the accepted motifs. But in their micromotifs, their individualized elements, each asserted his or her own ideas and methods of development. In detective fiction, for example, John D. MacDonald, who got his early training in the pulps, was an educator and social critic of considerable impact. One of his books, *Condominium*, made a substantial contribution to the literature directed against housing developers and developments and indiscriminate exploitation of land. Ross Macdonald was a cultural commentator who wanted to spread democracy and chip away at what he considered false and mischievous elitism in society. These two strong personalities would hardly sacrifice their individuality to motifs. Each was proud of his thoughts and of his style of writing them. Present-day author George C. Chesbro, who did not grow up in the pulps, wants to investigate the twilight psychological dream zone where people are brain-dead but body alive or body-dead and brain-alive. Conventional motifs will not allow him this investigation.

Throughout the conventional genre of crime fiction, writers have broken its bounds and are driving toward general fiction, where best-sellers have been all along. In doing that they are making more complex the micromotifs, and through this development they are enlarging the formulas, themes, types and motifs. They are a genre on the move, delving more deeply into the realities of life. They demonstrate that there is no such thing as a superficial novel, only superficial readers.

The elite, as usual, resist truth and reality. They have always demanded special treatment. They feed only on the top of a field of grass, leaving the rich carpet beneath the canopy for the larger population, the life-sustaining for most of us. Eating the top is easier and showier, and allows greater exposure of the neck and teeth. But the nutrients are lower to the ground. And we need to realize that just as the race is not always to the swift, nor lasting success to the flashy, the evolution of culture belongs to the populace, not to the top-croppers.

It is too easy for some of us to generalize and stereotype life and to be controlled by those generalizations. Just as it is dangerous to remember but not understand the past, it is destructive to act on the superficial knowledge of generalizations and stereotypes. Various kinds of mistakes and conflicts can be avoided with the realization that though one plus one may add up to two it does not add up to the same identity. A billion plus a billion adds up to two billion different organisms, identities and personalities—and expressions of those personalities. We must learn to read below the surface of seeming sameness. That is where the true meaning operates.

Chapter Fourteen

Windshield No Rear-View Mirror

We ask ourselves, finally, what are the potentials of human development, and what are the most effective ways of edging toward our goals?

Without being starry-eyed perfectionists we can assume that although the development has been slow, erratic and halting, humanity has made some positive development in the last 100,000 years. We seem a little less eager to bare our fangs than we used to be, or we do it in a somewhat different way.

We are more likely to be aware of our problems and have learned at least tenuously to address them. There is no doubt that technologically we have made some giant steps—though whether forward, backward or circularly may be an open question. In the process we have learned a great deal about ourselves—our strengths and weaknesses—and about the world around us. We may have learned that, to paraphrase Socrates, the enquiring life is the only one worth living, though in the 1980s it seemed that we had concluded that the only life worth living was greedy and self-indulgent.

Anyway, even the most sluggish minds among us are likely to be stimulated—we would call it making the adrenaline flow—by observing how much we can learn when assisted by all the devices around us, how much fun we can have when we utilize the fun-producing opportunities in our lives. Giant telescopes, searching microscopes, radio-carbon testing, machines to keep the human body alive—all are interesting. They open up new avenues, new areas and new worlds to investigate.

The brave new worlds are there before us, waiting for our visit. Our great task is to develop the mentality capable of handling the machines we will use. To do so we need a new orientation and calibration. We need to realize that our line of sight must be through the windshield of our hurtling machine looking forward rather than through the rear-view mirror, gazing backward. Looking backward only tells us where we have been. The view might bathe us in nostalgia and recreate a pleasant

194

though unreal experience, but it hardly prepares us for the new experience which is inevitable.

Looking forward, on the contrary, we can become fluent in all the media of communication of the future, in the possibilities open to us. If we concentrate on the past we remain bound to the past; if we are lucky we are fluent in that past. But only sharp perception can allow us to change the fluency in the past for fluency in the future; they are not coins traded at equal value on the market of human experience. The past sells for less on the living market than the future does. The past is a commodity that can only fade and shrink; the future can develop and grow.

It is a promising personal and real world to those who prepare for it by becoming fluent in its media of communication. It is well worth the cost. The future, an education, a life—all are too important to abuse or waste. The United Negro Fund uses as its motto, "The mind is a terrible thing to waste." Indeed it is. Similarly, opportunity is a terrible thing to abuse or waste. The investment is great, the potential unlimited. It is imperative that we realize the possible outcome.

Notes

Introduction

[1]Readings of Gestures:

(197) Touch Tips of right forefinger and thumb and bring to slightly open mouth with head tilted back a bit: food, or expression of hunger. Collected in all Arab countries noted in this list. Semiotic gesture.

(198) Extend forefinger and little finger from closed hand, and bring to mouth while head is tilted back a little: water, or expression of thirst. Collected in all Arab countries noted in this list. Semiotic gesture.

(199) Hold thumb side of right fist on mouth: expression of thirst. Saudi Arabia. Semiotic gesture.

(209) Hold extended right thumb near chin with heel of hand out: shame. Jordan, Syria. Semiotic gesture.

(210) Flip hands up and out before body and extend tongue: disbelief. Saudi Arabia. Semiotic, autistic gesture, or culture-induced gesture.

(213) Snap forefinger and thumb, then thrust out hand with forefinger extended: reference to past. Saudi Arabia. Semiotic gesture.

(214) Place hands together (palms) then separate them so that the palms are facing forward and hands are next to each other: teasing. Saudi Arabia. Semiotic gesture.

(216) Place extended forefinger sidewards over nose then move it across the nose several times with tongue extended: teasing. Egypt. Semiotic gesture.

(223) Place tip of forefinger beneath lower lip then flip the fingertip up so that it barely grazes the underside of the tip: teasing. Saudi Arabia. Semiotic gesture.

(224) Hook extended forefinger over ear (from back) then slowly move it over the ear to the front part: sign to person not to argue with signer. Saudi Arabia. Semiotic gesture.

(225) Place palms together so that fingers are pointing forward then twist hands in the opposite direction but still in contact: finished. Saudi Arabia. Semiotic gesture.

(226) Place thumb side of fist over mouth then twist the hand a half-turn: threat to *jinn* (spirits). Used by women in Saudi Arabia. Semiotic gesture.

(227) Extend left forefinger, then form an inverted V-configuration with right forefinger and thumb and place it over the lower part of the left forefinger near the thumb: insult, or "I'll ride you like a donkey." Saudi Arabia. Semiotic gesture.

(229) Place tip of right forefinger between eyebrows: shame, or "I can't do it." Saudi Arabia. Semiotic gesture.

(230) Make a circular motion around ear with forefinger: mother's threat to child to behave, or that she will deal with him later. Saudi Arabia. Semiotic gesture.

(231) Place tips of fingers and thumb together then hit them on cheek: threat to child to behave, or that she will deal with child later. Saudi Arabia. Semiotic gesture.

(232) Place tips of fingers and thumb together then hit them on distended cheek exhaling as the fingers hit: mocking, or what person is saying is nonsense. Saudi Arabia. Semiotic gesture.

(233) Hold stiff left forearm with hand closed then place palm of right hand on inside elbow: sign that signer has nothing, but said with anger. Saudi Arabia. Semiotic gesture.

(234) Place tips of left fingers and thumb together so that hand faces right then place tip of right forefinger directly on the left finger tips: obscenity, or insult directed at one's birth or parentage but specifically "You have five fathers." Saudi Arabia. Semiotic gesture.

(235) Place palms together so that fingers are in contact, then move all fingers back into palm except two middle fingers that remain extended: used by men to imply that they have slept with the woman to whom the gesture is made. Saudi Arabia. Semiotic gesture.

Chapter Four
[1]An earlier, different, version of this paper, by **Ray B. Browne** and **Arthur G. Neal**, appeared in *Journal of Popular Culture*, 25.1 (Summer 1991): 157-186.

Chapter Eight
[1]This article in a somewhat different form appeared first in *Journal of Popular Culture*, 24:3 (Winter 1990): 101-112.

Chapter Nine
[1]An early version of this paper appeared under the title, "The Repressive Nature of TV Esthetics Criticism," in *Journal of American Culture*, 6:3 (Fall 1983): 117-122.

Works Cited

Introduction

Barakat, Robert A., "Arabic Gestures," *Journal of Popular Culture*, VI, 4, 1973, 749-787.

Pugh, Simon. *Reading Landscape: Country-City-Capitol*. Manchester, England, 1990.

Singleton, Theresa A. "The Archeology of Slave Life," in Campbell, D.C., Jr., with Kym S. Rice, *Before Freedom Came: African-American Life in the Antebellum South*. Richmond, VA. 1991.

Chapter One

Castner, Henry W. *Seeking New Horizons*, Toronto, 1990.

Charbonnier, Georges. "Entretiens avec Claude Levi-Strauss," In *Les Lettres Nouvelles*, Vol. 10, 1961.

Daughty, Robin. "Nature Writing and Environmental Experience." In *Place Images in Media: Portrayal, Experience and Meaning*. Edited by Leo Zoon. Savage, MD. 1990.

Hart, John Fraser. *The Look of the Land*. Inglewood Cliffs, NJ 1990.

Lewis, Peirce. *Landscape*, 19, No. 2, 1975.

Marschack, Alexander. "The Art and Symbols of the Ice Age Man." In Rowly, David and Paul Heyer, *Communication in History: Technology, Culture, Society*. New York, 1990.

Newsweek, Fall-Winter, 1990; Jan. 7, 1991; Jan. 14, 1991.

Pugh, Simon. *Reading Landscape: Country-City-Capitol* Manchester, England, 1990.

Sagan, Carl. *The Dragons of Eden*. New York, 1990.

Siegel, Jeanne B. *How to Speak Furniture with an Antique American Accent*. Wilmette, IL, 1987.

Soderberg, Paul. *Art-Talk*, 1991, p. 17.

Truettner, William H. *The West as America: Reinterpreting Images of the Frontier*. Blue Ridge Summit, PA., 1991.

Zelinsky, Wilber. *Nation into State: The Shifting Symbolic Foundations of American Nationalism*. Chapel Hill, 1988.

Zonn, Leo. *Place Images in Media: Portrayal, Experience and Meaning*. Savage, MD, 1990.

Chapter Two

Brewer, James D. "Rap Lyrics and the Modification of Black Vernacular English," Lecture at the Far West PCA/ACA, Jan. 25, 1991.

Crowley, David and Paul Heyer. *Communication in History: Technology, Culture, Society*. New York, 1990.

Chapter Three

Arnold, Matthew. "Dover Beach." 1967.
Bloom, Allan. *The Closing of the American Mind.* New York, 1987.
Cawelti, John G. *The Six-Gun Mystique.* Bowling Green, OH, 1970.
Cheney, Lynne. *Humanities in America: A Report to the President, the Congress, and the American People.* Washington, 1988.
Hoggart, Richard. *The Uses of Literacy: Aspects of Working-Class Life and Entertainment.* London, 1957.
Inglis, Fred. *Popular Culture and Political Power.* London, 1989.
Spiller, Robert, Willard Thorp, Thomas H. Johnson, Henry Seidel Canby. *Literary History of the United States.* New York, 1953.

Chapter Four

Arnold, Matthew. "Functions of Criticism at the Present Time." 1869.
Bloom, Allan. *The Closing of the American Mind.* New York, 1987.
Boyer, Ernest L. "Toward a New Core Curriculum." *NEA Advocate* April/May 1978.
Grose, Francis. *A Classical Dictionary of the Vulgar Tongue.* London: 1785.
Hirsch, E.D. Jr. *Cultural Literacy: What Every American Needs to Know.* Boston, 1987.
Hutchinson, Thomas. In Ray Paul, *The Impact of Film: How Ideas Are Communicated through Cinema and Television.* New York: 1973.
Journal of Popular Culture Association of Japan No. 3, Kyoto, 1990.
Katz, Marilyn. *The Chronicle of Higher Education. May 23 May 1990.*
Perlman, Itzhak. *Newsweek* Fall/Winter, 1990: 49.
Reedy, George. *Chronicle of Higher Education, XXXVII* 19 Dec. 1990.
Rousseau, George S. *The Chronicle of Higher Education* 23 May 1990: A6-A9.
Seferis, George. *Summer Solstice.* 1966.
Schoen, Donald. "Generative Metaphor: A Perspective on Problem-Setting in Social Policy." *Metaphors and Thought.* Ed. A. Ortony. Cambridge: 1979: 254-283.
Smith, Melissa A. "The Russell Sage Foundation and the Southern Highland Division." *Rockefeller Archive Newsletter* Fall 1990: 12-13.

Chapter Five

Huer, Jon. *The Great Art Hoax.* Bowling Green, OH: 1990.
Lindauer, Martin S. "Comparisons Between Museum and Mass-Produced Art." *Empirical Studies of the Arts* 9(1), 11-22 (1991): 20.

Chapter Six

Reynolds, Davis S. *Beneath the American Renaissance: The Subversive Imagination in the Age of Emerson and Melville.* Cambridge: 1989.
Iacocca, Lee. *Iacocca: An Autobiography.* New York: 1985.

Chapter Seven

Iacocca, Lee. *Iacocca: An Autobiography.* New York: 1985.
Keillor, Garrison. *Lake Wobegon Days.* New York: 1985.

Chapter Eight

Bruccoli, Matthew. "Up from the Category Books." *Ross MacDonald's Inward Journey: Reflections on Ross MacDonald by 25 of America's Most Distinguished Authors.* Ed. Ralph B. Sipper. New York: 1984.

Cawelti, John G. *The Six-Gun Mystique*. Bowling Green, OH: 1970.
Hoggart, Richard. *The Uses of Literacy: Aspects of Working-Class Life and Entertainment*. London: 1957.

Chapter Nine
Laurent, Lawrence. "Wanted: The Complete Television Critic."
Warshow, Robert. *The Immediate Experience*. New York: 1964.

Chapter Ten
Browne, Ray B. *"A Night with the Hants" and Other Alabama Folk Experiences*. Bowling Green, OH: 1976.
Browne, Ray B. *Popular Beliefs and Practices from Alabama*. Berkeley: 1958.
Brunvand, Jan. *The Study of American Folklore*. New York: 1968.
Burke, Peter. *Popular Culture in Early Modern Europe*. New York: 1978.
Dundes, Alan. *Interpreting Folklore*. Bloomington, IN: 1980.
McNally, Jeffrey. *Folklife Center News* XII.3,4 Summer-Fall 1990.
Thompson, Stith. *Motif-Index of Folk-Literature. A Classification of Narrative Elements in Folktales, Ballads, Myths, Fables, Medieval Romances, Exempla, Fabliaux, Jest-Books, and Local Legends*. Rev. and Enlarged Edition. Bloomington, IN: 1966.
Williams, John. *Last Legacy: A Useful Family Herbal*. 1827. Ed. Ray B. Browne and Egil Ramstad, for Indiana Historical Society, 1967.
Xiyang, Tang. *Living Treasures: An Odyssey Through China's Extraordinary Nature Reserves*. New York: 1985.

Chapter Eleven
Cheney, Lynne. *Tyrannical Machines: Report on Educational Practices Gone Wrong and Our Best Hopes for Setting Them Right*. Washington: 1990.
Grella, George. *Twentieth Century Crime and Mystery Writers*. New York: 1985.
Levine, Arthur. *Education and National Affairs* 30 Sept. 1985: 7.

Chapter Twelve
Barth, Gunther. *Fleeting Moments: Nature and Culture in American History*. New York: 1990.
Barthes, Roland. *Mythologies*. New York: 1972.
Black Elk, Wallace and William S. Lyon. *Black Elk: The Sacred Ways of a Lakota*. San Francisco: 1990.
Bloom, Allan. *The Closing of the American Mind*. New York: 1987.
Brooks, Jeffrey. *When Russia Learned to Read: Literacy and Popular Literature, 1861-1917*. Princeton: 1985.
Cohn, Jan. "Redefining Literature." *Journal of Popular Culture* 23:3, 23-31.
Cortese, Anthony D. *Chronicle of Higher Education* 1 Aug. 1990: 11, 13.
Deetz, James. *In Small Things Forgotten: The Archeology of Early American Life*. Garden City: 1977.
Federation Review VIII No. 5.
Folklore Forum Vol. 21, No. 1 (1988): 41-55.
Gowans, Alan. *Learning to See*. Bowling Green, OH: 1981.
Handelman, Don. *Models and Mirrors. Towards an Anthropology of Public Events*. New York: 1990.

Hirsch, E.D., Jr. *Cultural Literacy: What Every American Needs to Know*. Boston: 1987.

Kagle, Steven E. *America: Exploration and Travel*. Bowling Green, OH: 1979.

L'Amour, Louis. *Education of a Wandering Man*. New York: 1989.

Lawlor, Patricia M. "Cultural Exchange Through Books." *Contemporary French Civilization* Fall/Winter 1985.

Lederman, Leon. *The University of Chicago Magazine* Dec. 1990: 14.

Liebes, Tamar and Elihu Katz. *The Export of Meaning: Cross-Cultural Readings of Dallas*. New York: 1990.

Madsen, Ray Paul. *The Impact of Film: How Ideas are Communicated Through Cinema and Television*. New York: 1973.

Nye, Russel B. *The Unembarrassed Muse: The Popular Arts in America*. New York: 1970.

Newsweek Fall/Winter 1990.

Pare, Richard. *Court House: A Photographic Document*. New York: 1987.

Rowson, Martin. *The Waste Land*. San Francisco: 1990.

St. George, Robert Blair. *Material Life in America: 1600-1860*. Boston: 1988.

Simonson, Rick and Scott Walker. *Multi-Cultural Literacy*. St. Paul: 1988.

Trachtenberg, Alan. *Documenting America, 1935-1943*. Ed. Carl Fleishchnauer and Beverly W. Brannan. Berkeley: 1988.

Turner, Victor. "The Spirit of Celebration." *The Celebration of Society: Perspectives of Contemporary Cultural Performance*. Ed. Frank Manning. Bowling Green: 1983. 197-201.

Vis-A-Vis, The Magazine of United Airlines. July 1990.

Wakeman, Edgar "Ned." Quoted in Ray B. Browne, "Mark Twain and Captain Wakeman." *American Literature, XXXIII* No. 3, Nov. 1961: 325.

Chapter Thirteen

Brunvand, Jan. *The Study of Folklore*. New York: 1968.

Marshall, Kathryn. *American Way* 1 Jan. 1991: 83.

Sampson, Robert. *Yesterday's Faces: Glory Figures*. Bowling Green, OH: 1983.

Thompson, Stith. *Motif-Index of Folk—Literature, A Classification of Narrative Elements in Folktales, Ballads, Myths, Fables, Medieval Romances, Exempla, Fabliaux, Jest-Books, and Local Legends*. Rev. and Enlarged. Bloomington: 1966.

www.ingramcontent.com/pod-product-compliance
Lightning Source LLC
Chambersburg PA
CBHW021053090426
42738CB00006B/324